Self-Liberation

Through Seeing with Naked Awareness

SAMANTABHADRA

Self-Liberation
Through Seeing with Naked Awareness

An Introduction to the Nature of One's Own Mind
from
The Profound Teaching of Self-Liberation in the Primordial State of the Peaceful and Wrathful Deities
A terma text of Guru Padmasambhava
expounding the view of Dzogchen, rediscovered by
Rigdzin Karma Lingpa

Foreword by
Namkhai Norbu

Commentary by
John Myrdhin Reynolds

Snow Lion Publications
Ithaca, New York USA

Snow Lion Publications
605 West State Street
P. O. Box 6483
Ithaca, NY 14851
(607) 273-8519
www.snowlionpub.com

ISBN 1-55939-144-8

Printed in Canada on acid-free, recycled paper.

Library of Congress Cataloging-in-Publication Data

Karma-gling-pa, 14th cent.
 [Rig pa no sprod gcer mthoṅ raṅ grol. English]
 Self-liberation : through seeing with naked awareness ; an introduction to the
nature of one's mind from the profound teaching of self-liberation in the primordial state of peaceful and wrathful deities ; a terma text of Guru Padmasambhava
expounding the view of Dzogchen ; rediscovered by Rigdzin Karma Lingpa ; foreword by Namkhai Norbu ; commentary by John Myrdhin Reynolds
      p.   cm.
 Originally published: Barrytown, N.Y. : Station Hill Press, ©1989.
 Includes bibliographical references and index.
 ISBN 1-55939-144-8 (alk. paper)
   1. Rdzogs-chen (Rñiṅ-ma-pa)—Early works to 1800. I. Reynolds, John Myrdhin,
1942-   II. Title.

BQ7662.4.k36613 2000
294.3'420423—dc21
                                                                  00-061885

This work is dedicated to the memory of
His Holiness Dudjom Rinpoche, Jigdral Yeshe Dorje
(1904–1987)

Contents

Foreword
Namkhai Norbu Rinpoche

In the eighth century of our era, the master from the country of Uddiyāna, Guru Padmasambhava, who was the individual principally responsible for establishing the teachings of the Buddhist Tantras in Tibet, gave to his group of disciples there many vast and profound teachings related to both Tantra and Dzogchen. But since the Tibetan people were not ready for all of these teachings, many of which were more directly suited to future generations, he had his consort, the Tibetan princess Yeshe Tsogyal, write them down and hide them in various places throughout the country. Such deliberately concealed texts are known as Termas or hidden treasures. Those among his original group of disciples who were reborn in later generations in order to rediscover these texts are known as Tertons, those who reveal hidden treasures. The appearance of Termas and Tertons during the following centuries, including the present one, has been a source of unending benefit and blessing for the Tibetan people and represents the continuing revelation of the highest teachings of the Tantras and Dzogchen.

In the fourteenth century of our era, there appeared a great Terton by the name of Nyida Sangye. His eldest son in turn became a great Terton by the name of Karma Lingpa. When he was fifteen years old, from a location on the mountain of Gam-po-dar, which looks like a dancing attendant deity, in eastern Dwagpo, he discovered many profound teachings, principally the *Zab-chos zhi-khro dgongs-pa rang-grol*, otherwise known as the *Kar-gling zhi-khro*.

This cycle of texts of the *Kar-gling zhi-khro* represents an introduction to the state of Dzogchen, the Great Perfection. Dzogchen is not the name of a religion, philosophy, school, or sect but the Primordial State of the individual. The essence of the teachings of all the Buddhas is the understanding of this state, which is the nature of one's own mind. Among different schools this Primordial State has many different names—Prajnāparimita, Tathāgatagarbha, Bodhichitta, or Mahāmudrā. Among Tibetan Buddhists of the old school, the Nyingmapas, and also among the Bonpos, it is generally known as Dzogchen, which means the Great Perfection. It is also called *tha-mal gyi shes-pa*, which means "ordinary awareness"; but this is not our ordinary mind incessantly thinking of this or that throughout the day. In Dzogchen we make a radical and fundamental distinction between mind (sems) and the nature of mind (sems nyid); and here ordinary awareness refers to the latter. The nature of the mind is like a mirror which has the natural and inherent capacity to reflect whatever is set before it, whether beautiful or ugly; but these reflections in no way affect or modify the nature of the mirror. It is the same with the state of contemplation: There is nothing to correct or alter or modify (ma bcos-pa). What the practitioner does when entering into contemplation is simply to discover himself in the condition of the mirror. This is our Primordial State. But in order to recognize it, we first need transmission from a realized master in the form of an introduction (ngo-sprod) to the state of presence and awareness (rig-pa), which is the capacity of the nature of mind. This introduction, a meeting face-to-face, is precisely the function of the present text, which reports the very words of Guru Padmasambhava introducing his disciples to such presence or awareness. Hence this text, which is the root text of the *Kar-gling zhi-khro* cycle, is called *Rig-pa ngo-sprod.* ˉy means of Rigpa we come to see everything with a direct immediate presence, denuded of the judgments and conceptual constructions that usually obscure our vision and obstruct our understanding. And in this way, we come to realize self-liberation (rang-grol). In the state of contemplation, when a thought arises, it is allowed to self-liberate into its own condition, without any effort or attempt at modification. Whereas the method of the Sūtras is the path of renunciation and the method of the Tantras is the path of transformation, the method proper to Dzogchen is the path of self-liberation, as is made clear in the teaching of Padmasambhava that we have here. This text, the *Rig-pa ngo-sprod gcer-mthong rang-grol*, which is part of the cycle of the *Zab-chos zhi-khro dgongs-pa rang-grol*, provides the essential view for this entire cycle of teachings relating to the six Bardos or intermediate states of existence. The *Kar-gling zhi-khro* is the most complete of all *Zhi-khro* (or Bardo) teachings and is widely known and used, especially among the Nyingmapa and the Kagyudpa schools. These teachings continue to generate activities for the benefit of beings, and in no way have they been exhausted.

In terms of my own personal experience as a young student in Derge in eastern Tibet, I received the transmission for the *Kar-gling zhi-khro* some five times. Principally I received this transmission from Khanpo Kunga Paldan (1878-1950), who was a master of my uncle Khyentse Rinpoche, Jamyang Chokyi Wangchuk (1910-1963). Originally a Sakyapa monk, Kunga Paldan was very non-sectarian (rip-med-pa) and became a disciple of the famous Nyingmapa master Dza Patrul Rinpoche. Having been ordained in the Sakyapa tradition, he then went to study at Dzogchen monastery, which is one of the principal and most famous Nyingmapa monasteries in Kham or eastern Tibet. It was founded by Padma Rigdzin (1625-1697) in 1685. The monastery received the patronage of the royal family of Derge and became one of the largest Nyingmapa monasteries in Tibet; it was like a large-scale city and it had thirteen different retreat centers. Here Kunga Paldan became the disciple of many eminent masters such as Patrul Rinpoche (1808-1887), Mi Pham Rinpoche (1846-1912), and Adzom Drugpa (1842-1924). Eventually he was invited to become a khanpo at Dzogchen Monastery, a position which is much like a professor at a western university. Normally at Dzogchen a khanpo holds office for three years and then retires in order to make a long retreat. This he did, retiring to Norbu yul-gyal, a snow mountain above the monastery, lying in the Zilthang mountains of Derge. On this mountain lived many hermits originally from the monastery below. The mountain had three levels: at the base was a thickly forested area; then came a barren rocky area above the timber line; and finally there was the topmost region of permanent snows. Kunga Paldan spent many years living both in the forest and in caves in the snow region. Eventually he returned to the monastery in order to teach, later retiring to his mountain retreat for the remainder of his life. It was my good fortune to be able to meet him through my uncle and have him be my principal teacher for these *Zhi-khro* practices.

In the present century, it was a Sikkimese Lama by the name of Kazi Dawa Samdup (1868-1922) who, with the help of his editor, a young American named W. Y. Evans-Wentz, first translated from the Tibetan into the English language the two texts of the *Bar-do thos-grol*, which are also part of this cycle called the *Zab-chos zhi-khro dgongs-pa rang-grol*. As a result of the efforts of Evans-Wentz, this translation became widely known in the West as "The Tibetan Book of the Dead" (bod-kyi gshin-yig), which was not the original title in Tibetan. Since then many Western scholars have read that translation and have commented on it, not the least of them the famous Swiss psychoanalyst, Dr. Carl Jung. However, the editor, who did not know the Tibetan language, introduced on his own many errors and misinterpretations into the translation and into his commentaries and notes to the translation. This led other Western scholars, including Dr. Jung, to further misinterpret the teachings found in the *Bar-do thos-grol* and related texts. It is unfortunate that these errors and misinterpretations continue to be perpetuated without correction, and that the so-called "Tibetan Book of the Dead" continues to be presented without the correct view which is the root-essence of the *Zab-chos zhi-khro Rig-pa ngo-sprod gcer-mthong rang-grol* and which is found in the text called the *Rig-pa ngo-sprod gcer-mthong rang-grol*. This latter text, even though it exists in another translation edited by Evans-Wentz, is not as well known in Western countries as *The Tibetan Book of the Dead* and is rather overlooked and neglected.

The translation of Buddhist texts from Tibetan, whether Sūtra, Tantra, or Dzogchen is not simply a matter of a scholar learning the Tibetan language and using a Tibetan-English dictionary. When one proceeds in this manner, it is very likely that the real meaning of the text will elude the translator, and this is especially the case with the Dzogchen teachings. It is necessary that the translator have some direct experience in the practice of the teachings. He must unite textual meanings with his own understanding of the Natural State (rnal-ma). Otherwise, not perceiving the real meaning, he is likely to fall into idle speculation over the significance of the words of the text. Thus we are fortunate that Vajranātha, an experienced yogin and practitioner, with indefatigable and earnest application, has translated this Dzogchen text from Tibetan into English. Where any points were obscure concerning the real meaning of the text, he consulted various lamas knowledgeable and experienced in the Dzogchen tradition. In the interest of clarity and with an eye to completeness he has enhanced the translation with notes and commentary (zin-bris).

Certainly many readers possessing fortunate karma will come to find themselves in a state of contemplation just by engaging the essential points of this profoundly instructive text, by thinking and reflecting upon its meaning, and by practicing it in their own mindstreams. It is our true hope and belief that this publication will serve as a cause for the uninterrupted happiness of countless beings.

Written on the sixth of January, 1987, in the city of Nea Makri in the country of Greece.

Translator's Acknowledgements

As translator I wish first to thank, much more than I can ever express in words, Dudjom Rinpoche for all his wisdom, kindness and inspiration when first introducing me to the vast and profound meaning of Dzogchen and for himself providing the consummate living example of these teachings. Also I wish to extend my everlasting gratitude to Namkhai Norbu Rinpoche for leading me farther along this path and for elucidating the many different dimensions of the Dzogchen teachings. Equally I wish to thank Thinley Norbu Rinpoche, Kangyur Rinpoche, Chatral Rinpoche, Prof. C.R. Lama, Lama Gonpo Tsedan, and Lama Tharchin for the various insights into Dzogchen which they shared with me. The translation in this present book was only possible because of the collaboration extended first by Lama Tharchin of Kongpo as the result of a seminar he presented in New York City in October of 1985, and subsequently by Namkhai Norbu Rinpoche in his going over the text, making corrections and suggesting revisions in the translations. The oral explanations of both of these Tibetan teachers have been incorporated into my commentary accompanying the translation.

I am also grateful for the help, financial and otherwise, extended to me by the Dzogchen Community of Conway and by the Dzogchen Community of Great Britain while I was engaged in completing this book, and to Nina Robinson for all her inspiration and encouragement. I am grateful as well to Bob Kohut, Susan Quasha and George Quasha for their many valuable suggestions, and especially to Larry Spiro for sharing with me his many insights into the relationship between psychotherapy and the spiritual path. Some of these have shaped the first Appendix in this book. Finally, my thanks are also extended to Māyā and to Arthur Mandelbaum for their efforts at oral translation during the seminar in New York with Lama Tharchin.

Vajranātha

Introduction

The Tibetan text which is translated here is a very important work for the understanding of the view of Dzogchen, which in Tibet is generally regarded as the highest and the most esoteric teaching of the Buddha. In Tibetan the title of the text is the *Rig-pa ngo-sprod gcer-mthong rang-grol*, which may be translated into English as "Self-Liberation through Seeing with Naked Awareness, being a Direct Introduction to the State of Intrinsic Awareness."[1] This is one of a large number of texts belonging to the cycle of Termas (gter-ma), or hidden treasure texts, entitled the *Zab-chos zhi-khro dgongs-pa rang-grol*, "The Profound Teaching of Self-Liberation in the Primordial State of the Peaceful and Wrathful Deities." This is the same Terma cycle to which belongs the justly famous *Bar-do thos-grol*, "Liberation through Hearing in the Intermediate State (between death and rebirth)," the so-called "Tibetan Book of the Dead." The present text represents the principal theoretical explanation (lta-khrid) for this entire Terma cycle of teachings, since it introduces and elucidates the meaning of intrinsic awareness or the state of immediate presence, known in Tibetan as *Rigpa* (rig-pa, Skt. vidya).

The authorship of the "Tibetan Book of the Dead" cycle of teachings has been traditionally attributed to the Buddhist Tantric master from the country of Uddiyāna, Guru Padmasambhava, who came to Tibet in the eighth century of our era.[2] He was invited to that country by the Tibetan king Tisong Detsan (742-797 CE) at the behest of the Buddhist scholar and abbot Śāntirakshita in order to subdue by means of his Tantric sorceries the hostile gods and demons who opposed the erecting of the first Buddhist monastery in Tibet at Samye (founded 779 CE). Thereafter, to an intimate circle of his

1

disciples he taught the Tantric methods of transformation known as Mahāyoga and Anuyoga, the culmination of which is the state of Dzogchen. Later other Dzogchen teachings belonging to the Mind Series (sems-sde) and the Space Series (klong-sde) were introduced into Tibet by the Indian master Vimalamitra and by the Tibetan translator Vairochana. The later followers of these three masters became known as the Nyingmapas or "the ancient ones." This lineage represents a continuous tradition (bka'-ma) which has been passed on from master to disciple over the centuries until the present. But there existed many teachings for which the Tibetan people of that time were not ready, so these were written down by Guru Padmasambhava and his consort, the Tibetan princess Yeshe Tsogyal, and concealed by them in temples, caves, and many other places in Tibet and the Himalayas. He prophesied that in later ages the reincarnations of his original group of disciples would recover these texts and propagate the teachings throughout Tibet. Thus the texts associated with this cycle of the "Tibetan Book of the Dead" were later rediscovered by the Tibetan master Karma Lingpa after their having lain concealed in a cave for many centuries. And for this reason, this Terma cycle is classified as a *sa-gter* or "earth treasure."[3]

As it says in the colophon of the blockprint of the *Bar-do thos-grol*, "These texts have been brought forth from the mountain sGam-po gdar on the banks of the gSer-ldan river by Rig-'dzin Karma gling-pa." The epithet Rigdzin (rig-pa 'dzin-pa), or in Sanskrit Vidyādhara, literally means "knowledge holder." But the knowledge referred to here is not mere intellectual knowledge such as a scholar might acquire through pursuing his researches in books; rather, it indicates the state of intrinsic awareness (rig-pa).[4] Although Rigdzin Karma Lingpa was among the great Tertons (gter-ston) or discoverers of hidden treasure texts, not much is known about his life. In the *Padma bka'-thang bsdus-pa*, a Terma text recovered by Urgyan Lingpa (1323-1360), Guru Padmasambhava is said to have prophesied the appearances in future ages of a number of important great Tertons: "The eight great incarnations as great Bodhisattvas shall be U-rgyan gling-pa in the center, rDo-rje gling-pa in the east, Rinchen gling-pa in the south, Padma gling-pa in the west, Karma gling-pa in the north, bSam-gtan gling-pa and Nyi-zla gling-pa and Zhig-po gling-pa (in the intermediate directions). These eight great Tertons shall appear and shall be my own emanations." As in the pattern of the mandala, here there are five principal Tertons associated with the five directions. Karma Lingpa was one of them and reprsented the Karma family in the north. The term Lingpa (gling-pa) means commander of a region or district, coming from the word *gling*, "region, island, continent."

According to the *gTer-ston brgya rtsa'i rnam-thar* and to the *rNying-ma'i chos-'byung* of Dudjom Rinpoche,[5] the Terton Karma Lingpa was the reincarnation or emanation (sprul-pa) of the translator Chog-ro Lotsawa (Chog-ro lo-tsa-ba kLu'i rgyal-mtshan), a contemporary of the Tibetan king Tisong Detsan (742-797). Then in the fourteenth century there appeared in Tibet a Terton and great adept (grub-chen) by the name of Nyida Sangye (Grub-chen Nyi-zla sangs-rgypas). From among all of the teachings concerning Phowa or the transference of consciousness, called "the practice of Phowa where one can insert a blade of grass (into the hole appearing at the top of the skull)" ('pho-ba 'jag zug-ma zhes-pa 'pho-ba gdams-pa),[6] it was this Terma teaching (gter chos) which became the most important and most widely diffused throughout Tibet. Then in the Fire-Monkey year (1356) at Khyerdrub (khyer-grub) in the upper part of Dwagpo (Dwags-po), which is a district to the southeast of Central Tibet, his eldest son was born. This son later became known as Karma Lingpa (1356-1405).

As a boy he practiced many different Tantric methods and developed without obstacle many powers, such as the six clairvoyant powers (mngon-shes drug), and so on.[7] Then at the age of fifteen there occurred an auspicious conjunction of events (rten 'brel): he received a prophecy together with certain favorable indications. Thus it came about that he discovered as hidden treasures (gter-ma) many profound teachings (zab chos), extracting them from the mountain of Gampodar (sgam-po gdar) which resembles in its form a dancing attendant deity (lha bran gar byed-pa 'dra-ba) in the eastern district of Dwagpo. In general, these treasure teachings (gter chos) belonged to two principal Terma cycles: the *Thugs-rje chen-po padma zhi-khro* and the *Zab-chos zhi-khro dgongs-pa rang-grol*. He entrusted his fourteen disciples with the entire cycle of the *Padma zhi-khro* and commissioned them to be the custodians of the teaching (chos-bdag). But he transmitted the cycle of the *Zab-chos zhi-khro dgongs-pa rang-grol* only to his own son Nyida Chorje (Nyi-zla chos-rje) and admonished him to deliver this cycle only to a single individual until the third generation. Because there did not occur the auspicious conjunction of events (rten 'brel ma 'grigs-pa'i rkyen gyis) of his meeting and uniting with the prophesied wife (gzung-ma) or secret consort (gsang yum) and, in addition, certain auspicious signs were not realized, he did not live for a very long time, but soon passed into Nirvāna (zhi-bar gshegs-pa).[8]

His son Nyida Chorje transmitted the cycle of *Zhi-khro* teachings to Namkha Chokyi Gyatso (Nam-mkha' chos kyi rgya-mtso) who represented the third generation mentioned in the prophecy. He primarily spread the precepts of the *Kar-gling zhi-khro*[9] in the provinces of central Tibet and in Eastern Tibet, especially in Dokham (mdo-khams), both the north and the south. The initiations, the scriptural authorizations, and the explanatory instuctions (dbang lung khrid) of this transmission are still intact. In particular, the *Bar-do thos-grol* teachings spread far and wide everywhere in Tibet. In general, it may be said that the *Kar-gling zhi-khro* is the most complete of any of the extant *Zhi-khro* teachings and has become very widely disseminated, especially among the Nyingmapas and the Kagyudpas, and now elsewhere throughout the world.

In the Nyingmapa school which preserves the most ancient traditions of Buddhist teachings in Tibet, Dzogchen is also known as Atiyoga, a term often interpreted to mean "the Primordial Yoga" (gdod-ma'i rnal-'byor). It represents the ninth and highest vehicle among the Nine Vehicles (theg-pa rim dgu) into which the teachings of the Buddha are classified in the Nyingmapa system.[10] But, although Dzogchen has usually been linked to the Nyingmapa school because of its role in Tibet of being the custodian of the traditions deriving from the Early Translation period (7-9 cen. CE), Dzogchen itself is not a school or a sect as such and its introduction into Tibet long antedates the rise of religious sects among Tibetan Buddhists.

The Tibetan term Dzogchen (rdzogs-pa chen-po), corresponding to the Sanskrit *mahāsandhi*, is usually translated as "the Great Perfection" and refers to the primordial state of the individual (kun-bzang dgongs-pa)[11] which is beyond time and conditioning—that is to say, it is one's inherent Buddha-nature and is synonymous with the nature of the mind. This nature of the mind (sems nyid) transcends the specific contents of mind, that is, the incessant stream of thoughts continuously arising in the mind which reflects our psychological, cultural, and social conditioning. This distinction between the nature of the mind (sems nyid) and the mind (sems) or thought process is crucial to the understanding of Dzogchen. We can make a similar distinction between the mirror which possesses the natural and inherent capacity to reflect whatever is set before it and the reflections that appear in the mirror. The capacity possessed by the nature of the mind to be aware is what is called *rig-pa*, which we translate as "intrinsic awareness" or "immediate presence." The opposite of *rig-pa* is *ma rig-pa* (Skt. avidyā), the absence of awareness, and this ignorance is the source of attachment and of all the suffering experienced in Saṃsāra, the cycle of transmigration.[12] This Rigpa is the central subject of the text we have here and its transmission serves as a direct introduction (ngo-sprod), as when meeting someone for the first time face to face, to this state of intrinsic awareness.

The well-known earlier translation of this same text serves as the center-piece in *The Tibetan Book of the Great Liberation* by W.Y. Evans-Wentz.[13] However, there are profound problems with that version, touching on the most fundamental issues of Dzogchen and, indeed, of Buddhism generally. For instance, no such concept as Evans-Wentz' "Knowing the One Mind, the Cosmic All-Consciousness" is actually found in the original Tibetan text or in the oral commentaries of the Tibetan Lamas on this text.[14] Evans-Wentz, who did not read any Tibetan himself, worked on the editing and explicating of this translation made by others at a time when next to nothing was known in the West about Dzogchen, and so he made a number of fundamental errors and arrived at basic misinterpretations as to the meaning of the text. This, in turn, led Dr. Carl Jung to come to a series of wrong conclusions regarding Dzogchen in particular and Tibetan spirituality in general. Thus I felt that the effort to make a new translation was both timely and worthwhile. The inadequacies of the earlier translation and, in particular, the misrepresentation of Dzogchen on the part of Evans-Wentz are dealt with in Appendix I.

The following translation was done in collaboration with Lama Tharchin of Kongpo. Subsequently, Prof. Namkhai Norbu of the Oriental Institute of the University of Naples was consulted with regard to the difficult problem of translating and interpreting the Tibetan technical terms employed in the Dzogchen texts. Deciphering the text also presented many problems. The Tibetan woodblock we used here for this translation, which was obtained some years ago in

Nepal, appears to have a number of scribal errors. Prof. Norbu has very kindly corrected them, and the resulting corrected version is included at the end of the book. The notes to the translation which will be found following it are put into the form of a running commentary rather than the usual scholarly apparatus. It was felt that this would make the notes much more accessible to the non-specialized reader, while drawing on the rich heritage of oral interpretation provided by Lama Tharchin, Prof. Namkhai Norbu, and a number of other learned Tibetan Lamas. In order to facilitate understanding the translation, I have provided an outline of its contents and divided the translation into twenty-eight sections. These and the sections of the commentary correspond accordingly. A glossary of Tibetan terms will also be found at the end of the book.

Vajranātha (John Myrdhin Reynolds)

Self-Liberation
Through Seeing with Naked Awareness

ༀ༅། །ྂ་མཚར་བ་དག་རྒྱས་པ་ཧྲཱ་སྤྲེལ། །སྐྱེ་འཆི་མི་མངའ་རྗེ་རྗེ་རི་སྲུ། །

དུས་གསུམ་རྒྱལ་ཀུན་ཕྲིན་ལས་མཛད། །པདྨ་འབྱུང་གནས་ལ་ཕྱག་འཚལ། །

PADMASAMBHAVA—THE LOTUS BORN GURU

Translation of the Text

1 Here is contained "Self-Liberation through Seeing with Naked Awareness," this being a Direct Introduction to the State of Intrinsic Awareness, ⁍
From "The Profound Teaching of Self-Liberation in the Primordial State of the Peaceful and Wrathful Deities." ⁍

2 Homage to the Trikāya and to the Deities who represent the inherent luminous clarity of intrinsic awareness. ⁍

3 Herein I shall teach "Self-Liberation through Seeing with Naked Awareness," which is a direct introduction to intrinsic awareness ⁍
From "The Profound Teaching of Self-Liberation in the Primordial State of the Peaceful and Wrathful Deities." ⁍
Truly, this introduction to your own intrinsic awareness ⁍
Should be contemplated well, O fortunate sons of a noble family! ⁍
SAMAYA ⁍   gya gya gya ⁍

4 Emaho! ⁍
It is the single (nature of) mind which encompasses all of Saṃsāra and Nirvāṇa. ⁍
Even though its inherent nature has existed from the very beginning, you have not recognized it. ⁍
Even though its clarity and presence has been uninterrupted, you have not yet encountered its face. ⁍
Even though its arising has nowhere been obstructed, still you have not comprehended it. ⁍

9

Therefore, this (direct introduction) is for the purpose of bringing you to self-recognition. ⸗

Everything that is expounded by the Victorious Ones of the three times ⸗

In the eighty-four thousand Gateways to the Dharma ⸗

Is incomprehensible (unless you understand intrinsic awareness). ⸗

Indeed, the Victorious Ones do not teach anything other than the understanding of this. ⸗

Even though there exist unlimited numbers of scriptures, equal in their extent to the sky, ⸗

Yet with respect to the real meaning, there are three statements that will introduce you to your own intrinsic awareness. ⸗

This introduction to the manifest Primordial State of the Victorious One ⸗

Is disclosed by the following method for entering into the practice where there exists no antecedent nor subsequent practices. ⸗

5   Kye-ho! ⸗

O my fortunate sons, listen! ⸗

Even though that which is usually called "mind" is widely esteemed and much discussed, ⸗

Still it is not understood or it is wrongly understood or it is understood in a one-sided manner only. ⸗

Since it is not understood correctly just as it is in itself, ⸗

There come into existence inconceivable numbers of philosophical ideas and assertions. ⸗

Furthermore, since ordinary individuals do not understand it, ⸗

They do not recognize their own nature, ⸗

And so they continue to wander among the six destinies (of rebirth) within the three worlds and thus experience suffering. ⸗

Therefore, not understanding your own mind is a very grievous fault. ⸗

Even though the Śrāvakas and the Pratyekabuddhas wish to understand it in terms of the Anātman doctrine, ⸗

Still they do not understand it as it is in itself. ⸗

Also there exist others who, being attached to their own personal ideas and interpretations, ⸗

Become fettered by these attachments and so do not perceive the Clear Light. ⁝

The Śrāvakas and the Pratyekabuddhas are (mentally) obscured by their attachments to subject and object. ⁝

The Mādhyamikas are (mentally) obscured by their attachments to the extremes of the Two Truths. ⁝

The practitioners of the Kriyā Tantra and the Yoga Tantra are (mentally) obscured by their attachments to sevā-sādhana practice. ⁝

The practitioners of the Mahāyoga and the Anuyoga are (mentally) obscured by their attachments to Space and Awareness. ⁝

And with respect to the real meaning of nonduality, since they divide these (Space and Awareness) into two, they fall into deviation. ⁝

If these two do not become one without any duality, you will certainly not attain Buddhahood. ⁝

In terms of your own mind, as is the case with everyone, Samsāra and Nirvāna are inseparable. ⁝

Nonetheless, because you persist in accepting and enduring attachments and aversions, you will continue to wander in Samsāra. ⁝

Therefore, your active dharmas and your inactive ones both should be abandoned. ⁝

However, since self-liberation through seeing nakedly by means of intrinsic awareness is here revealed to you, ⁝

You should understand that all dharmas can be perfected and completed in the great total Self-Liberation. ⁝

And therefore, whatever (practice you do) can be brought to perfection within the Great Perfection. ⁝

SAMAYA ⁝   gya gya gya ⁝

6   As for this sparkling awareness which is called "mind," ⁝
Even though one says that it exists, it does not actually exist. ⁝
(On the other hand) as a source, it is the origin of the diversity of all the bliss of Nirvāna and all of the sorrow of Samsāra. ⁝
And as for its being something desirable, it is cherished alike in the Eleven Vehicles. ⁝

With respect to its having a name, the various names that are applied to it are inconceivable (in their numbers). ⸸

Some call it "the nature of the mind" or "mind itself." ⸸

Some Tīrthikas call it by the name Ātman or "the Self." ⸸

The Śrāvakas call it the doctrine of Anātman or "the absence of a self." ⸸

The Chittamātrins call it by the name Chitta or "the Mind." ⸸

Some call it the Prajnāpāramitā or "the Perfection of Wisdom." ⸸

Some call it the name Tathāgatagarbha or "the embryo of Buddhahood." ⸸

Some call it by the name Mahāmudrā or "the Great Symbol." ⸸

Some call it by the name "the Unique Sphere." ⸸

Some call it by the name Dharmadhātu or "the dimension of Reality." ⸸

Some call it by the name Ālaya or "the basis of everything." ⸸

And some simply call it by the name "ordinary awareness." ⸸

7   Now, when you are introduced (to your own intrinsic awareness), the method for entering into it involves three considerations: ⸸

Thoughts in the past are clear and empty and leave no traces behind. ⸸

Thoughts in the future are fresh and unconditioned by anything. ⸸

And in the present moment, when (your mind) remains in its own condition without constructing anything, ⸸

Awareness at that moment in itself is quite ordinary. ⸸

And when you look into yourself in this way nakedly (without any discursive thoughts), ⸸

Since there is only this pure observing, there will be found a lucid clarity without anyone being there who is the observer; ⸸

Only a naked manifest awareness is present. ⸸

(This awareness) is empty and immaculately pure, not being created by anything whatsoever. ⸸

It is authentic and unadulterated, without any duality of clarity and emptiness. ⸸

It is not permanent and yet it is not created by anything. ⸸

However, it is not a mere nothingness or something annihilated because it is lucid and present. ⁝

It does not exist as a single entity because it is present and clear in terms of being many. ⁝

(On the other hand) it is not created as a multiplicity of things because it is inseparable and of a single flavor. ⁝

This inherent self-awareness does not derive from anything outside itself. ⁝

This is the real introduction to the actual condition of things. ⁝

8 Within this (intrinsic awareness), the Trikāya are inseparable and fully present as one. ⁝

Since it is empty and not created anywhere whatsoever, it is the Dharmakāya. ⁝

Since its luminous clarity represents the inherent transparent radiance of emptiness, it is the Sambhogakāya. ⁝

Since its arising is nowhere obstructed or interrupted, it is the Nirmānakāya. ⁝

These three (the Trikāya) being complete and fully present as one, are its very essence. ⁝

9 When you are introduced in this way through this exceedingly powerful method for entering into the practice, ⁝

(You discover directly) that your own immediate self-awareness is just this (and nothing else), ⁝

And that it has an inherent self-clarity which is entirely unfabricated. ⁝

How can you then speak of not understanding the nature of the mind? ⁝

Moreover, since you are meditating without finding anything there to meditate upon, ⁝

How can you say that your meditation does not go well? ⁝

Since your own manifest intrinsic awareness is just this, ⁝

How can you say that you cannot find your own mind? ⁝

The mind is just that which is thinking; ⁝

And yet, although you have searched (for the thinker), how can you say that you do not find him? ⁝

With respect to this, nowhere does there exist the one who is the cause of (mental) activity. ⁝

And yet, since activity exists, how can you say that such activity does not arise? ༔

Since merely allowing (thoughts) to settle into their own condition, without trying to modify them in any way, is sufficient, ༔

How can you say that you are not able to remain in a calm state? ༔

Since allowing (thoughts) to be just as they are, without trying to do anything about them, is sufficient, ༔

How can you say that you are not able to do anything with regard to them? ༔

Since clarity, awareness, and emptiness are inseparable and are spontaneously self-perfected, ༔

How can you say that nothing is accomplished by your practice? ༔

Since (intrinsic awareness) is self-originated and spontaneously self-perfected without any antecedent causes or conditions, ༔

How can you say that you are not able to accomplish anything by your efforts? ༔

Since the arising of discursive thoughts and their being liberated occur simultaneously, ༔

How can you say that you are unable to apply an antidote? ༔

Since your own immediate awareness is just this, ༔

How can you say that you do not know anything with regard to it? ༔

10 It is certain that the nature of the mind is empty and without any foundation whatsoever. ༔

Your own mind is insubstantial like the empty sky. ༔

You should look at your own mind to see whether it is like that or not. ༔

Being without any view that decisively decides that it is empty, ༔

It is certain that self-originated primal awareness has been clear (and luminous) from the very beginning, ༔

Like the heart of the sun, which is itself self-originated. ༔

You should look at your own mind to see whether it is like that or not. ༔

It is certain that this primal awareness or gnosis, which is one's intrinsic awareness, is unceasing, ༔

Like the main channel of a river that flows unceasingly. ༔

You should look at your own mind to see whether it is like that
or not. ⦂

It is certain that the diversity of movements (arising in the mind)
are not apprehendable by memories, ⦂

They are like insubstantial breezes that move through the atmosphere. ⦂

You should look at your own mind to see whether it is like that
or not. ⦂

It is certain that whatever appearances occur, all of them are
self-manifested, ⦂

Like the images in a mirror being self-manifestations that simply
appear. ⦂

You should look at you own mind to see whether it is like that
or not. ⦂

It is certain that all of the diverse characteristics of things are
liberated into their own condition, ⦂

Like clouds in the atmosphere that are self-originated and self-
liberated. ⦂

You should look at your own mind to see whether it is like that
or not. ⦂

11 There exist no phenomena other than what arises from the
mind. ⦂

Other than the meditation that occurs, where is the one who is
meditating? ⦂

There exist no phenomena other than what arises from the
mind. ⦂

Other than the behavior that occurs, where is the one who is
behaving? ÷

There exist no phenomena other than what arises from the
mind. ⦂

Other than the samaya vow that occurs, where is the one who is
guarding it? ⦂

There exist no phenomena other than what arises from the
mind. ⦂

Other than the fruition that occurs, where is the one who is
realizing (the fruit)? ⦂

You should look at your own mind, observing it again and again. ⁝

12 When you look upward into the space of the sky outside yourself, ⁝
    If there are no thoughts occurring that are emanations being projected, ⁝
    And when you look inward at your own mind inside yourself, ⁝
    If there exists no projectionist who projects thoughts by thinking them, ⁝
    Then your own subtle mind will become lucidly clear without anything being projected. ⁝
    Since the Clear Light of your own intrinsic awareness is empty, it is the Dharmakāya; ⁝
    And this is like the sun rising in a cloudless illuminated sky. ⁝
    Even though (this light cannot be said) to possess a particular shape or form, nevertheless, it can be fully known. ⁝
    The meaning of this, whether or not it is understood, is especially significant. ⁝

13 This self-originated Clear Light, which from the very beginning was in no way produced (by something antecedent to it), ⁝
    Is the child of awareness, and yet it is itself without any parents— amazing! ⁝
    This self-originated primordial awareness has not been created by anything—amazing! ⁝
    It does not experience birth nor does there exist a cause for its death—amazing! ⁝
    Although it is evidently visible, yet there is no one there who sees it—amazing! ⁝
    Although it has wandered throughout Samsāra, it has come to no harm—amazing! ⁝
    Even though it has seen Buddhahood itself, it has not come to any benefit from this—amazing! ⁝
    Even though it exists in everyone everywhere, yet it has gone unrecognized—amazing! ⁝
    Nevertheless, you hope to attain some other fruit than this elsewhere—amazing! ⁝

Even though it exists within yourself (and nowhere else), yet you seek for it elsewhere—amazing! ⁝

14 How wonderful! ⁝
This immediate intrinsic awareness is insubstantial and lucidly clear. ⁝
Just this is the highest pinnacle among all views. ⁝
It is all-encompassing, free of everything, and without any conceptions whatsoever: ⁝
Just this is the highest pinnacle among all meditations. ⁝
It is unfabricated and inexpressible in worldly terms: ⁝
Just this is the highest pinnacle among all courses of conduct. ⁝
Without being sought after, it is spontaneously self-perfected from the very beginning: ⁝
Just this is the highest pinnacle among all fruits. ⁝

15 Here is the teaching of the four great vehicles that are without error: ⁝
(First) there is the great vehicle of the unmistaken view. ⁝
Since this immediate awareness is lucidly clear, ⁝
And this lucid clarity is without error or mistake, it is called "a vehicle." ⁝
(Second) there is the great vehicle of the unmistaken meditation. ⁝
Since this immediate awareness is that which possesses clarity, ⁝
And this lucid clarity is without error or mistake, it is called "a vehicle." ⁝
(Third) there is the great vehicle of the unmistaken conduct. ⁝
Since this immediate primal awareness is that which possesses clarity, ⁝
And this lucid clarity is without error or mistake, it is called "a vehicle." ⁝
(Fourth) there is the great vehicle of the unmistaken fruit. ⁝
Since this immediate awareness is lucidly clear, ⁝
And this lucid clarity is without error or mistake, it is called "a vehicle." ⁝

16 Here is the teaching on the four great unchanging (essential points called) "nails." ⁝

(First) there is the great nail of the unchanging view: ፥
This immediate present awareness is lucidly clear. ፥
Because it is stable in the three times, it is called "a nail." ፥
(Second) there is the great nail of the unchanging meditation: ፥
This immediate present awareness is lucidly clear. ፥
Because it is stable in the three times, it is called "a nail." ፥
(Third) there is the great nail of the unchanging conduct: ፥
This immediate present awareness is lucidly clear. ፥
Because it is stable in the three times, it is called "a nail." ፥
(Fourth) there is the great nail of the unchanging fruit: ፥
This immediate present awareness is lucidly clear. ፥
Because it is stable in the three times, it is called "a nail." ፥

17 Then, as for the secret instruction which teaches that the three
    times are one: ፥
You should relinquish all notions of the past and abandon all
    precedents. ፥
You should cut off all plans and expectations with respect to the
    future. ፥
And in the present, you should not grasp (at thoughts that arise)
    but allow (the mind) to remain in a state like the sky. ፥
Since there is nothing upon which to meditate (while in the pri-
    mordial state), there is no need to meditate. ፥
And since there does not exist any distraction here, you continue
    in this state of stable mindfulness without distraction. ፥
In this state which is without meditation and without any distrac-
    tion, you observe everything with a naked (awareness). ፥
Your own awareness is inherently knowing, inherently clear, and
    luminously brilliant. ፥
When it arises, it is called the Bodhichitta, "the enlightened
    mind." ፥
Being without any activity of meditation, it transcends all objects
    of knowledge. ፥
Being without any distraction, it is the luminous clarity of the
    Essence itself. ፥
Appearances, being empty in themselves, become self-liberated;
    clarity and emptiness (being inseparable) are the Dhar-
    makāya. ፥

Since it becomes evident that there is nothing to be realized by means of the path to Buddhahood, ᣟ
At this time you will actually behold Vajrasattva. ᣟ

18 Then, as for the instruction for exhausting the six extremes and overthrowing them: ᣟ
Even though there exist a great many different views that do not agree among themselves, ᣟ
This "mind" which is your own intrinsic awareness is in fact self-originated primal awareness. ᣟ
And with regard to this, the observer and the process of observing are not two (different things). ᣟ
When you look and observe, seeking the one who is looking and observing, ᣟ
Since you search for this observer and do not find him, ᣟ
At that time your view is exhausted and overthrown. ᣟ
Thus, even though it is the end of your view, this is the beginning with respect to yourself. ᣟ
The view and the one who is viewing are not found to exist anywhere. ᣟ
Without its falling excessively into emptiness and non-existence even at the beginning, ᣟ
At this very moment your own present awareness becomes lucidly clear. ᣟ
Just this is the view (or the way of seeing) of the Great Perfection. ᣟ
(Therefore) understanding and not understanding are not two (different things). ᣟ

19 Although there exist a great many different meditations that do not agree among themselves, ᣟ
Your own ordinary present awareness is directly penetrating. ᣟ
The process of meditation and the one who meditates are not two (different things). ᣟ
When you look for the meditator who is meditating or not meditating, ᣟ
Since you have searched for this meditator and have not found him anywhere, ᣟ

At that time your meditation is exhausted and overthrown. ⁝
Thus, even though it is the end of your meditation, this is the beginning with respect to yourself. ⁝
The meditation and the meditator are not found to exist anywhere. ⁝
Without its falling under the power of delusion, drowsiness, or agitation, ⁝
Your immediate unfabricated awareness becomes lucidly clear; ⁝
And this unmodified state of even contemplation is concentration. ⁝
(Therefore) remaining in a calm state or not remaining in it are not two (different things). ⁝

20 Although there exist a great many different kinds of behavior which do not agree among themselves, ⁝
Your own self-originated primal awareness is the Unique Sphere. ⁝
Behavior and the one who behaves are not two (different things). ⁝
When you look for the one it is who behaves with action or without action, ⁝
Since you have searched for the one who acts and have not found him anywhere, ⁝
At that time your behavior is exhausted and overthrown. ⁝
Thus, even though it is the end of your conduct and behavior, this is the beginning with respect to yourself. ⁝
From the very beginning neither behavior nor the one who behaves have existed (as separate realities). ⁝
Without its falling under the power of errors and inherited predispositions, ⁝
Your immediate awareness is an unfabricated inherent clarity. ⁝
Without accepting or rejecting anything, just letting things be as they are without trying to modify them, ⁝
Such conduct or behavior alone is pure. ⁝
(Therefore) pure and impure action are not two (different things). ⁝

21 Although there exist a great many different fruits that do not agree among themselves, ⁝

The nature of the mind that is inherent awareness is (none other than) the spontaneously perfected Trikāya. ̊

What is realized and the one who realizes it are not two (different things). ̊

When you look for the fruit and for the one who has realized it, ̊

Since you have searched for the realizer (of the fruit) and have not found him anywhere, ̊

At that time your fruit is exhausted and overthrown. ̊

Thus, even though it is an end to your fruition, still this is the beginning with respect to yourself. ̊

Both the fruition and the one who has attained the realization are found to not exist anywhere. ̊

Without its falling under the power of attachments or aversions or of hopes and fears, ̊

Your immediate present awareness becomes spontaneously perfected inherent clarity. ̊

Understand that within yourself the Trikāya is fully manifest. ̊

(Therefore) this itself is the fruition of primordial Buddhahood. ̊

22 This intrinsic awareness is free of the eight extremes, such as eternalism and nihilism, and the rest. ̊

Thus we speak of the Middle Way where one does not fall into any of the extremes, ̊

And we speak of intrinsic awareness as uninterrupted mindful presence. ̊

Since emptiness possesses a heart that is intrinsic awareness, ̊

Therefore it is called by the name of Tathāgatagarbha, that is, "the embryo or heart of Buddhahood." ̊

If you understand the meaning of this, then that will transcend and surpass everything else. ̊

Therefore, it is called by the name of Prajnāpāramitā, that is, "the Perfection of Wisdom." ̊

Because it cannot be conceived of by the intellect and is free of all (conceptual) limitations from the very beginning, ̊

Therefore it is called by the name of Mahāmudrā, that is, "the Great Symbol." ̊

Because of that, in accordance with whether it is specifically understood or not understood, ̊

Since it is the basis of everything, of all the bliss of Nirvāna and of all the sorrow of Samsāra, ⁚

Therefore it is called by the name of Ālaya, that is, "the foundation of everything." ⁚

Because, when it remains in its own space, it is quite ordinary and in no way exceptional, ⁚

This awareness that is present and lucidly clear ⁚

Is called by the name of "ordinary awareness." ⁚

However many names may be applied to it, even though they are well conceived and fancy sounding, ⁚

With regard to its real meaning, it is just this immediate present awareness (and nothing else). ⁚

23 To desire something other than this ⁚

Is just like having an elephant (at home), but searching for its tracks elsewhere. ⁚

Even though you may try to measure the universe with a tape measure, it will not be possible to encompass all of it. ⁚

(Similarly) if you do not understand that everything derives from the mind, it will not be possible for you to attain Buddhahood. ⁚

By not recognizing this (intrinsic awareness for what it is), you will then search for your mind somewhere outside of yourself. ⁚

If you seek for yourself elsewhere (outside of yourself), how can you ever find yourself? ⁚

For example, this is just like an idiot who, going into a crowd of many people, ⁚

And having let himself become confused because of the spectacle, ⁚

Does not recognize himself; and, even though he searches for himself everywhere, ⁚

He continually makes the error of mistaking others for himself. ⁚

(Similarly) since you do not see the natural condition of the real disposition of things, ⁚

You do not know that appearances come from mind, and so you are thrust once again into Samsāra. ⁚

By not seeing that your own mind is actually the Buddha,
Nirvāna becomes obscured. ፧

With respect to Samsāra and Nirvāna, (the difference is simply
due) to ignorance or to awareness respectively. ፧

But at this single instant (of pure awareness), there is in fact no
actual difference between them (in terms of their essence). ፧

If you come to perceive them as existing somewhere other than
in your own mind, this is surely an error. ፧

(Therefore) error and non-error are actually of a single essence
(which is the nature of the mind). ፧

Since the mind-streams of sentient beings are not made into
something that is divided into two, ፧

The unmodified uncorrected nature of the mind is liberated by its
being allowed simply to remain in its own (original) natural
condition. ፧

If you are not aware that the fundamental error or delusion
comes from the mind, ፧

You will not properly understand the real meaning of the Dharmatā (the nature of reality); ፧

24 You should look into what is self-arising and self-originated. ፧

With respect to these appearances, in the beginning they must
arise from somewhere, ፧

In between they must remain somewhere, and at the end they
must go somewhere. ፧

Yet when you look (into this matter), it is, for example, like a
crow gazing into a well. ፧

When he flies away from the well, (his reflection) also departs
from the well and does not return. ፧

In the same way appearances arise from the mind; ፧

They arise from the mind and are liberated into the mind. ፧

The nature of the mind which (has the capacity) to know everything and be aware of everything is empty and clear; ፧

As is the case with the sky above, its emptiness and its clarity
have been inseparable from the very beginning. ፧

Self-originated primal awareness becomes manifest, ፧

And becoming systematically established as luminous clarity, just
this is the Dharmatā, the nature of reality. ፧

Even though the indication of its existence is all phenomenal existence (which manifests externally to you), ⁝

You are aware of it in your own mind, and this latter is the nature of the mind. ⁝

Since it is aware and clear, it is understood to be like the sky. ⁝

However, even though we employ the example of the sky to indicate the nature of the mind, ⁝

This is in fact only a metaphor or simile indicating things in a one-sided fashion. ⁝

The nature of the mind, as well as being empty, is also intrinsically aware; everywhere it is clear. ⁝

But the sky is without any awareness; it is empty as an inanimate corpse is empty. ⁝

Therefore, the real meaning of "mind" is not indicated by the sky. ⁝

So without distraction, simply allow (the mind) to remain in the state of being just as it is. ⁝

25   Moreover, as for this diversity of appearances, which represents relative truth, ⁝

Not even one of these appearances is actually created in reality, and so accordingly they disappear again. ⁝

All things, all phenomenal existence, everything within Samsāra and Nirvāna, ⁝

Are merely appearances (or phenomena) which are perceived by the individual's single nature of the mind. ⁝

On any particular occasion, when your own (internal) mind-stream undergoes changes, ⁝

Then there will arise appearances which you will perceive as external changes. ⁝

Therefore, everything that you see is a manifestation of mind. ⁝

And, moreover, all of the beings inhabiting the six realms of rebirth, perceive everything with their own distinct karmic vision. ⁝

26   The Tīrthikas who are outsiders see all this in terms of the dualism of eternalism as against nihilism. ⁝

Each of the nine successive vehicles sees things in terms of its own view. ⁝

Thus, things are perceived in various different ways and may be elucidated in various different ways. ⦂

Because you grasped at these various (appearances that arise), becoming attached to them, errors have come into existence. ⦂

Yet with respect to all of these appearances of which you are aware in your mind, ⦂

Even though these appearances that you perceive do arise, if you do not grasp at them, then that is Buddhahood. ⦂

Appearances are not erroneous in themselves, but because of your grasping at them, errors come into existence. ⦂

But if you know that these thoughts only grasp at things which are mind, then they will be liberated by themselves. ⦂

Everything that appears is but a manifestation of mind. ⦂

Even though the entire external inanimate universe appears to you, it is but a manifestation of mind. ⦂

Even though all of the sentient beings of the six realms appear to you, they are but a manifestation of mind. ⦂

Even though the happiness of humans and the delights of the Devas in heaven appear to you, they are but manifestations of mind. ⦂

Even though the sorrows of the three evil destinies appear to you, they are but manifestations of mind. ⦂

Even though the five poisons representing ignorance and the passions appear to you, they are but manifestations of mind. ⦂

Even though intrinsic awareness which is self-originated primal awareness appears to you, it is but a manifestation of mind. ⦂

Even though good thoughts along the way to Nirvāna appear to you, they are but manifestations of mind. ⦂

Even though obstacles due to demons and evil spirits appear to you, they are but manifestations of mind. ⦂

Even though the gods and other excellent attainments appear to you, they are but manifestations of mind. ⦂

Even though various kinds of purity appear to you, they are but manifestations of mind. ⦂

Even though (the experience) of remaining in a state of one-pointed concentration without any discursive thoughts appears to you, it is but a manifestation of mind. ⦂

Even though the colors that are the characteristics of things appear to you, they are but manifestations of mind. ⁞

Even though a state without characteristics and without conceptual elaborations appears to you, it is but a manifestation of mind. ⁞

Even though the nonduality of the one and the many appears to you, it is but a manifestation of mind. ⁞

Even though existence and non-existence which are not created anywhere appear to you, they are but manifestations of mind. ⁞

There exist no appearances whatsoever that can be understood as not coming from mind. ⁞

27 Because of the unobstructed nature of the mind, there is a continuous arising of appearances. ⁞

Like the waves and the waters of the ocean, which are not two (different things), ⁞

Whatever arises is liberated into the natural state of the mind. ⁞

However many different names are applied to it in this unceasing process of naming things, ⁞

With respect to its real meaning, the mind (of the individual) does not exist other than as one. ⁞

And, moreover, this singularity is without any foundation and devoid of any root. ⁞

But, even though it is one, you cannot look for it in any particular direction. ⁞

It cannot be seen as an entity located somewhere, because it is not created or made by anything. ⁞

Nor can it be seen as just being empty, because there exists the transparent radiance of its own luminous clarity and awareness. ⁞

Nor can it be seen as diversified, because emptiness and clarity are inseparable. ⁞

Immediate self-awareness is clear and present. ⁞

Even though activities exist, there is no awareness of an agent who is the actor. ⁞

Even though they are without any inherent nature, experiences are actually experienced. ⁞

If you practice in this way, then everything will be liberated. ⁞

With respect to your own sense faculties, everything will be understood immediately without any intervening operations of the intellect. ᠄

Just as is the case with the sesame seed being the cause of the oil and the milk being the cause of butter, ᠄

But where the oil is not obtained without pressing and the butter is not obtained without churning, ᠄

So all sentient beings, even though they possess the actual essence of Buddhahood, ᠄

Will not realize Buddhahood without engaging in practice. ᠄

If he practices, then even a cowherd can realize liberation. ᠄

Even though he does not know the explanation, he can systematically establish himself in the experience of it. ᠄

(For example) when one has had the experience of actually tasting sugar in one's own mouth, ᠄

One does not need to have that taste explained by someone else. ᠄

Not understanding this (intrinsic awareness) even Panditas can fall into error. ᠄

Even though they are exceedingly learned and knowledgeable in explaining the nine vehicles, ᠄

It will only be like spreading rumors of places which they have not seen personally. ᠄

And with respect to Buddhahood, they will not even approach it for a moment. ᠄

If you understand (intrinsic awareness), all of your merits and sins will be liberated into their own condition. ᠄

But if you do not understand it, any virtuous or vicious deeds that you commit ᠄

Will accumulate as karma leading to transmigration in heavenly rebirth or to rebirth in the evil destinies respectively. ᠄

But if you understand this empty primal awareness which is your own mind, ᠄

The consequences of merit and of sin will never come to be realized, ᠄

Just as a spring cannot originate in the empty sky. ᠄

In the state of emptiness itself, the object of merit or of sin is not even created. ᠄

Therefore, your own manifest self-awareness comes to see everything nakedly. ༔
This self-liberation through seeing with naked awareness is of
such great profundity., ༔
And, this being so, you should become intimately acquainted
with self-awareness. ༔
Profoundly sealed! ༔

28 How wonderful! ༔
As for this "Self-liberation through Seeing with Naked Aware-
ness" which is a direct introduction to one's own intrinsic
awareness, ༔
It is for the benefit of those sentient beings belonging to the later
generations of those future degenerate times ༔
That all of my Tantras, Āgamas, and Upadeśas, ༔
Though necessarily brief and concise, have been composed. ༔
And even though I have disseminated them at the present time,
yet they shall be concealed as precious treasures, ༔
So that those whose good karma ripens in the future shall come
to encounter them. ༔
SAMAYA ༔   gya gya gya ༔

This treatise which is an introduction to one's actual intrinsic
awareness or state of immediate presence ༔
Is entitled "Self-liberation through Seeing with Naked Awareness." ༔
It was composed by Padmasambhava, the Master from Uddiyāna. ༔
Until Samsāra is emptied of living beings, may this Great Work
of liberating them not be abandoned! ༔

(On the full moon day of the eighth month of the Wood-Ox year,
this Terma text entitled the *Rig-pa ngo-sprod gcer mthong rang-
grol*, belonging to the *Zab-chos zhi-khro dgongs-pa rang-grol* cycle of Rigdzin Karma Lingpa, was translated by Vajranātha in the
hope that it will enlighten and benefit all beings. New York, October 1985)

Sarva Mangalam

Outline of the Translation of the Text

I. Introductory Section (sngon-'gro)
   1. The title and its meaning
   2. The homage or verse of invocation
   3. The author's promise to begin where he states his purpose
   4. Direct introduction; the three statements of Garab Dorje
II. Principal Section (dngos-gzhi)
   A. Internal Awareness (nang rig-pa)
   5. Those who do not understand "mind"; mind vs. nature of mind
   6. Stabilizing one's understanding; mind as the source of all the diversity of phenomena; it has different names
   7. Consideration of the three times; mind and time; the extremes of eternalism and nihilism
   8. The Trikāya is wholly present as the nature of the mind which is the Base
   9. Mind-guidance (sems khrid) bringing one to self-recognition
   10. Metaphors to illustrate the nature of the mind
   11. Meditation (bsgom-pa) and conduct (spyod-pa)
   12. Self-observation of the mind; observing where thoughts arise, abide, and dissolve, and not finding that
   13. Paradoxes regarding awareness and the nature of mind
   14. The highest pinnacles of the view, meditation, conduct, and fruit
   15. The four great vehicles of the view, meditation, conduct, and fruit

29

Commentary to the Translation

(The numbered sections here correspond to the numbered sections in the foregoing translation).

1 The title of this text in Tibetan is *Zab-chos zhi-khro dgongs-pa rantg-grol/Rig-pa ngo-sprod gcer mthong rang-grol,* "Self-liberation through seeing with Naked Awareness, being a Direct Introduction to Intrinsic Awareness, from the Profound Teaching of Self-Liberation in the Primordial State of the Peaceful and Wrathful Deities."[1] This title is in three parts:

A. The first part gives the name of the literary cycle to which this text belongs, namely, the *Zab-chos zhi-khro dgongs-pa rang-grol* of the Terton Rigdzin Karma Lingpa (14 cen. CE)—that is to say, "the Profound Teaching (zab chos) of Self-liberation (rang grol) in the Primordial State (dgongs-pa) of the Peaceful and Wrathful Deities (zhi khro)."

The various texts belonging to the *Kar-gling zhi-khro,*[2] of which the text translated here is but one, do not represent the ordinary teachings of the Sūtra system of Buddhism, but are a cycle of special teachings relating to our experiences in the six Bardos or intermediate states (Skt. antarābhava). To be precise, this is a type of teaching known as *bar-do drug khrid,* "explanations giving guidance for the six Bardos."[3] Since this cycle of Terma texts derives from the teachings of Guru Padmasambhava and belong to the class of teachings known as Dzogchen, the entire collection is therefore called "a Profound teaching."

In Tibet, Dzogchen is regarded as the highest teaching of the Buddha. It is usually associated with the Nyingmapa school, although Dzogchen in itself, as pointed out in the introduction above, is beyond any such sectarian limitations. The Tibetan term Dzogchen (rdzogs-pa chen-po) means "the Great Perfection." It is so called because it is complete and perfect in itself (rdzogs-pa), there being nothing lacking in it, and be-

31

cause it is great (chen-po) in the sense that there is nothing greater than it or beyond it. The earliest sources for Dzogchen are the texts known as the Dzogchen Tantras. The teachings of the Buddha are found in the Sūtras and the Tantras. Why did the Buddha teach these diverse types of doctrines? His disciples differed in their capacities to understand His essential teaching and so, as an expression of His great compassion and His skillfulness in means, He taught each disciple at a level corresponding to his degree of comprehension in order that he might understand and be able to practice the teaching. Thus there are found many different kinds of teachings attributed directly to the Buddha and collected together in the Sūtras and the Tantras.

The Nyingmapa system has classified all of these teachings of the Buddha into Nine Yanas or vehicles to enlightenment (theg-pa rim dgu). The first vehicle is that of the Śrāvakayāna (nyan-thos-pa'i theg-pa), "the vehicle of the Listeners," who are the Hīnayāna practitioners or disciples. This path is indicated principally in the discourse that the Buddha gave at the Deer Park near Sarnath which is known as "the First Turning of the Wheel of the Dharma." Here He expounded the Four Holy Truths and the Noble Eightfold Path. These teachings are thoroughly elaborated in the Hīnayāna Sūtras. The second vehicle is that of the Pratyekabuddhayāna (rang rgyal-ba'ı theg-pa), "the Vehicle of the Solitary Buddhas." The Śrāvakas are "listeners" (nyan-thos-pa) because they need to hear (nyan-thos) the oral instructions of the Buddha in order to find the correct path, whereas the Pratyekabuddha (rang rgyal-ba) finds the path on his own (rang) and then lives a life of solitary meditation practice, avoiding communication and contact with humanity. These two vehicles comprise the Hīnayāna or lesser vehicle to enlightenment.

The third vehicle is that of the Bodhisattvayāna (byang-chub sems-dpa'i theg-pa), "the Vehicle of the Enlightened Beings." A Bodhisattva (byang-chub sems-dpa') becomes one by virtue of the Bodhichitta (byang-chub sems), "the thought of enlightenment," which is the resolute intention ɩo attain the enlightenment of a supremely perfect Buddha, not just for his own benefit, but for the sake of liberating all sentient beings from Samsāra. For this reason, this path is known as the Mahāyāna or the greater vehicle to enlightenment. These teachings are found in the Mahāyāna Sūtras which contain the discourses of the Buddha given at the Vulture Park near Rajgir and also elsewhere. These discourses represent the Second and the Third Turnings of the Wheel of the Dharma, where the Buddha expounded the "Perfection of Wisdom" and the "Mind-only" teachings respectively. Out of this developed the two philosophical schools known as the Mādhyamika (dbu-ma-pa), which taught the middle way avoiding all extreme views, and the Yogāchāra of Vijnānavādin (sems-tsam-pa), which principally taught the "mind-only" doctrine. The teachings of the Hīnayāna and the Mahāyāna collectively are known as the Sūtra system (mdo-lugs), and are said to have been revealed by the historical Buddha Sakyamuni, who is the Nirmānakāya aspect of Buddhahood.

The outer or lower Tantras (phyi rgyud) comprise the next three vehicles in this scheme of classification. The methods elucidated in these Tantras employ elaborate rituals and purifications. The fourth vehicle is that of the Kriyā Tantra (bya-ba'i rgyud), where the practice is mainly external, requiring an abundance of ritual activity (bya-ba). The fifth vehicle is that of the Charyā Tantra (spyod-pa'i rgyud), which is partially external and partially internal in terms of practice, and where there are many rules regarding conduct or behavior (spyod-pa). The descriptions found in the Kriyā Tantra and the Charyā Tantra of how Buddhahood is attained is the same as the account found in the Mahāyāna Sūtras. The sixth vehicle is that of the Yoga Tantra (rnal-'byor-pa'i rgyud), where practice is mostly internal and an actual union (rnal-'byor) of the meditation deity and the practitioner is experienced. The teachings found in these outer Tantras are said to have been revealed by Vajrasattva, the Sambhogakāya aspect of the Buddha. Collectively, the teachings of the Tantras, both outer and inner, are known as the Vajrayāna, or the diamond-like vehicle to enlightenment. They are also known, in contrast to the Sūtra system above, as the Tantra system (sngags-lugs), or literally "the Mantra system."

The inner or higher Tantras (nang rgyud) comprise the three highest vehicles: the Mahāyoga, the Anuyoga, and the Atiyoga. The seventh vehicle, the Mahāyoga, which is subdivided into the Tantra section (rgyud-sde) and the Sādhana section (sgrub-sde), employs elaborate mandalas and puts the emphasis on the Generation Process (bskyed-rim) or stages of creation. This is a process of gradual transformation, so that the visualization of the deity and the mandala are created or generated in successive stages. The method of the Tantras is properly that of transformation, the alchemical transmutation of the poison of the passions within the vessel of one's own body into the elixir of enlightened awareness (ye-shes). This process culminates in the realization of the experience of the inseparability of clarity and emptiness (gsal stong dbyer-med). The newer schools of Tibetan Buddhism: the Sakyapa, the Kagyudpa, and the Gelupa, relying upon the later transla-tions of Indian Tantric texts, speak of the Anuttara Tantras, and these are said to correspond more or less to the older classification called Mahāyoga Tantras.

The eighth vehicle, the Anuyoga, puts the emphasis on the Perfection Process (rdzogs-rim) or stages of perfection, which makes extensive use of the yoga of the channels and the energies (rtsa rlung). This process brings the practitioner to the realization of the inseparability of bliss and emptiness (bde stong dbyer-med). Here the method of transformation differs from that in Mahāyoga, in that it may either be gradual or nongradual.

The ninth and highest vehicle, the Atiyoga, is also known as Dzogchen (rdzogs-pa chen-po, Skt. Mahāsandhi), which, as we said above, means the Great Perfection. Here in Atiyoga the elaborate visualizations of mandalas, as well as the internal yoga of the channels and energies, and so on, are no longer necessary, for the emphasis is put on how to enter directly into the state of contemplation (ting-nge-'dzin, Skt. samādhi) and the ensuing realization of the inseparability of awareness and emptiness (rig stong dbyer-med). Among the Dzogchen Tantras, there are found three series of teachings:

1. The *Semde* (sems sde) or "Mind series" provides a rather intellectual approach, a step by step explanation of how to enter into the state of contemplation, and is rather similar to the Mahāmudrā system of the Anuttara Tantras.

2. The *Longde* (klong sde) or "Space series" is more direct in its approach; the stages occur simultaneously rather than sequentially as they do in the Mind series.

3. Finally there is the *Upadeśa* (man-ngag gi sde) or "Secret Instruction series" which assumes that one already knows how to enter into contemplation, and so it gives advice on and methods for continuing in the state of contemplation. All of these teachings which are found in the Dzogchen Tantras are said to have originated with the Primordial Buddha, the Dharmakāya aspect of Buddhahood.

How have these teachings of Dzogchen come down to us at the present time? There are three principle ways in which this may occur:

1. *Kāma* (bka'-ma) is a continuous "tradition" which goes back to the enlightened masters of the past, such as Padmasambhava, Vimalamitra, Vairochana, and so on, and has been transmitted down through the centuries in an unbroken lineage of masters and disciples. Therefore it represents a distant or long lineage of transmission (ring brgyud).

2. *Terma* (gter-ma) or "a hidden treasure" is a teaching given by an enlightened master in a previous age, this usually being Guru Padmasambhava; then it was written down and subsequently hidden away, to be rediscovered at a later time. One who discovers such a hidden treasure text is known as a Terton (gter-ston); and since the

Termas were rediscovered at a much later time and closer to the present, they represent a short lineage of transmission (nye brgyud).

3. *Dag-nang* (dag-snang) or "pure vision" is a term designating the inner experiences of individual masters.

The collection of texts which we have here, the *Kar-gling zhi-khro*, are Terma. They are attributed to Guru Padmasambhava (8 cen. CE) in terms of their origin and were recovered later by the Terton Karma Lingpa (14 cen. CE); thus they are *sa-gter* or "earth treasures."

Why is this Terma cycle called the *Zab-chos zhi-khro dgongs-pa rang-grol?* We have already explained above that, since the teachings found here belong to Dzogchen or the Great Perfection system, they are called "profound teachings." What is the method or path specific to Dzogchen? Whereas the Sūtra system represents the path of renunciation (spong lam) and the method of the Tantras is the path of transformation (sgyur lam), the procedure which is proper to Dzogchen is the path of self-liberation (rang-grol lam). This is the practice we find described in the text, rather than something else called meditation. The translation "meditation" for *dgongs-pa* misses the mark. Meditation (bsgom-pa) involves meditation upon something, whether that be the visualization of a deity or thinking that the inherent nature of all phenomena is empty. Meditation is dualistic in its nature; it exists in time and is conditioned because it involves the working of the mind. But the Primordial State of the individual (dgongs-pa) is beyond time and conditioning and the activities of the mind. Thus the significance here is "self-liberation in the Primordial State (dgongs-pa rang-grol)". Being in this state is known as "contemplation"; so when the word *dgongs-pa* is a verb, we can translate it as "to contemplate." We must keep in mind the clear and essential distinction between contemplation and meditation. "Contemplation" is entering into and remaining in a state of pure presence or intrinsic awareness (rig-pa), whereas "meditation" involves the activities of the mind and the erecting of mental constructions. Having entered into the state of contemplation, any thoughts which then arise are allowed to self-liberate into their own condition (rang sar grol). This is the method of Dzogchen.

Then, in particular, the Peaceful and Wrathful Deities (zhi khro lha) refer to the visionary experiences which may occur to one in the Bardo of Reality (chos-nyid bar-do), after one has died and passed away from this present life. The essential point here is to recognize that all of these apparitions and experiences arising in the Bardo, whether they be peaceful or terrifying, are in actuality the manifestations of the energy of one's own Primordial State. These manifestations are spontaneously self-perfected from the very beginning (lhun-grub). If we recognize them (ngo-shes-pa) as being that, then we will attain liberation at that instant into the clarity of our Primordial State, which is called the natural Clear Light ('od gsal). If not, we will again be caught in the network of illusions, our own thoughts, and thus be driven relentlessly by the winds of our karma into transmigration, the beginningless cycle of birth and death and rebirth which is Samsāra.

B. The next part of the title, *rig-pa ngo-sprod*, tells us the function of this particular text, among all of the texts belonging to the cycle of the *Kar-gling zhi-khro*. This text is an introduction (ngo-sprod) to intrinsic awareness (rig-pa). Properly, the way in which we enter into Dzogchen is for the Lama or master to give us an introduction to the nature of our own mind and to its inherent capacity for presence or awareness. The master is able to do this because he or she has had direct personal experience of the state of contemplation, and so by means of symbols and explanations the master indicates to us the real meaning of presence. In this way we come to clearly distinguish between what is the nature of the mind (sems nyid) and what is mind (sems), that is to say, our thought processes, the endless sequence of discursive thoughts (rnam-rtog) which continuously arise within us. What is the difference here? There is the traditional metaphor to help us understand this. The nature of the mind is like a highly polished mirror, whereas individual thoughts which arise are like the reflections in this mirror. Rigpa, which we translate as "presence" or "intrinsic awareness," is similar to the capacity of the mirror to reflect whatever arises before it, whether that be beautiful or ugly. The opposite of Rigpa is *ma rig-pa*, ignorance or the absence of awareness. With intrinsic awareness we live in the condition of the mirror, so to speak, whereas with ignorance we live in the condition of the reflections, thinking that whatever appears before us is substantial and real. From ignorance we enter again into the cycle of transmigration.

The text here is an Upadeśa, the secret or private instruction of a master to his disciple. In the text, Guru Padmasambhava is speaking directly to us in order to bring us into an immediate experience of Rigpa, of intrinsic awareness. This is "a direct introduction," not a philosophical treatise; it does not marshall up one argument after another in support of some sectarian viewpoint. In this context, the term "view" (lta-ba) does not refer to some particular sectarian or philosophical position, such as a school might have, but rather it refers to our way of seeing. In Dzogchen, our view or way of seeing is far more important than practicing meditation. Meditation is limited by the mind, but the direct introduction to intrinsic awareness takes us to what lies beyond the limitations of the mind. Nevertheless, Rigpa or intrinsic awareness can be known directly in our own personal experience as pure presence; however, in itself it is outside of and beyond conceptions made by the mind (spros-bral). This intrinsic awareness is not just a knowing of something. In Tibetan the term for this kind of awareness is *shes-pa*, "to be aware, to know something." For example, we may know very well that if we eat poison, it will make us sick and even kill us; and yet through distraction or inattention, through a lack of awareness, we could eat poison and die. This is the difference. The term *rig-pa* indicates something far more fundamental and radical; it is not just a knowledge of something. Where there is an aware knowing, an awareness with knowledge, this is indicated by the terms *shes-rig*.

   C. The final part of the general title gives the specific title of this text: *gcer mthong rang-grol*, "self-liberation (rang-grol) through seeing (mthong) nakedly (gcer)," that is to say, the way of seeing things just as they are in themselves without our vision being obscured and distorted by judgments and conceptual constructions. These judgments and conceptions derive from our social and cultural conditioning in this life and from inherited predispositions refuting from karma in past lives. What we are introduced to and what comes into view here is intrinsic awareness; but only in the state of contemplation is intrinsic awareness revealed in all its nakedness (rig-pa rjen-pa). This is intrinsic awareness denuded of all obscurations, whether these be emotional obscurations (nyon-mong-pa'i sgrib-pa) or intellectual obscurations (shes-bya'i sgrib-pa). Freeing oneself of all obscurations, then everything can be seen nakedly with an unimpeded clarity. At this point we live in the state of the mirror and not in the condition of the reflections, and we see everything from the standpoint of the mirror. In this way, what ever is seen (mthong) without any conceptual elaborations intervening (gcer) is allowed to liberate itself (rang grol) into its own inherent condition, which is emptiness, without any effort or modification on our part. When discursive thoughts arise, they are allowed to self-liberate without correction or interference (ma bcos-pa). Everything is seen as it exists in a state of being just as it is in itself (ji-bzhin nyid).

2 Every Tibetan text properly has three parts: I. the preliminary section (sngon 'gro); II. the principal section (dngos-gzhi), which is the main body of the text; and III. the concluding section (rjes). The preliminary section consists of three essential items: 1. the title (mtshan ston-pa) of the text; 2. the verses or words of offering (mchod-par brjod-pa) which is an invocation paying homage to the Masters and the Deities; and 3. the declaration of the author's intention and purpose (rtsom-par dam-

bca'-ba), which is a promise to his readers where he informs them what he is about to say. The meaning of the title has been discussed above.

Here the homage or words of offering are quite brief: *Rig-pa rang-gsal sku gsum lha la phyag 'tshal-lo.* The author pays homage (*phyag 'tshal* literally means "to make a prostration") to the Trikāya or Three Bodies of the Buddha (sku gum) and to the Deities (lha), these latter being in particular the one hundred Peaceful and Wrathful Deities. However, the Trikāya and the Deities are not regarded as being something external to ourselves, such as is the case with the conventional notion of God in the West. Here the term Trikāya refers to the Primordial State of the individual, which has three aspects: its Essence (ngo-bo), which is emptiness (stong-pa nyid), its Nature (rang-bzhin), which is luminous clarity (gsal-ba); and its Energy (thugs-rje)[4] which, is uninterrupted and unobstructed (ma 'gag-pa) and all-pervading (kun-khyab). Thus, with respect to the nature of the mind, Buddhahood is already fully realized and manifest. Indeed, it has been so since the very beginning and never otherwise. However, due to the accumulated layers of obscurations, both emotional and intellectual, it has gone unrecognized until this time. The Essence of the mind which is emptiness is the Dharmakāya. Its nature which is luminous clarity is the Sambhogakāya. Its Energy which is uninterrupted is the Nirmānakāya. In this context "mind" means the nature of the mind (sems nyid) which in terms of Dzogchen is synonymous with the Bodhichitta. In the view of Dzogchen, Buddhahood is not only inherent in the mind of a sentient being, but fully manifest as the Trikāya here and now.[5]

Moreover, the Deities in question here are actually manifestations or reflections of our own Primordial State; they represent the inherent creative potency (rang rtsal) of the nature of the mind. They manifest spontaneously in self-perfection (lhun-grub) and are an expression of our pure vision of things. For example, at the time of the Bardo experience, our five skandhas, which are the five aggregates of our human experience, manifest to us as the five Dhyāni Buddhas, the eight consciousnesses manifest as the eight great Bodhisattvas, and so on. We should recognize all of them as being emanations or projections (sprul-pa) of our own mind. Thus, in terms of the Trikāya and the Deities, when we do homage, or go to refuge in them for that matter, we are not worshipping some external God or Deity, but turning toward our own inherent Buddha-nature.

3 Now follows the author's promise to begin (rtsam-par dam-bca') and here the title of the text is repeated once more. Buddhist tradition distinguishes individuals of three levels of capacity, namely, superior (rab), intermediate ('bring-po), and inferior (tha-ma). Thus, with re-

spect to understanding the meaning of the title, an individual of superior capacity will immediately understand the contents of the entire text by merely hearing the title alone. A person of intermediate capacity, upon hearing the title, will understand to what category or class the text belongs. And a person of inferior capacity will only hear the words in the title and will therefore require a lengthy and full explanation. Traditionally, in Tibet one did not just walk into the library of a monastery, pull a book off the shelf at random, and begin reading. On the contrary, the student required the permission and authorization of a qualified Lama or master before reading a spiritual book. Such an authorization or *lung* took the form of the master reading the text aloud to the student. When this *lung* was completed, usually it would be followed by an explanation (khrid) of the text. And indeed many of these recondite texts cannot be understood without the explanation of a Lama who, first of all, is heir to a long lineage of oral tradition, and second, has had some direct experience and realization of what the text speaks. Through this authorization (lung) and explanation (khrid) given by the Lama, the student receives the transmission of the text which goes back through time to the original author. Therefore, we speak of the Dharma as having two aspects, traditional knowledge (lung) and direct understanding through personal experience (rtogs-pa).

Here the author, Guru Padmasambhava, admonishes us, "Therefore this introduction to your own intrinsic awareness (rang gi rig-pa ngo-sprod) should be contemplated well, O fortunate sons of a noble family (legs-par dgongs cig skal-ldan rigs kyi bu)." As we have said above, the word *dgongs-pa* usually means the Primordial State, but here it is a verb and so it is best translated as "to contemplate." It does not mean "to meditate," which is mental activity, the work of the mind; rather, it refers to being in the state of intrinsic awareness (rig-pa). But this does not mean that while one is in a state of contemplation, being totally present and aware, that mental activities, such as reasoning and intellectual analysis, cannot occur. In this case here, when we are listening to the teaching of the Dharma, in order to come to an understanding of the teaching, it is necessary to exercise the intellect.

We who are reading or listening to this text are "the fortunate ones" (skal-ldan) because our fortunate karma has brought us into contact with a master and with these teachings in our present life. "Sons of a noble family" (rigs kyi bu), or in Sanskrit *kulaputra* is a term used in the Sūtras by the Buddha when addressing His disciples who are Bodhisattvas at the time of their listening to His teachings. By producing the Bodhichitta, the resolute intention to attain enlightenment for the sake of liberating all sentient beings, they have entered into the family or clan (rigs) of the Buddhas. The word "sons" refers to both male and female practitioners. In the view of the Mahāyāna, all of us who have made the commitment to attain enlightenment are Jinaputras, "the children of the Victorious Ones."

The word *samāyā*, which concludes this section, is Sanskrit and signifies "I promise" or "This is my promise." It refers to the promise made by Padmasambhava to his disciples and also to us who belong to the later generations of the Kali Yuga. The Tibetan word *gya* means "seal" (rgya). This teaching is sealed with the Samāyās of the Body, Speech, and Mind of the Guru; therefore, the word "sealed" is repeated three times.[6] Moreover, this text is sealed because it is secret. A secret teaching is given in confidence and in privacy between a master and his disciples, and so it is not to be spoken of idly to others who are not interested participants in its practice. The interjection "Emaho!" means "how marvelous!"

4 Now the author proceeds to inform us of his purpose. The first line reads, "It is the single nature of mind that encompasses all of Samsāra and Nirvāna" ('khor 'das yongs la khyab-pa'i sems gcig-po).[7] Here "mind" (sems) is not our ordinary thought process, but rather the nature of the mind (sems nyid), which like the mirror has the capacity to reflect whatever is set before it, whether beautiful or ugly, whether belonging to Samsāra or Nirvāna. Whether we find ourselves in the enlightened state of a Buddha or in the unenlightened state of an ordinary sentient being, what is present in both cases is the nature of the mind; that is, the primordial foundation or base (ye gzhi), encompassing both awareness (rig-pa) and the absence of awareness (ma rig-pa). Thus the nature of the mind is the more general term, whereas Rigpa, meaning intrinsic awareness or immediate presence, is like the capacity of the mirror to reflect. There exists the possibility of its opposite: ignorance or the absence of awareness. In Dzogchen it is said that there is a single foundation or base, but two paths, that of awareness and that of ignorance, and as a consequence there are two fruits, existence as a Buddha and existence as an ordinary sentient being. Hence, Rigpa, intrinsic awareness, is the actual subject matter of this text, as is pointed out in its title *Rig-pa ngo-sprod*, "a direct introduction to one's own intrinsic awareness." In the context of Dzogchen, it is precisely this "introduction" that is the function of the Guru or master: to indicate, to point out directly the nature of our own mind as intrinsic awareness. The subject matter in this teaching by Padmasambhava is something to be found at the heart of our immediate experience; it is not some sort of hypothetical metaphysical entity to be discovered through philosophical speculation.

Speaking of this mind, Padmasambhava says that its inherent nature, which is intrinsic awareness, has existed from the very beginning (ye nas rang-bzhin yin), that is to say, it is not created at some point in time. But it has gone unrecognized (ngo ma shes-pa) because of our ignorance or lack of awareness in all of our previous lives. It is like a precious self-luminous gem which, over countless centuries, has become encrusted with layer upon layer of dross. These various layers of obscuration are both emotional and intellectual. The emotional obscurations (nyon-mong pa'i sgrib-pa) consist principally of our negative and selfish passions, such as anger, greed, jealousy, pride, and so on. The intellectual obscurations (shes-bya'i sgrib-pa) consist in our misperceiving and having erroneous ideas about reality. At the present time, even though this clear presence or awareness (gsal rig) has been unceasing and uninterrupted, yet we have not directly met with it face to face (zhal ma mjal). And even though its arising is nowhere obstructed, impeded, or interrupted ('gag med ci yang 'char), still we do not apprehend or recognize it (ngos ma zin). These three lines above in the text refer to the nature of the mind in terms of its Essence (ngo-ba) which is emptiness (stong-pa nyid), its Nature (rang-bzhin) which is luminous clarity (gsal-ba), and its Energy (thugs-rje) which is unobstructed and uninterrupted ('gag med) and all-pervading (kun khyab).

This Upadeśa or secret instruction of the Guru has the purpose of bringing us to self-recognition (rang ngo shes-pa), which means the recognition of our own inherent intrinsic awareness (rang gi rig-pa). The teachings of the Buddha have been traditionally divided into the eighty-four thousand gateways for entering into the Dharma. Why this precise number? There are twenty-one thousand gateways belonging to the Vinaya which were expounded as antidotes to the poison of greed and attachment ('dod-chags), there are twenty-one thousand gateways belonging to the Sūtras which were expounded as antidotes to hatred and anger (zhe-dangs), and there are twenty-one thousand gateways belonging to the Abhidharma which were expounded as antidotes to delusion and confusion (gti-mug). Finally, there are twenty-one thousand gateways which were expounded as antidotes to all three of these poisons which are the root passions. Thus the total of eighty-four thousand is obtained. All of the teachings which have been expounded by the Jinas of the three times of past, present, and future are incomprehensible if we do not understand this single point which is intrinsic awareness. Jina (rgyal-ba) is a title of the Buddha meaning "the Victorious One," and He is so called because of His victory over the four Māras at the time of His enlightenment. Thus He is one who has triumphed over the cycle of death and rebirth and has entered into the condition of the deathless. Here the Buddha of the three times means not just Dīpankara, Sakyamuni, and Maitreya, as is often depicted in Buddhist iconography, but all of the Buddhas who manifest throughout the infinities of time and space. The Buddha Sakyamuni taught these eighty-four thousand gateways to the Dharma in order that we would come to understand our own nature and the nature of existence. He did this for the benefit of beings alone and had no other reason for doing so.

Nonetheless, even though there exist unlimited numbers of scriptures, the real meaning (don) has not been expounded elsewhere by the Buddha—but it is found in the three statements that introduce one to his own intrinsic awareness (rig pa ngo-sprod tshig gsum). These are the famous "Three Statements which Strike the Essential Point" (tshig gsum gnad brdeg). According to the Buddhist tradition of Tibet, the first human teacher of Dzogchen was the Nirmānakāya Garab Dorje (Skt. Prahevajra) who appeared as a precocious and miraculously endowed child in the country of Uddiyāna, somewhere to the northwest of India. The great Buddhist scholar Manjuśrīmitra, having heard of this master, came from western India to Śītavana and, after the exchange of only a few words, he was converted to the view of Dzogchen. Sometime later, when Garab Dorje had passed into Nirvāna, his disciple uttered many loud lamantations, exclaiming, "The sun has set upon the world; what are we to do?" At that moment Garab Dorje manifested himself in the center of the sky within a sphere of rainbow light, and he uttered these three statements which represent his last testament (zhal 'chems). Thereafter Manjuśrīmitra classified the texts he had received and transmitted them to Śrīsimha. From Śrīsimha the teachings were transmitted to Padmasambhava, Vimalamitra, and Vairochana the translator.[8]

These three Statements succinctly sum up the essential points of the Dzogchen teachings. They are:

1. Direct introduction to one's own nature
   (ngo rang thog-tu sprad-pa);
2. Directly discovering this unique state
   (thag gcig thog-tu bcad-pa);
3. Directly continuing with confidence in liberation
   (gdeng grol thog-tu bca'-ba).

Dudjom Rinpoche explains these three as follows:

This fresh immediate awareness of the present moment that transcends all thoughts relating to the three times is itself that primordial awareness (ye-shes) which is self-originated pure presence or awareness (rang-byung rig-pa).

This is the direct introduction to one's own nature. Whatever phenomena of Samsāra or Nirvāna may manifest, all of them represent the potency of one's own intrinsic awareness (rig-pa'i rtsal). Since there is nothing that goes beyond just this, one should continue in the state of this singular and unique awareness. Therefore, one must discover directly this unique state, and there exists nothing other than this. Whatever gross or subtle thoughts arise, by one's merely recognizing their nature, all of them will arise and be liberated simultaneously in the vast expanse of the Dharmakāya where emptiness and awareness are inseparable. Therefore, one should continue directly with confidence in their liberation.[9]

These three Statements epitomize all the myriads of volumes of Dzogchen. All texts are relative compared to this essential meaning; they are merely explanations of different methods of how to enter into the state of contemplation, so that we can come to experience intrinsic awareness directly for ourselves. The fundamental point here is our knowledge of this and not some old and venerable tradition. This knowledge transcends time and history. The first statement refers to a direct introduction to our own nature which is intrinsic awareness. This in fact is what the author is doing here in this text; Guru Padmasambhava introduces us directly to the nature of our own mind by means of this Upadeśa teaching. This introduction by the Guru is how one enters into Dzogchen. There are no specific practices which are prerequisite or preliminary to this introduction, nor are there required practices which must be pursued following the introduction. Thus it says in the text that this introduction to the manifest Primordial State of the Victorious One (rgya-ba'i dgongs-pa mngon-sum ngo-sprod) is a method for entering into practice where there is neither an antecedent nor a subsequent practice (snga phyi med-par 'jug tshul). This entering into intrinsic awareness by way of direct introduction is sufficient, because intrinsic awareness (rig-pa) is the essential and inherent quality of the Primordial State of Buddhahood (rgyal-ba'i dgongs-pa), wherein the Trikāya exist in full manifestation (mngon-sum), as explained previously. This intrinsic awareness is beyond time and conditioning; it is beyond mind.

5   Now the principal section of the text begins. The Tibetan word "kye-ho!" means "listen!" First the author tells us about those who do not understand the real condition of the individual. To understand what is meant by the nature of the mind is the most important consideration.

Here a distinction is made between what is loosely and conventionally called "mind" (sems) and what is actually the nature of mind (sems nyid). Where this distinction has not been understood, the confusion has given rise to many different philosophical systems (grub-mtha'). However, the nature of mind transcends all of these conceptual limitations and is, therefore, inconceivable (bsam gyis mi khyab). And since ordinary sentient beings do not recognize it, they do not recognize their own nature (rang ngo rang gis ma shes-pa) which is intrinsic awareness, and so they wander endlessly throughout the six destinies of rebirth within the three worlds. The six destinies ('gro drug)[10] are rebirth among the Devas (gods), among the Asuras (titans), among human beings, among animals, among the Pretas (hungry ghosts), and among the denizens of hell; and the three worlds or three dimensions of existence (khams gsum) are the Kāmadhātu or Desire World, the Rūpadhātu or Form World, and the Arūpyadhātu or Formless World. The Desire World is inhabited by beings, such as those in the six destinies of rebirth listed above, who are dominated by sensuous desires and by their passions. The Form World and Formless World represent higher states of consciousness where sensuous desire has been transcended.[11] Why do sentient beings endlessly wander through these destinies and worlds in the cycle of death and rebirth which is Samsāra? Because they do not recognize their own intrinsic awareness and understand its significance. This was the primordial error, and its consequence was the fall of beings into transmigration. When did this fall first occur? From time without beginning. It was not an event that occurred in history, but rather it was the primordial and ever present precondition for the existence of time and history. Transmigration is the fate of ordinary beings (so-so'i skye-bo tha-mal-pa) who are obscured by ignorance and hence are dominated by their selfish passions.

But spiritually evolved beings, not just ordinary individuals, likewise do not understand the nature of the mind and do not recognize intrinsic awareness. The Śrāvakas or Hīnayāna disciples (nyan-thos-pa)[12] whose aim is to realize the state of the sage-like passionless Arhat, as well as the Pratyekabuddhas (rang rgyal), who aim to attain realization in solitude, only understand the nature of the mind in terms of the Anātman doctrine (bdag med). The understanding that no eternal or abiding self exists in persons is the ultimate realization attained in the Hīnayāna Sūtra system. The ātman (bdag) is the notion of a self, the idea of an "I" or "ego" as the core of our personality and mental life. It is conceived of as an unchanging entity having its own specific individual character. But in actual fact, this entity is merely a fiction imposed on an ever-changing stream of consciousness. However, according to the Hīnayāna, although this notion of a self or ego is empty and, therefore, unreal, still the dharmas or momentary phenomena into which our mental experiences can ultimately be analyzed are thought to be real. Momentary states of consciousness, which incessantly succeed each other in the mind, as well as their contents in terms of momentary phenomena or dharmas, are taken to be realities. But this view is dualistic in terms of subject and object. These two types of practitioners of the Hīnayāna may understand the doctrine of Anātman, but they do not understand the real condition of things just as they are in themselves (ji-bzhin nyid du ma rtogs). They cling resolutely to certain concepts and engage themselves in mental analyses (yid dpyod), and so they become caught up in the activities of the mind, which is conditioned and exists in time. Thus they are unable to see things clearly. Even though the Śrāvaka and the Pratyekabuddha have tried to free themselves from the domination of the passions, still they are limited by many subtle intellectual obscurations. The fundamental obscuration is that of dualism and these Hīnayāna practitioners are obscured by their attachment to the reality of subject and object.[13]

As explained previously, the Nyingmapa system classifies the teachings of the Buddha into Nine Vehicles to enlightenment. The Śrāvakas and the Prayekabuddhas represent the first two vehicles which together comprise the Hīnayāna. The third vehicle is that of the Bodhisattvas, those who are followers of the Mahāyāna Sūtras. These three lower vehicles comprise the Sūtra system. However, even those who follow the Mahāyāna may become fettered to their attachments and will not see things clearly because they entertain many ideas about emptiness. Having ideas about something, even emptiness, is in fact an activity of mind, and all activities of mind exist in time and are conditioned. Thus the Mādhyamikas, whose view according to the Tibetans represents the highest realization to be found within the Sūtra system, are obscured by their attachment to the extremes of the Two Truths, the Relative Truth as opposed to the Absolute Truth (bden gnyis mtha' la zhen-pas bsgrib). They have the tendency to get at emptiness through reasoning and mental analysis, which, as we have said, are activities of mind.

But equally the viewpoints of the adherents of the Tantra system are obscured and lead them into dualism. The practitioners of the Kriyā Tantra, the Charyā Tantra, and the Yoga Tantra —these three vehicles representing the outer Tantras —are obscured by their attachments to sevā-sādhana practice (bsnyen grub). In their generation of the deity during the course of the visualization known as the Generation Process (bskyed-rim), there arises an attachment to the notion of a deity. This is the case whether this deity is visualized in the sky in front of oneself like a great lord before his servant, as one does in Kriyā Tantra and Charyā Tantra, or actually transforms oneself into the deity, merging the symbolic being and the wisdom being into inseparable union, as one does in Yoga Tantra. Here there exists very much a notion of dualism.

Even the practitioners who follow the three highest vehicles of Mahāyoga, Anuyoga, and Atiyoga, which comprise the inner Tantras, can go astray into dualism. The practitioners of Mahāyoga and Anuyoga may become obscured by their attachment to Space and Awareness (dbyings rig zhen-pas bsgrib). If they do not understand that these two are actually inseparable from the very beginning, and think that they are two different things which are to be brought into union, it will be impossible for them to realize Buddhahood. To make a real distinction between these two is to fall into deviation (gol-sa).[14] Thus the viewpoints of all of the eight lower vehicles may obscure and miss the mark.

There is no real difference between Samsāra and Nirvāna[15]—since the nature of mind is like a mirror that can reflect whatever is set before it, whether beautiful or ugly, whether pure vision or impure karmic vision. From the Base, which is the Primordial State of the individual, there diverge two paths: from awareness arises Nirvāna, from ignorance or lack of awareness, Samsāra. In either case the nature of the mind remains the same, unadulterated and unchanged in its own condition. Just as we speak of it as being primordially pure (ka-dag), we speak of appearances, whether pure or impure, as being expressions or manifestations of its spontaneous self-perfection (lhun-grub). Thus the text says that Samsāra and Nirvāna are inseparable ('khor 'das dbyer-med). When the text refers to one's own mind (rang sems), this actually means the nature of the mind. Of course, in terms of our ordinary conditioned mind (sems), impure and pure vision, Samsāra and Nirvāna, are quite different. And because the conditioned mind persistently clings to dualism, to attachments and aversions, we continue to wander aimlessly within the cycle of existence.

Nonetheless, from the standpoint of Dzogchen, the Primordial State of the individual, it is an error to think that there are things to do—these are the active dharmas (byas chos); or that there are things not to do—these are the inactive dharmas (bya bral chos). Thinking in this manner is the very reason why we are caught up in Samsāra. Apart from the understanding of intrinsic awareness, both active dharmas and inactive dharmas represent errors. Grasping at and clinging to duality (gnyis 'dzin) in whatever practice we do, no matter how wholesome and altruistic, is still an error, although the practice in itself is not necessarily erroneous. It is of paramount importance that we understand the principle involved in all of this. That principle is Rigpa or intrinsic awareness. When we practice, if we continually harbour expectations of future results, then there will be no hope of attaining Buddhahood. Therefore, when we practice, we should have no fear of continuing to wander in Samsāra and no expectation of attaining Nirvāna. The point is to be wholly present in whatever we do, whether this be Dharma practice or the activities of everyday life.

Since Dzogchen, the Great Perfection, is complete in itself, it is the key to transcending the limitations of our existence. Therefore, we can practice any dharma, engage in any spiritual practice, and still do so from a Dzogchen point of view. We can make use of all the methods which are found in the eight lower vehicles, such as the methods of purification found in the Sūtras and the methods of transformation found in the Tantras, and do so from the perspective of Dzogchen. Dzogchen is beyond all limitations, so we need not limit ourselves by rejecting certain methods *a priori*. Thus it says in the text, since that intrinsic awareness which sees things nakedly, unencumbered by judgments and conceptual constructions, is revealed to be the method of self-liberation (rig-pa gcer mthong rang grol du bstan-pas), all spiritual practices, can be undertaken and understood as being the method of self-liberation; and everything that manifests is complete in itself as the Great Perfection. "Samāyā gya gya gya" again means "I promise" and "sealed with the Samāyā vows of Body, Speech, and Mind."

6   Having initially introduced us to intrinsic awareness and having also indicated who does not recognize it, Padmasambhava now leads us to a firmer understanding. This sparking awareness (rig rig thur-thur-po) which is called "mind" (and here this means *sems nyid*), even though we may assert that it exists (in the sense of an entity), it does not exist in that way. Nevertheless, it is the source and origin of all of the diversity (sna-tshogs) which we experience as the sorrows of Samsāra and as the bliss of Nirvāna. Whether impure vision or pure vision, the nature of the mind is the source (byung-ba) of all phenomena. Thus it is spoken of in all of the vehicles to enlightenment (theg-pa bcu gcig)[16] as existing and as something to be cherished, for without it there is neither the attaining of Buddhahood nor the wandering in Samsāra. It is the original and primordial basis of everything.

Moreover, this "mind" which is the source of all things is given many different names by both Buddhists and non-Buddhists. In general, we have been calling it the nature of the mind (sems nyid).[17] This Tibetan word could also be translated as Mind (sems) itself (nyid). The particle *nyid* is often reflexive, meaning "itself, oneself," but it is also used to make abstract nouns like the English particles "-ness" and "-ity." Thus, the translation "the nature of the mind" is both accurate and unpretentious. Also it has a parallel to the term *chos nyid* (Skt. Dharmatā), "the nature of reality." Some Tīrthikas (mu-stegs-pa) or Hindus call it by the name Ātman or the Self (bdag). This has reference to the Upanishads and the Vedānta philosophy in particular. The Śrāvakas who follow the Hīnayāna Sūtras call it the doctrine of Anātman or no self (bdag), as explained above.[18] Among the followers of the Mahāyāna Sūtras, the Yogāchāras or Chittamātrins call it Chitta or Mind (sems), while the Mādhyamikas call it the Prajñāpāramitā or the Perfection of Wisdom (shes-rab pha-rol tu phyin-pa).[19] Others call it the Tathāgatagarbha or embryo of Buddhahood. Among the followers of the Tantras, some call it by the name of Mahāmudrā or the Great Symbol (phyag-rgya chen-po), others call it the Unique Sphere (thig-le nyag-gcig)[20] which is a Dzogchen term, or call it the Dharmadhātu or dimension of existence (chos dbyings), or call it the Ālaya or basis of everything (kun gzhi). Again, others simply call it ordinary awareness (tha-mal gyi shes-pa).[21]

7 When we are introduced to this intrinsic awareness, the method for entering into it involves three considerations (don gsum 'jug tshul), which are then explained. These considerations refer to the three times. In terms of intrinsic awareness, thoughts which have occurred in the past were empty and thus they have left no trace, like clouds in the sky that pass from view. Thoughts in the future will arise and be fresh and unconditioned by anything. And in the present moment, intrinsic awareness remains in its own natural condition without constructing anything in terms of concepts and judgements, without any changes, corrections, or modifications (bzo-med rang-lugs gnas-pa).[22] We are totally present in the immediate moment, the here and now (da-lta), without constructing any sense of time, past and present or future. This condition of being is beyond time, since presence or awareness (rig-pa) is beyond mind, the linear succession of thoughts that creates time. In terms of the Foundation or Base (gzhi), there exists neither the presence nor the absence of the three times, because intrinsic awareness is primordially pure from the beginning (ka-dag).

When speaking of intrinsic awareness we should not let ourselves fall into an extreme view either of eternalism or of nihilism. On the one hand, it is not a permanent entity or substance (rtag-pa ma yin) and it is not created or made by anything (cir yang grub med). And on the other hand, it is not something which is destroyed or becomes annihilated (chad-pa ma yin), nor is it a mere nothingness, because it is lucid and present (gsal-le hrig-ge-ba). Again, on the one hand, it is not a single entity or substance (gcig tu ma yin) because, in terms of the diversity of things, it is present and clear (du-mar rig cing gsal). Yet, on the other hand, it is not many or multiple because it is uncreated, inseparable, and of a single flavor (ma grub dbyer-med ro-gcig).[23] Thus, intrinsic awareness transcends these two fundamental types of metaphysical dualism: eternalism and nihilism, on the one hand, and the one and the many, on the other hand. Intrinsic awareness (rig-pa) cannot be contained within such conceptual limitations. We cannot speak of it as being either way. The nature of the mind transcends all metaphysical and either/or categories and speculations. Furthermore, this inherent self-awareness (rang-rig) does not derive from anything outside of itself; it is not created from some antecedent cause whether natural or supernatural. And the direct experience of this presence or awareness is the actual introduction (don gyi ngo-sprod) to the natural condition of things (dngos-po'i gnas-lugs).

8   Within this Rigpa or intrinsic awareness, the Trikāya (sku sum), what we usually understand as "the Three Bodies of the Buddha, " are wholly present and inseparably united from the very beginning. They are present in the sense of being fully realized and manifest; they are inseparable in the sense that they are in actuality not three different things but only three aspects of a single nature of the mind. We only distinguish them in a conventional sense for purposes of communication and discussion. The Sanskrit term *kāya* (sku) literally means "body," but just as in our own personal experience, our physical body and our immediate environment interpenetrate and form a single field of activity, so *kāya* also has the sense of "the dimension of existence." Thus the three dimensions of the existence of the Buddha are the Dharmakāya which is all-pervasive and omnipresent; the Sambhogakāya which manifests in Akanistha, the highest plane of existence; and the Nirmānakāya which manifests to ordinary sentient beings in time and history. Collectively these three are known as the Trikāya.

From the standpoint of Dzogchen, the Trikāya is not something which is attained or realized at some point in time, nor is it something which is latent or undeveloped in the individual which must be nurtured and cultivated in order to be brought into manifestation, such as a seed containing the entire tree in potential. For the Trikāya is already fully present from the very beginning in the nature of the mind. Since in its essence the nature of the mind is empty and is not made out of anything, it is the Dharmakāya. Yet it is not a dark, cold void. Since its nature is clear luminosity, the inherent translucent radiance of emptiness (stong-pa'i rang mdangs gsal-ba), it is the Sambhogakāya. And since its arising is nowhere obstructed, impeded or interrupted ('gag med cir yang 'char), it is the Nirmānakāya. When we speak of the base (gzhi), the Primordial State of the individual, we are speaking of these three aspects: its Essence, its Nature, and its Energy—and as the Trikāya which is the base (gzhi'i sku gsum), they are primordially present and of a single essence.

9   When we are introduced by means of this powerful method for entering into practice ('jug tshul btsan thabs), we discover our own immediate inherent awareness (da-lta rang gi shes-pa) at this precise moment which is itself outside the three times. Its inherent clarity is entirely unfabricated (ma bcos rang gsal); it is a pure intelligence, totally present and aware, unconditioned by any judgments or conceptions. The nature of the mind is just this.

The master Padmasambhava now asks us a series of questions in order to stimulate our realization of awareness and our understanding of it. Such guidance is known as *sem-ti* (sems khrid), "guiding the mind." Such guidance takes the form of a dialogue between the master and his disciple in order to introduce the latter to the experience of self-recognition. At the present moment we are experiencing this immediate self-awareness (da-lta rang gi shes-pa) and its nature is unfabricated self-clarity (ma bcos rang gsal). In view of what is indicated here, how can we say that we do not understand what is meant by the nature of the mind? Yet when we observe ourselves during meditation practice, we do not find anyone there who is meditating (sgom rgyu ci yang med-pa), since the mind is not some material entity which has qualities like shape, color, and so on. When there is no one meditating and nothing to meditate upon, how can we say that our meditation does not go well?

Since our manifest intrinsic awareness (rig-pa mngon-sum) is just this which has been indicated here by the Master, how can we say that we do not find our own mind (rang sems ma rnyed)? In view of this uninterrupted clarity and awareness (gsal rig rgyun-chad med-pa), how can we say that we do not see the face (or essence) of our own mind (sems ngo ma mthong)? Who is it who is thinking "Where is the mind?" However, the mind is just there as it is and nothing else. We may think that we ourselves are the one who is thinking by means of this mental process (yid kyis bsam-mkhan), but when we search for this one and do not find him anywhere, how can we say that we do not find the essence of our own mind? This very unfindability of the one it is who thinks (bsam-mkhan) or meditates (sgom-mkhan) is precisely the point. The essence of the mind is just there as it is (ji-bzhin nyid).

Thus there is nothing to do, nothing to modify or correct. So how can we say that our actions are performed rightly or wrongly. Because ultimately there is nothing to be done except leaving the mind in the state of being just as it is in itself (ji-bzhin nyid), we should allow intrinsic awareness to remain in its own condition without attempting to modify or correct it in any way (ma bcos rang sar bzhag-pa). That is sufficient. So how can we say that we have no capacity for entering into the calm state (gnas su ma btub)? Since just letting it be as it is, without making any effort or trying to do anything about it (byar-med cog-ge zhag-pa), is sufficient, how can we say that we do not have the capacity to meditate? We do not need to do anything, but just leave the mind where it is. Some say that they have accomplished something and some say that they did not accomplish anything. Yet since clarity and awareness and emptiness (gsal rig stong gsum) are inseparable and everything is spontaneously self-perfected, how can we say that we have not accomplished anything by means of our practice (gsal rig stong gsum dbyer-med lhun-grub la bsgrubs-pas ma 'grub)? Since everything in the universe is the reflection or potency of awareness (rig-pa'i rtsal), what is there to be accomplished here? Since everything is self-originated and spontaneously self-perfected without any antecedent causes or conditions, how can we say that we do not have the capacity to accomplish anything by our efforts (rgyu rkyen med-par rang-byung lhun-grub la rtsol-bas ma nus)? Since the arising of discursive thoughts and their being liberated occur simultaneously (rtog-pa shar-grol dus mnyam), how can we say that we do not have the capacity to apply the proper antidote (gnyen-pos ma thub)? But in fact we do not need to apply some antidote, as is done in the case of the Sūtra system methods, because, as soon as a discursive thought arises, it is allowed to liberate, like a cloud dissolving in the sky. Since immediate awareness (da-lta shes-pa) is just this presence and nothing else, how can we say that we know nothing of it?

10 The author now employs a series of similes to illustrate the nature of the mind and invites us to look within ourselves and to observe whether or not it is like that. The nature of the mind is empty and without any base (sems nyid stong-pa gzhi med). Our own mind is intangible and immaterial (rang sems dngos-med)—it is like the clear empty sky devoid of clouds.[24] Yet this mind is not just a mere nothingness because, as self-originated gnosis or primal awareness (rang-byung ye-shes), it is luminous clarity and has been so since the very beginning (ye nas gsal-ba). This clarity is like the heart of the sun which is itself self-originated. We should observe our own mind to see if it is like that or not. The clarity of intrinsic awareness is always present, just as the sun is present in the sky, although its visible orb may be obscured by the

clouds. Without this presence of the sun, even though it is invisible behind the clouds, our world would have no illumination at all.

This primal awareness which is intrinsic awareness or immediate presence (rig-pa'i ye-shes) is unceasing and uninterrupted, like the main channel of a great river. The diversity of movements of thoughts and memories which arise in the mind are not something that can be grasped tangibly and apprehended. They are like insubstantial breezes moving through the atmosphere (dngos-med bar-snang ser-bu). Whatever appearances are self-manifestations (rang snang), in the same way as reflections in a mirror are self-manifestations—they simply appear and are nothing other than what they are. And in this way, the qualifications of things become liberated into their own condition (rang sar grol-ba). Like the clouds in the sky that simply appear and then disappear again, they are self-originated and self-liberated, leaving no traces behind.

11 Having spoken extensively concerning the view, now the author considers the meditation, the conduct, and the fruit. There exist no phenomena other than what arises from mind (sems las ma gtogs gzhan na chos med). What appears and what does not appear, all of this arises from mind. Since everything arises in the mind, what is the difference between conduct or behavior and the one who behaves (spyod-pa spyod rgyu)? Concerning the samāyā vows, they also are held in the mind. What is the difference between the samāyā vow and the one who guards it (dam-tshig bsrung rgyu)? Finally, since nothing can be realized or attained from anything outside of the mind, what then is the difference between the fruit and the one who realizes it ('bras-be sgrub rgyu)?

12 We must look again and again at our own mind (yang ltos yang ltos rang gi sems la ltos). When we look upward into the sky which is outside of ourselves, what do we see? There exists no mind there which has emanated from somewhere or which is projected to somewhere else. There is no place from which discursive thoughts emanate or to which they go. And when we look inward into our own mind which is the space inside of ourselves, what do we see? We find that there does not exist any projectionist who projects thoughts by somehow thinking them (rtogs-pas 'phro-ba'i phro-mkhan mi 'dug). Looking again and again into our mind, we find that there is no place from which thoughts arise ('char-sa med), no place where they remain (gnas-sa med), and no place to which they go ('gro-sa med). Moreover, there cannot be found anyone who causes them to arise, to remain, or to pass away. The mind has no locatable source for the arising of thoughts, yet, nonetheless, its nature is luminous clarity. Not finding any source from whence thoughts arise, our own subtle mind (rang ses phra) which lies

below the usual hubbub of thoughts becomes lucidly clear without any projections of thoughts occurring ('phro med-pa'i gsal-le-ba). And since this luminous clarity, this natural Clear Light of our own intrinsic awareness, is empty, it is the Dharmakāya. It is like the sun rising in a cloudless sky. Even though this mind does not possess any particular shape or form, such as is possessed by a concrete object, nevertheless, it can be fully known.

13 Now the author proceeds to cite a number of paradoxes: This self-originated Clear Light (rang-byung 'od-gsal) is uncreated and unborn from the very beginning (gdod nas ma skyes). Yet, it is the child of intrinsic awareness which is itself without any parents (pha ma med-pa'i rig-pa'i khye'u). And since it is unproduced and uncreated, we speak of it as self-originated primordial awareness (rang-byung ye-shes). This Tibetan term *ye-shes* (Skt. jnāna, which is a cognate of the Greek word *gnosis*) is often translated as "wisdom," but this is not the meaning here. It is a primal or primordial (ye nas) awareness (shes-pa). It is a direct intuition, nondual in nature; it is that awareness which exists before the perception process comes into operation that makes the distinction between subject and object and that identifies and labels an object as being this thing or that. This process of perception ('du-shes) is actually a quite complex series of events involving the collocation and synthesis of a large number of psychic factors. Normally this process occurs so rapidly that it appears to us that, as soon as we see the object, we recognize it. And although we think that this perception is instantaneous, it is actually a process that takes place in time, albeit in an exceedingly brief moment of time: whereas, on the contrary, *ye-shes* is primordial (ye nas), something outside of the temporal sequence that is the product of mental activity.

Thus, this awareness does not undergo the experience of birth, nor does there exist any cause to bring about its death. Although it is clearly visible, there is no one who sees it. Although it has wandered throughout all of Samsāra from time without beginning, it has come to no harm. That is to say, having existed in lifetimes throughout countless cycles of time, our Tathāgatagarbha or inherent Buddha-nature has never been damaged or corrupted by sin or error. On the other hand, our Tathāgatagarbha has never been effected or caused to evolve into a new or higher condition because of all this wandering throughout all these different dimensions of existence. Our original Buddha-nature does not evolve or improve with experience or with the lessons learned in each lifetime; it simply is as it is from the very beginning. It is not affected by our karma, by our past experiences, by our accumulations of merit and knowledge. It remains just as it is, just as it always has been. It is the Alpha and the Omega; it is the Base, the Path and the Fruit. It does not move anywhere out of itself. Even though it sees Buddhahood, it does not go anywhere in pursuit of it. Its nature remains the same whether we are an enlightened Buddha or an ignorant sentient being. It is astonishing that it exists at all! Athough it exists in everyone everywhere, it goes unrecognized. And strangely, there are some who hope to attain some other fruit than this. Although it is our very own being (rang nyid yin), we seek elsewhere outside of ourselves for it. We should give up this erroneous notion that Buddhahood is something to be attained or acquired. It is not to be found somewhere else outside of ourselves, nor is it to be found only in some very distant future after countless lifetimes of practice. It is to be found nowhere else except in our own mind. How wonderful (e-ma)!

In the Phalayāna, "the fruitional vehicle," which is another name for the Vajrayāna, the origin and the goal are the same. The Base which is the foundation for the Path and the Fruit which is its goal are identical. The Path is not a matter of striving for or of attaining something that we do not at present possess. Buddhahood has been with us from the very beginning, even though it has gone unrecognized due to accumulated layers of obscuration. The Path does not bring about any changes in the Base. On the contrary, the Path is merely the process of removing these obscurations, so that we come to recognize who we really are and rediscover that precious treasure which we have had in our possession all along. In our practice, we should be without any expectations and fears (re dogs med-pa) with regard to the Path and its results, because the primordial Base which is Buddhahood itself is inherent within us. So how can we have any fears of losing or of not ever finding something which is identical with our own innate nature and has been with us all along?

When they consider enlightenment, some people think that they will have to abandon something in terms of their ideas or behavior. Others think that they must acquire something first. This is all wrong. All that is needed is our immediate present awareness (da-lta'i shes rig). This awareness is knowledgeable (shes rig); we know why it is that we do practice. This awareness is made into our view, into our meditation, and into our behavior or conduct. We do not have to look for the fruit of Buddhahood elsewhere than in this intrinsic awareness. According to the Sūtra system of the Mahāyāna, the Fruit is defined as the realization of the Trikāya, the Three Bodies of the Buddha. But this is the view proper to the Hetuyana, "the causal vehicle," which makes a distinction between the point of origin and the goal, between the cause and the effect. It is the distinction between the seed, which holds everything in potential, and the blossoming tree where everything is in full manifestation. But according to Dzogchen, at the time when this primordial awareness (rig-pa'i ye-shes) is present, the qualities of the Trikāya are fully manifest, naturally and spontaneously. Thus, in Dzogchen, Buddhahood is like the mighty Garuda bird that springs forth from its egg fully grown and soars into flight. It is mature, possessing all its qualities, right from the very beginning. When the Trikāya becomes manifest, there is no difference between intrinsic awareness (rig-pa) and the Trikāya—the Trikāya exists as the qualifications of intrinsic awareness. This is the real fruit. There is nothing else than this, no other Buddhahood.

14 This immediate present awareness (da-lta'i shes rig) is the highest pinnacle of all views (lta-ba'i kun gyi yang rtse) because immediate awareness is luminous clarity without any materiality (dngos-med gsal-ba). It is the highest pinnacle of all meditations because, being without any particular object of meditation, it is all-encompassing and free of all limitations and unconditioned by conceptions (dmigs med brdal kun dang bral-ba). It is the highest pinnacle of all conducts because, being uncontrived and unfabricated, it is spoken of widely in the world. It is the highest pinnacle of all fruits because, without being sought after, it is spontaneously perfected from the very beginning (ma btsa ye nas lhun-grub).

15 The author, having spoken of intrinsic awareness as the highest pinnacle of all views, meditations, conducts, and fruits, now declares it to be the greatest of all vehicles, the total vehicle. Specifically, he speaks of the four great vehicles which are without error (ma nor-ba'i theg chen bzhi). Intrinsic awareness is inherently unmistaken and without error; errors arise due to ignorance and to mind. Immediate awareness (da-lta'i shes-pa) is lucidly clear (gsal-le-ba), just as a perfect mirror refects whatever is before it. As it is with the view, so it is with the meditation (bhai-ba), the conduct, and the fruit. This luminous clarity (gsal-ba) is a pure inerrant intelligence.

16 Next the author alludes to the four great unchanging "nails" (mi 'gyur-ba'i gzer chen bzhi). The term "nail" (gzer) means the essential point (gnad). Intrinsic awareness is the essential point upon which everything else hangs. There are the four great unchanging nails of the view, the meditation, the conduct and the fruit because this immediate present awareness is lucidly clear. Thus, whatever we think or do, whether in practice or in daily life, is infused with this presence and awareness.

17 Then there follows the secret instruction which teaches that the three times are one (dus gsum gcig tu bstan-pa'i man'ngag). In relation to the past, we must relinquish all notions rooted in the past and abandon all

precedents which we have followed. With respect to the future, we must abandon all plans and all expectations. And with respect to the present time, without grasping at or following after thoughts which arise, we should allow our minds to remain in the condition of the sky ('dzin-med nam-kha ngang la gzhag). Just as clouds appear in the sky and then of themselves disappear again without in any way affecting or modifying the nature of the sky, so in the same way discursive thoughts may arise, but they in no way affect or modify or change the nature of the mind. Therefore, there is nothing upon which to meditate, for meditation is an activity of mind which, of necessity, involves the arising of thoughts. So we find ourselves in a state which is beyond meditation, a state of nonmeditation (bsgom-med). And even though thoughts may arise, we are not distracted (yengs-med) by them. Since our mindfulness is undistracted, our state of contemplation becomes stable (yengs med dran-pas brta). While being in this state of contemplation without meditation and without distraction (bhai-med yengs-med ngang). We are able to observe everything with a naked awareness (gcer gyis ltos) undistorted and unencumbered by judgments and preconceptions.

This self-awareness (rang rig), when it arises, is inherently knowing (rang shes), inherently clear (rang gsal), and radiantly brilliant (lhang-nge-ba), like the triumphant sun at dawn which illuminates the entire sky in every direction; and it is called the Bodhichitta. As we have indicated previously, in the context of Dzogchen and especially in the Semde series of teachings, Bodhichitta refers to the Primordial State of the individual, the quality or capacity of which is known as intrinsic awareness. This Sanskrit word Bodhichitta in its Tibetan translation byang-chub sems is interpreted according to Dzogchen to mean byang, "pure" from the very beginning (ka-dag), which indicates the Essence of the mind which is emptiness and the Dharmakāya; chub, "perfected," that is, spontaneously self-perfected (lhun-grub), which indicates the Nature of the mind which is luminous clarity and the Sambhogakāya; and sems, "mind," signifying compassion or energy, indicating the unobstructed all-pervading Energy of the mind which is the Nirmānakāya. Thus Bodhichitta is not only the seed or potentiality for Buddhahood in every sentient being, as is the case in the Mahāyāna Sūtras, but Buddhahood fully realized: the Trikāya perfectly manifest as the qualifications of the nature of the mind.

Going beyond any meditation, intrinsic awareness actually transcends all objects of knowledge. It cannot itself be the object of meditation. And being without any distraction, it is the inherent clarity of the state of the Essence (no-bo nyid) which is emptiness. Clarity and emptiness are not two different things, just as the empty daytime sky and its illuminatedness are not two different things. The inseparability of appearance and emptiness represents self-liberation, and the inseparability of clarity and emptiness is the Dharmakāya.[25] Since it is evident that there is nothing to be realized by means of a path to Buddhahood, at the time when we realize this, it is said that we shall actually see the face of Vajrasattva, the Sambhogakāya aspect of Buddhahood.[26]

18 Then there follows the instructions for exhausting and overthrowing the six extremes (mtha' drug zad sar skyal-ba'i gdams-pa). The six extremes refer to such views as, for example, asserting the existence or nonexistence of something, or asserting that it is eternal or may suffer annihilation, and so on. Although there exist many different views regarding the mind, which, in fact, disagree greatly among themselves, what we call the mind in this context is our own intrinsic awareness (rang rig sems) which is self-originated primordial awareness (rang-byung ye-shes). With respect to our view which, as we have said previously, is our way of seeing, we must look within ourselves, observing and making an examination to see if there is any difference between the observer and the process of observing (lta bya lta byed). These are not two different things. When we observe our mind, perching for the observer (lta-mkhan), we will not find anyone who is the observer. At that moment, realizing this unfindability, our view will become exhausted and is overthrown (lta-ba zad sar skyel-ba). Although this realization puts an end to our view, it is the beginning of self-awareness. Thus we have discovered for ourselves that the view (lta-ba) and the one who is viewing (lta-rgyu) do not exist anywhere as discreet and separate entities. On the other hand, because we have not fallen excessively and one-sidedly into a view of emptiness and the belief that nothing has existed from the very beginning, our own immediate present and knowing self-awareness (da-lta'i rang rig shes-pa) becomes lucidly clear and intelligent (gsal-le-ba), like the clear empty illuminated sky uncluttered by clouds. In this situation where we find ourselves in the condition of the mirror, so to speak, whether we have understanding or whether we lack understanding, this no longer represents a case of duality (rtogs dang mi rtogs gnyis-med).

19 Next the author gives us the instruction for how our meditation becomes exhausted and is overthrown. Although there exist many different kinds of meditation which disagree greatly among themselves, our ordinary present awareness (rang rig shes-pa tha-mal) is directly penetrating (zang-thal). The meditator and the process of meditating are not two different things (bhai bya bhai byed gnyis-med). Even though we search for the meditator (bhai-ba'i mkhan-po), we do not find him

anywhere. Discovering this unfindability, at that very moment our meditation will become exhausted and is overthrown (sgom-pa zad sar 'khyol-ba). Thus, even though this is the end of our meditation, it is the beginning of self-awareness. Without our coming under the influence of agitation, drowsiness, and confusion, our immediate unfabricated awareness (da-lta ma bcos shes-pa) becomes lucidly clear (gsal-le-ba). This unmodified state of even contemplation (ma bcos mnyam-par bzhag-pa) is concentration or dhyana (bsam-gtan). Thus, whether we remain in a calm state or do not remain in a calm state, this no longer represents a case of duality (gnas dang mi gnas gnyis-med).

20 Now our behavior comes under consideration. Although there exist many different kinds of behavior, this inherent present primordial awareness (rang rig ye-shes) is the state of the Unique Sphere (thig-le nyag-gcig). In this case, behavior and the one who behaves are not two different things (spyod bya spyod byed gnyis-med). When we observe our action or inaction, and search for the one it is who behaves or acts (spyod-mkhan), we will not find him anywhere. Discovering this unfindability, our behavior will become exhausted and is overthrown (spyod-pa zad sar 'khyol-ba). Even though this is the end of our behavior, it is the beginning of self-awareness. Neither the action nor the one who is acting have existed as discreet separate entitles from the very beginning (spyod-pa bya rgyu ye nas med). So, without our falling under the influence of erroneous inherited predispositions (bag-chags 'khrul-pa), our immediate awareness (da-lta'i shes-pa) becomes unfabricated self-clarity (ma bcos rang gsal). Without accepting or rejecting anything, we just allow things to be as they are without trying to modify them. This is behavior or conduct which is truly pure (rnam-pa dags-pa'i spyod-pa). Whether our actions are pure or impure, this no longer represents a case of duality.

21 Finally, the fruit is considered. Although there exist many different fruits and results, the nature of the mind, which is inherent self-awareness (rang rig sems nyid) in terms of its capacity, is none other than the spontaneously self-perfected Trikāya (sku gsum lhun-grub). Realization and the one who realizes it are not two different things (bsgrub bya sgrub byed gnyis-med). When we observe the mind and search for the one who has attained realization (bsgrub-mkhan), we do not find him anywhere, neither within nor outside oneself. Discovering this unfindability, at that very moment the realization of the fruit will become exhausted and is overthrown ('bras-bu zad sar 'khyol-ba). And even though it is the end of our seeking the goal, yet it is the beginning of self-awareness. Both the fruition and the one who is attaining it ('bras-bu sgrub rgyu) are found to not exist anywhere as discreet and separate

entities. Without our falling under the influence of attachments and aversions, or hopes and fears, our immediate present awareness (da-lta'i shes rig) becomes fully manifest within us. This is the ultimate fruition which is primordial Buddhahood, that is to say, the Buddhahood which has existed within us fully manifest from the very beginning (ye sangs-rgyas-pa'i 'bras-bu nyid).

22 Intrinsic awareness is free of all intellectual extremes (mtha' bral), such as the ideas of eternalism and nihilism (rtag chad med-pa). Thus we speak of a middle way which does not fall into any of these extreme views. There is nothing we can assert positively or negatively regarding the ultimate nature of the essence of the mind (sems kyi ngo-bo). We cannot say that it is something which has always existed from all eternity (rtag-pa), nor that it is something which will be annihilated in the future (chad-pa). Both Saṃsāra and Nirvāṇa are reflections or manifestations of the energy or potency (rtsal) of the mind. It is not that Saṃsāra and Nirvāṇa exist or do not exist in absolute terms—such views are party to the eight extremes (mtha' brgyad). Rather it is a matter of how we understand and perceive reality. If we have understanding, we are an enlightened being, whereas if we do not have understanding, we are an ordinary ignorant being who is caught up in the cycle of transmigration. The essence of awareness is just this.

We speak of Rigpa or intrinsic awareness as uninterrupted mindful awareness (dran rig rgyun-chad med-par rig-pa), but this presence or intrinsic awareness has been given many different names over the ages. Since emptiness possesses a core or heart which is intrinsically aware, it is called the Tathāgatagarbha, the embryo of Buddhahood, which is our own inherent Buddha-nature. Since it transcends and surpasses everything else, it is called the Prajñāpāramitā, the Perfection of Wisdom. Because it cannot be comprehended by the intellect and is from the very beginning free of all limitations, it is called the Mahāmudrā, the Great Symbol. Since it is the basis of all the bliss of Nirvāṇa and of all the sorrow of Saṃsāra, it is called the Ālaya, the basis of everything. Because this awareness is present and lucidly clear (shes-pa gsal-le hrig-ge), being ordinary and in no way exceptional, it is called ordinary awareness (tha-mal shes-pa). But no matter how many different names are applied to it, in terms of its real meaning, it is just this immediate present awareness (da-lta'i shes rig).

23 To desire some spiritual goal other than this awareness is like having an elephant at home, and yet be off searching for its tracks in the jungle. Or again, it is like trying to measure the entire universe with a tape measure. This universe is called three-thousandfold (stong gsum) because, according to Buddhist tradition, it contains some one-thousand

times one-thousand times one-thousand world systems similar to our
own earth and inhabited by intelligent life-forms. If we do not understand that everything originates from mind, it will not be possible for
us to attain Buddhahood. Not recognizing the nature of this intrinsic
awareness, we then search for our mind elsewhere. If we do not understand that Buddhahood is our own mind and search for it outside of
ourselves, then we will not find it. Mind is the single basis of both the
bliss of Nirvāna and the sorrow of Samsāra. Seeking for it elsewhere is
like the idiot who goes out into a crowd of people for entertainment,
but becoming disoriented, he does not recognize himself. Not looking
at himself he frantically looks at others and continually mistakes others
for himself. In the same way, if we do not understand that all appearances are manifestations of the energy of the mind (rig-pa'i rtsal), we
mistakenly think that these appearances are real and through this we
enter into transmigration. If we do not perceive the natural condition
of the real disposition of things (dngos-po gshis kyi gnas-lugs ma
mthong), not being aware that appearances are manifestations of mind
(snang-ba sems su ma shes), we are thrust again into Samsāra.

If we do not understand that in actuality our own mind is the Buddha
(rang sems sangs-rgyas ma mthong), then Nirvāna becomes obscured.
The only difference between Nirvāna and Samsāra is the presence of
awareness (rig-pa) or the absence of awareness (ma rig-pa). Whether
there is Nirvāna or Samsāra, the nature of the mind remains the same.
The essence of liberation and of delusion is the same; it is the nature
of the mind. The mind is one, not two, whether there is pure or impure
vision, whether there is Nirvāna or Samsāra. If we come to perceive
Nirvāna and Samsāra as being somewhere else than in our own mind
this is an error. Nevertheless, error and non-error are of a single essence
(ngo-bo gcig)—they both equally derive from mind. The mind-streams
of sentient beings ('gro la sems rgyud)[27] do not divide into two separate
channels called Nirvāna and Samsāra; they do not fall into two separate sections (gnyis su ma grub). The nature of the mind, without any
attempt at modifying or correcting thoughts which arise (sems nyid
ma bcos), liberates these same thoughts by allowing them to remain in
their own natural condition (rang sar bzhag-pas grol). If we leave the
mind in a state of being just as it is (ji-bzhin nyid) without trying to
correct or modify it, that is liberation.

24 Having discussed the mind and the thoughts that arise in it, which is
the inner or internal side of things, the author proceeds to speak of
external appearances (phyi'i snang-ba). "Appearances" (snang-ba) as
a term does not only mean phenomena visible to sight, but all phenomena which arise to the various senses. The real error in terms of our

existence in the world is our lack of awareness, our not knowing what is the mind ('khrul-pa de nyid sems su ma rig). Not having previously understood the real meaning of the Dharmatā, the nature of reality (chos nyid don), we must now look into ourselves (rang gis rang a blta) at what is self-arisen and self-originated (rang shar rang byung). Initially we may think that appearances must arise from somewhere at the beginning, then in between they must remain somewhere, and finally at the end, they must go somewhere. But when we look into this, observing our own mind, we find that it is like a crow gazing into a well at his own reflection. He thinks that he sees another crow there and, flying away again, his reflection departs with him. In the same way, all appearances arise out of the mind (snang-ba sems las shar-ba). It is the source of all our experience internal and external. Appearances arise from the mind and are liberated into the mind (rang gis sems las shar zhing sems su grol).

The nature of the mind, whereby we know everything and are aware of everything (sems nyid kun shes kun rig), is empty and luminously clear. Just as is the case with the sky, its emptiness and its clarity have been inseparable (gsal stong dbyer-med) from the very beginning.[28] Our manifest self-originated primal awareness (rang-byung ye-shes mngon-sum) arises as luminous clarity and that, becoming systematically established in an orderly fashion, is the Dharmatā, the nature of phenomena (chos nyid). There is a parallelism here. Internally there are thoughts or mind (sems) and the nature of the mind (sems nyid), and externally there are appearances (snang-ba) and the nature of reality or of phenomena (chos nyid). Even though the sign of its existence (yin-pa'i rtags) is all of phenomenal existence (snang srīd thams-cad), that is to say, whatever appears and whatever exists, still we are aware of things only in our mind (rang gis sems su rig). All phenomena, everything in the entire universe, are like the objects which are set before the mirror and this mirror is the nature of the mind. Since this latter is aware and clear (rig cing gsal), we come to understand that it is also like the sky. However, although we use this example of the sky as a means to indicate the nature of the mind, still this is only a simile which illustrates things in a one-sided way. The nature of the mind is empty, clear and aware everywhere, whereas the sky is neither aware nor intelligent. The real significance of the mind cannot be defined by such similes and metaphors.

25 This great diversity of appearances which represents relative existence (snang-ba kun-rdzob sna-tshogs) is not real in any absolute sense (bden-par ma grub) and will only disintegrate. All phenomenal existence, everything within Samsāra and Nirvāna (snang srīd 'khor 'das thams-

cad), are appearances which are seen in our own single nature of the mind (rang gi sems nyid gcig-pu'i mthong snang), like reflections appearing in a mirror.[29] At any particular moment, within the continuity of our own mind-streams (rang gi sems rgyud), there occur changes, and from this originate appearances which we perceive as external changes (phyi ru 'gyur-ba de'i mthong snang 'byung). Accordingly, everything which we perceive is an appearance of mind (thams-cad sems kyi mthong snang). Even the six destinies of rebirth ('gro-ba rigs drug) are just different appearances arising to vision. Each destiny or realm of rebirth has its own particular kind of karmic vision (las snang), depending on the cause of that destiny. All of us here in this lifetime are experiencing human karmic vision because we all possess in common the cause for such a vision. Therefore, we share this common vision. But this is not so with beings in other destinies of rebirth whose vision possesses different causes. For example, when we humans look at a river in summer, it appears to us to consist of cool and refreshing water. But to a Deva, who possesses a different kind of vision, the river seems to consist of fragrant sweet-tasting divine nectar. On the other hand, to a Preta or hungry ghost it seems to be a sluggish stream of foul-smelling excrement, and to a denizen in hell it seems to be a river of molten lava. In this way, external appearances are perceived by living beings in such a way as is determined by internal karmic causes. The same river is perceived quite differently by beings in different dimensions of existence.

But when our mind is transformed, all external appearances are transformed. If these two, Samsāra and Nirvāna, arise to us as reflections of our mind, then when our mind is transformed, when impure karmic vision is transformed into pure vision, the one will seem to change into the other. Instead of the usual chaotic mess which is the world around us, we perceive everything as the pure mandala of the Buddha. This is the principle of Tantra: transformation. This, of course, indicates something much more radical and profound than a superficial visualization of a wish-fulfillment fantasy—it is a radical transformation at the very root of the mind. But here in this context, the meaning is a bit different. In the Tantras a great deal of diligence and effort in meditation is required, a great deal of practice in clear visualization. But in Dzogchen, there is nothing to be transformed, nothing to be visualized such as beautiful mandalas and magnificent deities, nothing at all to be constructed by the mind, because all appearances are already spontaneously self-perfected from the very beginning.

All this is very easy to say. But external appearances seem to us to be very much real, very solid and substantial. It seems that there must be something actually out there and not just empty space, incredibly cluttered up with phantom projections of the mind. Why do appearances seem to be so solid and real? We must understand that it is the mind that grasps at appearances, at their reality and their substantiality (bdag'dzin). But these seemingly solid appearances are empty, being only space; they are nothing in themselves, save in the context of their relations to everything else. As distinct concrete isolated entities with their own individual reality they are nothing. And in terms of this, there is no error in them—rather the error lies in our grasping at them as real (bda 'dzin). It is this grasping that leads to attachments and aversions; this is the problem and not the things in themselves. But if we can come to understand that no matter how long we search, no matter how far we wander in this quest, we will not find anyone there who is doing the grasping, then we will discover liberation in that very fact. Whatever arises and whatever is liberated are only appearances of mind (sems kyi snang-ba).

26 On the other hand, the outsiders (the Europeans) and the Tīrthikas (the Hindus) see all of this question in terms of the duality of eternalism and nihilism (rtag chad gyis su mthong). For example, the nihilist asserts that what we call the mind or consciousness does not exist because it cannot be measured by his senses or by his laboratory instruments, the mind not having any discernable shape, color, mass, and so on. Equally there is no karma or rebirth because there is nothing measurable that survives the death of the material body. It should follow that everything in life is purely accidental and without purpose and meaning. This nihilistic viewpoint arises in the West in the form of the philosophy of materialism. In contrast, the eternalist asserts that there exists some abiding entity or substance which is unchanging and eternal, whether this is called the immortal soul, or God, the Creator of heaven and earth, the universal One Cosmic Mind.[30]

Moreover, each of the eight lower vehicles sees the matter in terms of its own view. Perceived in different ways, it is also explained and elaborated in different ways, and eventually each vehicle has come to develop a vast literature of its own. And yet, as indicated previously, each of these eight lower vehicles has the possibility of becoming afflicted and obscured by dualistic views. These dualistic views can be exceedingly subtle and so may go unrecognized; they will enter into the composition of the fundamental metaphysical assumptions that we have about the nature of reality. It is due to this radical unconscious dualism that we grasp at things and become attached to them, and thus errors ('khrul-pa) come into existence.

What are we to do then? Even though these appearances of which we are aware in the mind (sems su rig) do indeed arise and are perceived by us, if there is no grasping ('dzin-pa med) at them, no following after them and becoming attached to them, then in that lies the way to Buddhahood. But when we do grasp at these appearances taking them to be real self-existing entities and becoming attached to them, even though they are in themselves without any errors, errors then come into existence, and we find ourselves in the condition of Saṃsāra. However, if we become aware that the thoughts that apprehend or grasp at things are only mind ('dzin rtog sems su shes), then we will be able to allow these thoughts to become liberated by themselves (rang gis grol). It is not appearances in themselves that are the cause of the trouble, but our own grasping and attachment.

27 It is necessary to recall and be mindful that everything which arises is a manifestation of mind (sems kyi snang-ba). Even though an entire universe comes into manifestation, it is only an appearance of mind. Even though all sentient beings who inhabit this universe come into manifestation, they also are only appearances of mind.[31] In the same way, all of the delights of heaven and all of the sorrows experienced in the three evil destinies are but appearances of mind. Also, the five passions, good intentions, obstacles due to demons and evil spirits, attainments of realization, purity, one-pointed concentration, and states that are without definable characteristics or conceptual elaborations (mtshan-med spros-bral ngang) are all but appearances of mind. Even our experience of intrinsic awareness which is self-originating primal awareness is only an appearance of mind.

This continuous and uninterrupted arising of appearances represents the obstructed energy of the nature of the mind (sems nyid ma 'gags). Whatever appearances arise, these are like the waves upon the great ocean; yet the waves and the waters of the ocean are not two different things. Just as waves arise from the ocean and again return into it, so appearances are liberated of their own accord into the condition of the mind (sems kyi ngang du grol).

However many different names we apply to it, in terms of its real meaning the nature of the mind does not exist as other than a singularity; but this singularity (gcig-po de yang) is without any foundation and devoid of any root (gzhi med rtsa bral). Mind has no particular direction or location in space; we cannot say that it is in or is not in any direction. Nor can we say that it is just empty because there exists the transparent radiance of its own clarity and awareness (rig cing gsal-ba'i mdangs). On the other hand, clarity and emptiness have been inseparable from the very beginning. Immediate self-awareness is clear and present (da-lta rang gi shes-pa gsal hrig-ge). Not even Manjuśrī has the words to sufficiently express the profundity of the meaning of this. It is like a dumb man who suddenly tastes sugar for the first time. How can he express and describe his initial experience to others? We cannot say or point out anything concrete about emptiness. It has no definable characteristics and yet we can experience it. Whether we are a brilliant and learned scholar or just an ignorant uneducated cowherd, we can get the taste of it and that itself is liberation.

Actions certainly exist, but when we look into ourselves, we do not find any agent there who is the actor (byed-po mi shes). On the other hand, even though they are without any inherent nature (rang-bzhin med), experiences are still actually experienced (nyams su dngos su myong). If we understand this and practice accordingly, then everything becomes liberated on its own (kun grol) and everything is understood directly by the sense faculties without any intervening operations of the intellect (blo brtu med-par rtogs). But to realize this, it is necessary for us to practice. For example, even though the oil is inherent in the sesame seeds, if we do not press them first, we will not obtain the oil. Or again, even though milk is the cause of butter, if we do not churn it, we will not obtain any butter. Thus, in the same way, even though Buddhahood is inherent in every sentient being, if we do not practice, we will never realize Buddhahood. However if one does practice, even a humble cowherd can realize liberation.

And although we do not know how to explain this experience of intrinsic awareness, yet we can establish ourselves in it. We know the taste of sugar because we have actually had it in our mouth, but it is not really possible to explain that taste to others. They will have to taste it for themselves. Even a brilliant scholar, such as a pandita knowing Sanskrit, can fall into error through not understanding the nature of intrinsic awareness. It is not enough just to be learned and eloquent in explaining the Nine Vehicles. What is essential here is the direct experience of Rigpa or intrinsic awareness. Otherwise it will be like spreading rumors or telling tales of things and events which we have never seen personally. People like this have not even approached Buddhahood for a moment.

There is no higher view than that of Dzogchen. It is said to be like a great and mighty Garuda, the king of birds, who can move swiftly everywhere in the world in the twinkling of an eye. If we do not have such a vast and profound view, choosing rather to cage ourselves in restrictions and limitations, we cannot hope to fly free and reach the heights of Buddhahood. Those individuals having only mediocre and inferior capacities cannot reach these heights, for they are like chickens flapping about in the barnyard who do not have the ability to fly away. However, while our view should be vast and wide-ranging like the mighty Garuda, our behavior and conduct should be highly refined. This is the way it is with the Boddhisattva. As Guru Padmasambhava himself said, "Although my view is as vast as the sky, still my conduct is as refined as white flour."

When we actually come to understand the nature of the mind and its capacity for intrinsic awareness, then there is no way that our virtuous or vicious actions can affect us. This is because all of our merits and our sins (dge sdig)[32] become liberated into their own condition (rang sar grol), dissolving like clouds in the sky that leave no traces. At the time when we recognize our own intrinsic awareness (rang rig ngo-shes-pa) and realize the actual fruition of this, and not just an initial recognition, then we will not experience karmically the results of our actions. This is because we have transcended all duality, all notion of Samsāra and Nirvāna. At this point there exists no distinction between ourselves and the primordial Buddha because we have realized the Primordial State. This state is called Samantabhadra (kun tu bzang-po), "supremely excellent in every way," that is to say, the ultimate good, because it surpasses and transcends all relative considerations of good and bad. It transcends good and evil. Therefore, when we find ourselves in such a state, for us there exists no expectation of attaining Nirvāna and no fear of falling into Samsāra. When we understand the empty nature of our own mind (rang sems stong-pa ye-shes rtogs), then the consequences of merit and sin will not be realized. In the state of emptiness, there exists no objective merit or sin (stong-pa nyid la dge sdig yul ma grub). As it says in the text, the empty sky will not support an ocean, nor even a spring of water.

The nature of the mind is like a mirror; merits and sins are like the reflections in this mirror; and reflections in no way affect or modify the nature of the mirror. When we are in a state of contemplation, we are living in the condition of the mirror. At the time when all phenomena (chos-can kun) are exhausted and pass into the nature of reality (chos nyid zad-pa),[33] then our virtuous and vicious deeds will cause no benefit or harm to us. There is no basis for effect—all limitations, all frames of reference, all solid ground having been eliminated. But if we do not understand the nature of the mind and intrinsic awareness through direct personal experience, it will be a very dangerous situation for us. Indeed, it is not sufficient merely to understand these teachings intellectually; one must first practice and attain realization from this practice. Otherwise the virtuous and the vicious acts we commit in this life will create and accumulate karma, leading us again inevitably into transmigration. From the present time until we realize the ultimate exhausting of all phenomena into the nature of reality, our behavior must be refined; it must be heedful and scrupulous (bag-yod). Otherwise our view is only so much empty intellectual talk.

True, the nature of the mind, being like a highly polished mirror, is beyond cause and effect, but this fact does not abrogate for us the principle of karma, the law of cause and effect. On the contrary, it is only when we are actually in the state of contemplation, the primordial state of total integration, that we are beyond the operations of cause and effect. Short of that state our relative existence in the world in terms of body, speech, and mind is still very much under the dominion of karma. And this is no less true when our facile cleverness convinces us of the contrary, because what we think with our intellect, no matter how erudite, is still but the working of conditional mind. To jump up from our meditation seat thinking, "Wow, I'm in the state! I'm a Mahāsiddha!," and then run around doing whatever we like without regard for whom we hurt, exploit or deceive, is not Dzogchen, but just plain stupidity. And Dzogchen is not a path for stupid people. In itself, Dzogchen may be without limitations and without rules, but people lacking the capacity for awareness and for taking responsibility for what they do require limits and rules.

We must not let our view fall into behavior such that the view becomes a mere rationalization for our actions, nor let our behavior fall into the view such that behavior becomes a rigid expression of ideology without reference to the actual circumstances around us. But the really demonic or perverted view is the self-justifying one that both good and bad actions are empty and meaningless, whereby it does not matter at all what we do since there are no karmic consequences to our actions. However, this view is only an idea, a delusion of clever intellect, and does not represent our being in the state of contemplation. It is at our peril that we use this convenient sense of "emptiness" as an excuse for not accumulating meritorious karma. We must make inseperable the two accumulations—of merit and of wisdom. It is often said that all sentient beings are in reality Buddhas. But how did they become ordinary deluded sentient beings? It is due to the two obscurations: that resulting from the passions and that resulting from wrong knowledge. When these two layers of obscuration are thoroughly purified and eliminated, one becomes a Buddha. For this reason, we need both the seed of merit and the fruit of wisdom.

In the context of Buddhist practice, we speak of the three kinds of vows (sdom-pa gsum). In terms of the Hīnayāna, the path of renunciation, there exist the rules found in the Vinaya for monks and nuns and lay people: these vows or śīlas (tshul-khrims) tell us what we should not do. The principle here is ahimsā or non-violence, not harming others by our actions. In terms of the Mahāyāna, the path of purification, there exist the vows of the the Bodhisattva. These vows called samvaras (sdom-pa), in contrast to the above Hīnayāna śīlas, are positive and affirmative in their phrasing. The principle here is the performing of actions in order to help and benefit others, not just avoid harming them. In terms of the Vajrayāna, the path of transformation, the root is initiation, and this is maintained by the samāyā commitments (dam-tshig). Having once received initiation or empowerment, we must keep the samāyā vows and guard them well. These represent the commitment to do the practice. However, all of these Tantric vows may be condensed into the Samāyās of the Body, Speech, and Mind: all appearances are the deity, all sounds are the mantra, and all thoughts and memories are the Dharmatā. Thus, the principle of samāyā is having pure vision (dag snang).

But in terms of Dzogchen, there exist no such rules or vows. When the Indian Buddhist master Atīśa came to Tibet in the eleventh century, he met the famous Tibetan translator Rinchen Zangpo. Atīśa asked him how he practiced the Tantras which he had translated, and the latter replied that he practiced them meticulously one after the other. But Atīśa told him that this was not the correct way. He pointed out to the translator that all of the Tantras could be condensed and integrated into a single Upadeśa and one need only practise that in order to maintain all of the transmissions which he had received. The same is true with Dzogchen. If we really understand this single teaching here which comes directly from Guru Padmasambhava, we can attain liberation. But we must grasp this vital core (srog shing) of the teaching. No matter what we are doing, which ever among the four modes of behavior—walking, sitting, lying down, or eating, we must always hold ('dzin) to awareness (rig), never forgetting, never losing this awareness. This is the real meaning of Rigdzin (rig-'dzin), one who is totally aware. In Dzogchen, there is only one rule—always be aware in whatever we do, never be distracted (ma yengs cig)!

When our own intrinsic awareness becomes manifest (rang rig mngon-sum), everything is seen nakedly (gter mthong), unencumbered and undistorted by conceptual constructions and the workings of the mind. In the state of contemplation, the state of total awareness and presence, whatever thoughts and appearances arise are allowed to remain in their own condition without any attempts by the mind to modify or correct them, and in this way they self-liberate. To be precise, their very arising is simultaneously their self-liberation. There is no duality between arising and liberating, no interval between these events, no intervention by the mind or thought process. This self-liberation through seeing nakedly is clearly a teaching of the greatest profundity, and we are fortunate to have the rare opportunity to become acquainted with it.

28 Now there comes the concluding section of the text. The author, Padmasambhava, tells us that the teaching found here was given especially for the benefit of sentient beings of later generations who will appear in these degenerate times (snyigs-ma'i dus), and this means us in particular. It is for our benefit that all of his Tantras, Āgamas, and Upadeśa have been revealed.[34] After being written down by his disciple, the lady Yeshe Tsogyal, they were subsequently concealed as hidden treasures (gter-ma) in order to be rediscovered in future times by those whose karma had ripened (ma 'ongs las 'phro-can), that is to say, by the future reincarnations of the members of his original group of disciples in Tibet. Samāyā gya gya gya—this is his promise to us. The colophon of the text which follows this repeats the title of the text and gives us the author's name, Padmasambhava, the Master from Uddiyāna.

These notes were compiled and put into the form of a continuous commentary to the translation of the text by the translator, relying in particular on the oral comments of Lama Tharchin and in general on the writings and teachings of Namkhai Norbu Rinpoche.

Vajranātha,
Strode House, South Devon
February, 1986

Appendix I

The Views on Dzogchen of
W. Y. Evans-Wentz and C.G. Jung

1. The Life and Writings of W. Y. Evans-Wentz

An earlier translation of this text will be found in *The Tibetan Book of the Great Liberation* by W. Y. Evans-Wentz.[1] However, there are many serious errors in this translation, particularly in terms of its interpretation and comparison with other spiritual systems. It is therefore appropriate here to discuss the Evans-Wentz version, especially in view of the fact that it has enjoyed a rather wide circulation and is responsible for a number of misunderstandings regarding the meaning of Dzogchen, including that of Dr. Carl Jung.

The purpose here is not to denigrate the pioneer role of Evans-Wentz in the study of the literature of the Nyingmapa and Kagyudpa schools of Tibetan Buddhism. He worked on these texts in Gangtok and Darjeeling (1919, 1935) in collaboration with Tibetan Lamas who were familiar with the oral traditions of interpretation of Tibetan texts. Moreover, at the time when Evans-Wentz was writing, European scholars had little knowledge of the vast extent and the historical importance of Tibetan literature. In general, these scholars looked down upon anything that was connected with the Tantras, which they regarded as a decadent and sex-obsessed form of Hinduism which had crept into and corrupted the once chaste body of Buddhism.[2] Under much the same impression concerning the Hindu origin of the Buddhist Tantras, Evans-Wentz asked Sir John Woodroffe, an English magistrate of the High Court in Calcutta and at the same time an authority on the Shākta system of Hindu Tantra, to write an introduction to *The Tibetan Book of the Dead* which he was preparing for publication. In line with this, Evans-Wentz also introduced a terminology into the translations which was largely derived from Hinduism. Thus, for example, the consorts or female aspects of the Buddhas are called Shaktis, "Powers," in this way reversing the polarity of the whole Buddhist system. Under the influence of the Hindu philosophy of Vedānta, as well as the beliefs of modern day Theosophists, Evans-Wentz made many mistakes in a field that was largely unknown to him, his field of academic research and expertise having lain elsewhere in Celtic folk-lore studies. But despite this academic training at Oxford, Evans-Wentz appears somewhat naive in his tendency to believe so much of what he read of a Theosophical nature.

71

Nevertheless, with enthusiasm he tried to penetrate intellectually this unknown world of Tibet and make Tibetan Buddhist beliefs plausible to an unbelieving and increasingly materialistic West.[3]

At the risk of appearing to argue *ad hominem*, I must say something about the career of Evans-Wentz and the influences, both spiritual and intellectual, that led him to misinterpret Dzogchen and Tibetan Buddhism in the way he did. His biography is given more extensively elsewhere.[4] Evans-Wentz never visited Tibet itself, never lived as a Buddhist monk, and did not spend three years in Darjeeling studying under his Lama, Kazi Dawa Samdup, as is sometimes claimed.[5] In fact, he spent barely a few months, all told, among the Tibetans in Darjeeling and Sikkim. The extant letters of both Evans-Wentz and Dawa Samdup indicate that this Lama did not play the role of a personal Guru to Evans-Wentz. In the letters there are no references to any "secret teachings" which Evans-Wentz was supposed to have received. The writings of Evans-Wentz also clearly indicate this, as we shall see shortly. Quite the contrary, Evans-Wentz occasionally attempted to foster his own views and interpretations on the Lama, as was the case, for example, with his Theosophical interpretation of reincarnation.[6] Also, according to the accounts of the Lama's own son, there was no evidence that Evans-Wentz actually participated in pūjās or Buddhist ceremonies on a daily basis or arose early in the morning in order to practice meditation.[7] His letters and diaries show only a rather formal relationship with the Lama.

Nor did Evans-Wentz, as he himself freely admitted, ever know or read any Tibetan. The Tibetan texts themselves which he collected were first translated by Tibetan Lamas knowing English into what amounted to a rough translation, and then these were reworked and edited by Evans-Wentz over a number of years. During this time he also composed lengthy introductions and copious footnotes to the translations, which formed a kind of running commentary to them. Ultimately, this resulted in the publication of a series of four books:

The Tibetan Book of the Dead (1927)
Tibet's Great Yogi Milarepa (1928)
Tibetan Yoga and Secret Doctrines (1935)
The Tibetan Book of the Great Liberation (1954)

In these books, the actual translations form only a small part, while the bulk of them is taken up, overwhelmingly so, by the material written by Evans-Wentz himself. Thus, we tend to overlook and forget who were the actual translators of the Tibetan texts.

How did Evans-Wentz come to collaborate with these Lamas? Evans-Wentz was a very eccentric, albeit charming figure, a compulsive traveler and a sober, indeed puritanical, romantic. Wandering restlessly about Europe, the Near East, and Asia, he came to think of himself as a gypsy-scholar, and he certainly was that. Even as a young man, he was outraged by any public display of sexuality, and on one occasion, during his under-graduate days at Stanford University, he was part of a project that made a survey of and attempted to reform the moral character of "the fallen women" or prostitutes of Oakland, California. During his travels in Italy and southern Europe, he was appalled by what he regarded as the open sensuality and hedonism of the Latin peoples. In his later years he was much given to denouncing the lack of public morals in the life he saw about him. He remained a life-long bachelor. Indeed throughout his life he re-mained in essence "an innocent abroad," that very peculiar turn-of-the-century American combination of naive idealistic innocence and stern puri-tanism, reminiscent of a character out of a Henry James novel. He was a type very common in the Theosophical circles of those days, characterized by alienation between spirit and flesh.

Evans-Wentz was born on February 2, 1878 in Trenton, New Jersey. His father was a German immigrant (Wentz), his mother of American Quaker stock (Evans). He later hyphenated these two names when he was a student at Oxford. In his early years, he was much given to reading the Bible, and this gave the peculiar Biblical diction and tone to the translations he edited. Weary of the hypocrisy of conventional American Christianity, he read extensively in the new Theosophical literature which just then was appear-ing.

The Theosophical Society was founded in New York City in 1875 by a Russian immigrant of Spiritualist interests, Madame Helena Petrovna Blavatsky, and two American lawyers, Col. Henry Steele Olcott and Wil-liam Q. Judge. Madame Blavatsky, when living in India during the follow-ing decade, claimed that she was in direct telepathic communication with certain Mahātmās or Masters of Wisdom residing in remote Tibet. In re-sponse to a series of questions posed by an English journalist, A. P. Sinnett, handwritten letters from these mysterious Mahātmās in Tibet began to appear, letters which allegedly materialized miraculously in various places about the house and garden where the Madame was staying in Simla. In these letters, appropriately known as the Mahatma Letters, a system of Ancient Wisdom was delineated, revealing the past occult history of the human race and this planet. Now generally known by the name Theosophy, Madame Blavatsky and A. P. Sinnett first called this system "Esoteric Bud-dhism," and she asserted that this was the real Buddhism of Tibet. Later, while residing in Europe, she composed by means of automatic writing a lengthy re-formulation of this system, which was soon published as *The Secret Doctrine* (1888). This work was alleged to be a translation, with elaborate commentaries, of the oldest book in the Tibetan canon of scriptures, *The Stanzas of Dzyan*. This short text, said to derive from certain high initiates of Lemuro-Atlantean times, gives in rather gnomic verses an account of the origin of the world and the evolution of humanity from an occult standpoint. She was never able to produce this exceedingly ancient Tibetan manuscript for examination by Orientalists and other scholars.[8] However, one of the principal themes of this Theosophical system is reincarnation, and it was this idea which first attracted Evans-Wentz to Theosophy. The belief in reincarnation had once also existed among early Christian groups, but at the Second Council of Constantinople in 553 CE, this doctrine was expelled from the body of Christianity and declared heretical. It was largely due to the writings of Madame Blavatsky and other Theosophists that the idea of reincarnation was popularized in Europe and America.

His father having become a successful real estate developer in Florida, Evans-Wentz followed him there in 1900, and, going into business himself, he quickly made a fortune. In 1905 Evans-Wentz sold these properties and invested in southern California real estate. For the remainder of his life, he was able to live off the income from these American rentals. In 1901 he went to San Diego, California for the first time and visited Point Loma, which had become the headquarters of the American Section of the Theosophical society under the leadership of the formidable Katherine Tingley. She had taken control of the American Section after the death of William Q. Judge in 1896. At the urging of Mrs. Tingley, Evans-Wentz entered Stanford University, taking a B.A. in English in 1906 and M.A. in 1907. That same year he entered Jesus College, Oxford, where he read Social Anthropology and where Sir John Rhys was his tutor in Celtic studies. Although he himself did not personally wander throughout Celtic lands interviewing peasants about their beliefs regarding the fairy people, he read thoroughly all of the existing accounts of those researchers who had done so.[9] The results of his own compilation from these sources were published later as *The Fairy Faith in Celtic Countries* (1911). In its initial form, this book was submitted for a doctorate at the University of Rennes in Brittany. In 1910 Oxford awarded him a B.Sc. and in 1931 it awarded him a D.Sc. in Comparative Religion.

World War I found him in Egypt where he remained for some three years. T. E. Lawrence, the famous Lawrence of Arabia, a friend from his days at Oxford, obtained government permission for him to leave Egypt and sail for Ceylon. The following year, 1918, found him in South India at Adyar, south of Madras, at the international headquarters of the Theosophical Society which was a rival of the one at Point Loma. Here he met with the equally formidable Annie Besant, the president of the Theosophical Society. At the time, she and C. W. Leadbeater, a former Anglican clergyman, were preparing Jiddu Krishnamurti to assume his future role as the Messiah, the next World Teacher who would be the incarnation of the Buddha Maitreya. Some years later, Krishnamurti renounced this august role and went his own way, precipitating a major schism in the Theosophical Society. Evans-Wentz also went his own way in 1919, visiting Amritsar, Simla and Birbhadura near Rishikesh where he met Swāmi Satyānanda. This figure, more than anyone else, played the role of Guru in his spiritual development.

Finally, in the same year, Evans-Wentz arrived in Darjeeling where he met the superintendent of police in that town, an officer by the name of Sardar Bahadur Laden La. This Sikkimese gentleman later came to translate into English a portion of the Terma of Urgyan Lingpa, entitled the bKa'-thang gser-phreng, which is the largest existing biography of Guru Padmasambhava. He entrusted this translation to Evans-Wentz in 1935, and it in due time appeared as one of the translations in The Tibetan Book of the Great Liberation (1954).[10] But on this occasion S. B. Laden La gave him a letter of introduction to the headmaster of the Mahārāja's Bhutia Boy's School in Gangtok, Sikkim, because Evans-Wentz, having acquired a number of Tibetan books in the Darjeeling bazaar, was in need of a translator for them. This headmaster was none other than the same Lama, Kazi Dawa Samdup, who for several years previously had been the teacher and translator for Alexandra David-Neel, the French scholar of things Tibetan, who claimed to have spent several years inside of Tibet while in disguise.[11]

For the next two months, together with his eager American student, the Lama went through the Tibetan texts of the Bar-do thos-grol and some shorter Kagyudpa texts on Mahāmudrā and Nāro chos drug. On his own, the Lama was a scholar and a linguist, having just published an English-Tibetan Dictionary (1919) and a translation, Srīchakrasambhara Tantra (1919), in Sir John Woodroffe's Tantrik Texts series.[12] In addition, the Lama was translating the biography of Milarepa, the rJe-btsun bka'-'bum. The Lama was subsequently appointed Lecturer in Tibetan at the University of Calcutta and died not long afterward in 1922. After his death, his family presented the above manuscript to Evans-Wentz, who, after editing it, saw it published as Tibet's Great Yogi Milarepa (1928). The shorter texts which the Lama had translated were published in Tibetan Yoga and Secret Doctrines (1935). Thus it is to this Sikkimese Lama, rather than to Evans-Wentz, that the honor of being the first translator of Nyingmapa and Kagyudpa texts into English belongs.

Over all, it appears that Evans-Wentz spent relatively little time with this Lama—enough time perhaps for the translations to be made because the Lama was quite conversant with English, but hardly enough time to actually enter into and pursue the meditation practices of which these texts speak. A scant two months after arriving in Darjeeling, Evans-Wentz was back at the ashram of Swāmi Satyānanda, determined to compare these abstruse Tibetan teachings which he had just obtained with those of the more familiar Hatha Yoga system of Hinduism. Following a regime of ascetic training devīsed by the Swāmi, attired as a Sādhu and living in a grass hut, Evans-Wentz practiced āsnas and prānāyāma. This training under the Swāmi was thoroughly Hindu, though he did consult the Swāmi and solicit his opinions on the contents of the translations which referred to yogic practices.[13] What is important to note here is that Evans-Wentz did *not* practice under the guidance of a qualified Lama either the Six Yogas of Nāropa or Mahāmudrā or Dzogchen or any other Tibetan Buddhist practice for that matter. The only practice attested to in his diaries are Hindu. But even here he did not remain long with Swāmi Satyānanda.

In June of 1920 he was off visiting Amarnāth, Kedarnāth, and other sites, as well as buying property in Puri. In October of 1920 he briefly visited the Lama again in Darjeeling. By New Year of 1921 he was back at Puri, where he met with Srī Yukteshwar Giri and many other prominent Swāmis whom he consulted in order to elucidate certain metaphysical and theological questions which perplexed him. He applied the Hindu Vedāntist explanations which he received here to interpret the rough translations which he had obtained from Lama Dawa Samdup.[14] After a stay in the Nilgiris in South India in order to study the Todas, a Dravidian buffalo-herding people, he was off to Colombo in Ceylon to debate the Roman Catholics over the question of reincarnation. After visiting China, he returned to the West Coast and San Diego. Here he reported on the situation at Adyar to Katherine Tingley who was at that time in the midst of a raging feud with Annie Besant over control of the world-wide Theosophical movement. In 1924 he was again at Oxford where he edited the Milarepa translation for future publication. But not since his last meeting with Lama Kazi Dawa Samdup in 1920 did he consult any Tibetan Lama on interpreting the translations he had received. In 1928 he was back in Ceylon and then Puri, with frequent visits to Swāmi Satyānanda near Rishikesh. In 1931 he was back in California, where he met Swāmi Paramahamsa Yogānanda whose own Guru, Yukteshwar Giri, Evans-Wentz had met some years before in Puri. Thereafter these two remained life-long friends. Eventually the Swāmi established his own ashram and the Self-Realization Fellowship (SRF) near Los Angeles, a city the Swāmi came to characterize as "the Benares of the West."

In 1934 Evans-Wentz was back in India. For a short time in 1935, he resided in Darjeeling and Ghoom. It was here that he employed two Tibetan Lamas, Sumdhon Paul and Lobzang Mingyur Dorje, to translate for him another short text from the *Tibetan Book of the Dead* cycle (the text I have retranslated here). This occasion was the last direct personal contact that Evans-Wentz had with any Tibetan Lamas. In 1936 he purchased a remote piece of property near the Himalaya hill station of Almora, where he had the intention of eventually establishing an ashram. Nearby was the ashram of an English Yogi, Srī Krishna Rem (Ronald Nixon), whose views were similar to those of Evans-Wentz. With the onset of World War II he left India and arrived back in San Diego in June of 1941.

Years later he offered the use of his property in Almora to Anagarika Govinda, who had returned in 1947 from a six month journey in western Tibet with his wife. Thereafter the couple resided in a house on this property for many years. Lama Anagarika Govinda (b. 1898), a German artist and poet, had come to India and Ceylon many years before and became a practicing Buddhist in Ceylon under the guidance of a German Buddhist monk belonging to the Theravadin school. In 1936 he met a Gelugpa Lama, Tromo Geshe Rinpoche, during the latter's pilgrimage in India. From that time onward, Govinda considered himself no longer a Theravadin but a Tibetan Buddhist, although he continued using the Theravadin title "anagarika" (which means a lay practitioner who wears white robes). He had not been an ordained monk, and subsequently he married an Indian actress and talented photographer, Li Gotami. Being a German national, he was interned by the British government of India during the war years, 1940 to 1945, at Dehra Dun. During this time, at the suggestion of a fellow internee, a German Swāmi, he wrote a book presenting his own personal interpretation of Vajrayāna Buddhism, subsequently published as *The Foundations of Tibetan Mysticism* (1959). However, no original Tibetan sources, textual or oral, were used in the writing of this book, and its contents bear no relation to the actual foundation practices and teachings of Tibetan Buddhism which are known as Ngondro and Lamrin.[15] After release from internment and his brief visit to Tibet, an account of which is given in *The Way of the White Clouds* (1966), he adopted the title of Lama and declared himself a member of the Kagyudpa order of Tibetan Buddhism. In Germany a quasi-Masonic order based on this Lama's teachings and writings was organized, called the Arya Maitreya Mandala.

Having been presented by Evans-Wentz with his own collection of Tibetan xylographs and manuscripts which he had left behind in India, Govinda clearly saw the need for a revision of the translation of *The Tibetan Book of the Dead*, which was faulty and inaccurate in many regards. Govinda corresponded with Evans-Wentz on this matter and with the latter's agreement prepared an extensive list of corrections, but the publisher, Oxford University Press, refused to make any extensive changes due to the cost involved in typesetting the whole book all over again.[16] Thus, instead of a revised edition meeting the standards of modern Tibetan scholarship, the book was reprinted with all the original mistakes and misunderstandings. It was left to others to bring out a more accurate translation.[17]

Back in the United States, Evans-Wentz settled into a working class hotel in downtown San Diego, the Keystone Hotel, and lived there for the next twenty-three years of his life. Working in the nearby public library, he edited the translations found in *The Tibetan Book of the Great Liberation*, published in 1954. He grew very close to Paramahamsa Yogānanda who often invited him to meetings and lectures at the Self-Realization Fellowship. This Swāmi whose *Autobiography of a Yogi* (1946) has circulated widely in America, was a leading advocate in the West of Advaita Vedānta and he asked Evans-Wentz to write a foreword to this book. In those years he also actively contributed articles to various Theosophical publications. In the last few months of his life, at the invitation of Yogānanda, Evans-Wentz took up lodgings at the latter's ashram in Encinitas, California. Here he died on July 17, 1965, at the age of eighty-eight.

2. The Tibetan Book of the Great Liberation

The final volume of his Tibetan series, *The Tibetan Book of the Great Liberation* was the product of the last period of his life. The actual translation to which he referred by this title and which I have retranslated here, represents only a small portion of the entire book. The bulk of the book is composed of commentaries and explanations by the editor. There is a preceding section giving an epitome of the life of Padmasambhava, translated by S. B. Laden La. But it was the second section, Book II, "The Yoga of Knowing the Mind," etc., that he considered to be the most important of all his works. As he had felt for most of his life that all existence is mind, this translation only appeared to confirm his preconceptions, and he thought of it as representing the quintessence of all his work, his final statement and testament. But working over the drafts of this, the last book in the series, while living in semi-retirement in San Diego, in an environment where all of his friends were Theosophists and neo-Vedāntists, only strengthened and confirmed in him a view of Tibetan Buddhism which was fundamentally neither Tibetan nor Buddhist, but Theosophical and Vedāntist.

In the case of the text we have here, Evans-Wentz employed two Lamas, Lama Sumdhon Paul and Lama Lobzang Mingyur Dorje, to translate it for him. Both of these Lamas had been close disciples of Geshe Sherab Gyatso, the Mongolian Gelugpa Lama, who had some years previously founded Ghoom monastery at Ghoom, a mountain village a few miles south of Darjeeling. Both of these Tibetans had taught at the Government High School in Darjeeling and thus surely had a command of the English language. Nevertheless, the religious education and training of both of these Lamas was strictly within the Gelugpa tradition, and so it is rather unlikely that they would have had much direct acquaintance with the Dzogchen teachings and with the rather special, if not arcane, terminology they employ. The technical terms peculiar to Dzogchen, as well as the special meanings given in the Dzogchen context to a number of common Buddhist terms, will not be found in the Sarit Chandra Das *Tibetan-English Dictionary* (1902), the bulk of which was actually compiled by Lama Lobzang Mingyur Dorje. Although certainly representing a monumental effort, if we look at the sources consulted in the compiling of this dictionary, it is clear that no Dzogchen texts are cited as sources, with the possible exception of the *Bar-do thos-grol*.[18] Thus, although these two Lamas might be aware of the literal or conventional meaning of the words in the text, the translation as it is presented does not penetrate to the real meaning of Dzogchen. This is despite the claim made by Evans-Wentz that "the translators and Editor believe, however, that the rendering herein contained faithfully conveys the real meanings which an educated Lama would derive from a careful study of the treatise in its original form."[19]

The second point, which is even more critical, is that Evans-Wentz, in his lengthy introductions and in his copious footnotes, approaches Tibetan Buddhism from the standpoint of Theosophy, that is to say, the modern neo-theosophy and occultism of Madame Blavatsky. This is combined with some knowledge of Neo-Platonic philosophy and modern popularized Advaita Vedānta. The latter two he cites again and again as sources for his exegesis of the text. In this way he comes to impose on the rough translation he obtained from his Tibetan informants a conceptual construction, an odd mixture of ancient and modern, which has little relation to the actual meaning of the texts in Tibetan. All of this leads him to assert erroneously that the essential teaching of Dzogchen is the existence of a metaphysical entity which he calls "the One Mind."

Thus in his Introduction to *The Tibetan Book of the Great Liberation* he says:

> Here in Book II in the Yoga of Knowing the Mind in its Nakedness . . . is set forth an epitome of the root teachings of Mahāyāna transcendentalism concerning Reality. In common with all schools of Oriental Occult Sciences, the Mahāyāna postulates that the One Supra-Mundane Mind, of Universal All-Pervading Consciousness,

transcendent over appearances and over every dualistic concept born of the finite or mundane aspect of mind, alone is real. Viewed as Voidness, it is the Become, the Unborn, the Unmade, the Unformed, the predicateless Primordial Essence, the abstract Cosmic Source where all concrete or manifested things come and into which they vanish into latency. Being without form, quality, or phenomenal existence, it is the Formless, the Qualityless, the Non-Existent. As such it is the Imperishable, the Transcendent Fullness of the Emptiness, the Dissolver of Space and Time and of Sangsāric (or mundane) mind, the Brāhman of the Rishis, the Dreamer of Māyā, the Weaver of the Web of Appearances, the Outbreather and the Inbreather of infinite universes throughout the endlessness of Duration....

In its totality, the Universal Essence is the One Mind manifested through the multitudinous myriads of minds throughout all states of Sangsāric existence.... Unenlightened man, being far from Full Awakening, believes himself to be possessed of an individual mind uniquely his own; and this illusion-based belief has given rise to the doctrine of the soul. But the Tibetan Teachers declare that the One Cosmic Mind alone is unique; that, on each of the incalculable myriads of life-bearing orbs throughout space, the One Cosmic Mind is differentiated only in an illusory sense, by means of a reflected, or subsidiary, mind appropriate to, and common to, all living things thereon, as on the planet earth. Though there be but a single speaker, his voice may be broadcasted to all the millions of Earth's inhabitants and be heard by each one of them individually.... It is because mankind's minds, or consciousnesses, are collectively one that all mankind see the same world of phenomenal appearances.... Earth's multitude of human and sub-human creatures, each of them like a single cell, collectively constitute the body of one great multi-celled organism, mentally illuminated by the One Cosmic Mind.... [20]

One may well admire the spiritual enthusiasm of Evans-Wentz in all this, enthusiasm which is quite genuine. However, there is no equivalent in the actual Tibetan text for his "the One Mind." The phrase *sems gcig-po* occurs in one place where it means "It is the single (nature of) mind which encompasses all of Samsāra and Nirvāna" ('khor 'das yongs la khyab-pa'i sems gcig-po). This is its only occurrence. What is meant here is not some sort of Neo-Platonic hypostasis, a universal *Nous*, of which all individual minds are but fragments or appendages. Rather, what is meant by this phrase in the context of the text is that, whether one finds oneself in the state of

Samsāra or in the state of Nirvāna, it is the nature of mind (and here *sems* means *sems nyid*) which reflects with awareness all experiences, no matter what may be their nature. This occurs much in the same way as a mirror reflects whatever objects come before it, whether these be ugly or beautiful. The text is not postulating the real existence of a plurality of individual minds, infinite in number, nor the real existence of a single Over-Mind into which all our individual mind-streams will eventually merge, like rivers flowing into the ocean, at the end of our spiritual careers on earth, with an accompanying loss of our individuality.[21]

3. *The Buddhist Concept of Nirvāna*

After postulating the existence of this One Mind, Evans-Wentz proceeds to speak of our ultimate spiritual goal as a returning to and absorption in this One Mind. He writes:

> As our treatise on knowing the One Mind teaches, it is by knowing himself... that man yogically merges his microcosmic mundane consciousness in the Supra-Mundane All-Consciousness; ceasing to be man, he becomes Buddha; the circumscribed becoming the uncircumscribed, the universalized, the Cosmic.... Mind in its microcosmic aspect is variously described by the unenlightened, some calling it the ego, or soul.... Realization of the One Mind through introspectively attaining the understanding of the true nature of its microcosmic aspect innate in man, is equivalent to the attainment of Brāhmanical Moksha, the Mahāyānic Nirvāna, the Full Awakening of Buddhahood.... Evolution is a purely mental process. This microcosmic mind of man fashions for himself ever new mansions; and, in the process of evolution, there is a continuous expansion of mind until at-one-ment with the One Mind has been attained.... In the One Mind is the summation of the whole of consciousness, the ineffable at-one-ment of all the One Mind's microcosmic aspects. In transcending the microcosmic mind of the human ego, man transcends himself; he becomes a conscious participator in the all-embracing Universal Mind, the Over-Mind, the Cosmic Consciousness....[22]

Here there is a fundamental misunderstanding of the Buddhist conception of Nirvāna. But Evans-Wentz is not alone in this, for even in so reliable a source as the *Oxford Illustrated Dictionary* (1962) the following definition is given for Nirvāna: "In Buddhist theology, extinction of individual existence and absorption into the Supreme Spirit. . . . " It is questionable whether or not we can apply the term "theology" to Buddhism, since Buddhists do not believe in a God who is the creator of the universe and who reveals himself in history to intervene on the side of his chosen nation as against other nations. Nor does Nirvāna, in the Buddhist context, mean rebirth in heaven after death, nor union with God, nor the merging of oneself with some sort of Universal Mind or impersonal Absolute.

Etymologically, Nirvāna comes from a Sanskrit root meaning "to blow out," such as when one might blow out the flame of a candle; this gives it the sense of "extinction." But extinction of what? In the Hīnayāna Sūtras it means the extinction of our outflows or pollutants (zag-bcas, Skt. āsrava), such as sexual desire, craving for existence, and so on— that is, our passions (nyon-mong-pa, Skt. kleśa). This is how the Hīnayāna Sūtra system conceives of the Nirvāna of an Arhat or perfect saint. When the causes of rebirth are removed, these passions and pollutants, then one is reborn no more. An Arhat (dgra-bcom-pa), which is the final goal of the Hīnayāna path, is explained etymologically to mean one who has slain (bcom-pa) his enemies (dgra), these enemies being the passions. Having done so, he realizes a state of perfect peace. It is the passions that propel us into action and the creating of karma, and thus we are led again into transmigration. It is these same passions that inevitably lead to anxiety and frustration in our lives, and therefore they create suffering. This sense is reflected in the Tibetan translation of the Sanskrit word Nirvāna as *mya-ngan las 'das-pa*, "passing beyond suffering." This of course puts Nirvāna in a rather negative perspective, namely, escape from all the sorrows and problems experienced in the world.

According to the Hīnayāna view, the extinction of one's desires means that the causes of rebirth have been annihilated, and one will be reborn no more in this world. The Buddha realized this condition while in contemplation beneath the Bodhi Tree. Then, with the death of His material body, which had persisted after His enlightenment only because of residual karma, He passed into final Nirvāna and was seen in this world no more. Does this mean that the individuality of that person known in history as Śākyamuni Buddha was totally extinguished, like a fire going out when its fuel is exhausted? In many Hīnayāna writings, this would seem to be the case.

But this is not so with the explanations found in the Mahāyāna Sūtras, as for example, the *Saddharmapundarīka* or *Lotus Sūtra*. Although the realization of the Arhat who has extinguished all his passions is admitted as valid, still this is not considered to be his ultimate goal. Why is this? Even though the Arhat has eliminated his obscurations due to the passions

(Skt. kleśa-āvarana), he is unconsciously still afflicted by subtle intellectual obscurations (Skt. jneya-āvarana), and so, after an exceedingly long period of dormancy in a state of cosmic unconsciousness, these subtle propensities awaken him again into existence. Therefore, the Arhat has not really liberated himself from Samsāra.

According to the Mahāyāna view, the ultimate goal is that of Buddhahood itself, and this realization of Buddhahood is known as Bodhi or "enlightenment." Etymologically the Sanskrit word Buddha means "one who has awakened" to the actual nature of reality. In its Tibetan translation, sangs-rgyas, the term Buddha is interpreted to mean one whose mind has awakened (sangs-pa) and expanded (rgyas-pa) like a lotus blossom opening its petals above the murky waters of a pond. The word Bodhi, "enlightenment," derives from the same Sanskrit root as Buddha, namely, "to awaken, to wake up." Thus this term emphasizes the positive and affirmative side of Buddhahood, the realization of enlightenment, whereas the term Nirvāna emphasizes the negative aspect, the liberation from Samsāra. It is a matter of looking at things from a slightly different point of view. Moreover, according to the Mahāyāna, Bodhi is equated with the realization of omniscience (Skt. sarvajnā): the Buddha is one who knows all things, both in their individual aspects and in their ultimate nature as emptiness.

In the Hīnayāna system, the Buddha has a more restricted soteriological role in relation to humanity and the cosmos. He is the World-Teacher who reveals the path to liberation from Samsāra, but only one such Buddha can appear within a single kalpa or cycle of time. There will not be another Buddha until the advent of Maitreya some five thousand years hence. The only escape from suffering open to us as human beings now in the Kali Yuga is the Nirvāna of the Arhat; but, according to some accounts, there has not been an Arhat for the last two thousand years. However, according to the Mahāyāna system, there existed not only our historical Buddha, Sakyamuni, some two thousand five hundred years ago, but even at this present moment throughout the universe, in all world-systems inhabited by intelligent life-forms, there are countless numbers of Buddhas being born, attaining enlightenment, teaching the Dharma, and passing away into Nirvāna. This process is unceasing. There are as many Buddhas as there are stars in the night sky. Buddhahood is the principle of enlightenment and so it is not something restricted or limited in its manifestation to a single historical moment or a period of time.

Since Buddhahood is the principle of enlightenment, it is something which exists at the core of every single sentient being. There exists no sentient being who does not possess the potentiality for Buddhahood in seminal form, what is called our inherent Buddha-nature or Tathāgatagarbha. This being so, why then pursue something lesser, if we all possess the potentiality for supreme enlightenment? And so we can well ask why did the Buddha teach this lesser goal of the Arhat? It was because the Hīnayāna system was especially well suited to the cultural and historical conditions prevailing at the time in northern India. There were many other spiritual disciplines existing at the same time as the Buddha was teaching, such as those of the Jainas, the Ajiviakas, the Sāmkhyas, and so on. Most of these were ascetic paths which stressed the absolute necessity of renouncing the worldly life of the householder and of adopting an ascetic life-style, at times entailing extreme austerities and mortification of the flesh. Some of these groups of ascetics became organized into orders of wandering mendicants or bhikshus. The ultimate goal of these spiritual paths was the total annihilation of all desires, in the belief that this would bring about an end to suffering and the necessity for rebirth. In order to teach the people of northern India who held beliefs like this, the Buddha had to speak in such a way and use such concepts as they could understand.

And moreover, when He did speak of attaining the full enlightenment of a Buddha, there were many among His listeners, actually the majority of His disciples in those days, who despaired of their ever reaching such a distant and exalted goal. Thus the Buddha taught for them a lesser goal, that of the Arhat. In doing this the Buddha was like a wise caravan guide leading the merchants across a great waterless desert. Gradually the merchants begin to despair of ever reaching their ultimate goal and come to fear that they will die of thirst in the desert and never reach their ultimate destination. Thus their wise guide leads them to an oasis where they can rest and refresh themselves before setting out on their journey with renewed vigor. In the same way, the Arhat, awakening from his long repose, takes up the career of a Bodhisattva and eventually he attains the enlightenment of a fully manifest Buddha. But since he has attained the state of an Arhat previously, he does not need to be reborn again on earth, but can pursue his spiritual career exclusively on the higher planes of existence.

In the Buddhist context, Nirvāna is usually contrasted with Samsāra. Samsāra ('khor-baa, "cycle") means the cycle of birth, death, and rebirth. This cycle represents the totality of cyclical existence; all of the states of existence within Samsāra are conditioned by causes and are therefore transient and impermanent. Consequently, there is no ultimate salvation to be had anywhere within this cycle of conditioned existence. This cycle has existed since time without beginning, and so we cannot speak of some point in time when it was created. Just as we sentient beings have lived before in many diverse forms, in a long series of previous lives having no beginning, so in the same way, before our present universe there existed many other such universes, a long series of universes infinite in extent. Although in terms of time and history, there is no beginning to this cycle, still we can speak of Samsāra as having a cause, and that cause is ignorance. It is because of ignorance that we continue to wander aimlessly, driven relentlessly on by the winds of our karma, lifetime after lifetime, universe after universe, in this unending cycle of birth and death and rebirth.

What is ignorance? It is not knowing what is our real condition, our Primordial State. Not knowing who we really are, not recognizing our real nature, we become attached to appearances and pursuing them, we get caught up again in transmigration. Ignorance only begets ignorance. Our liberation from this beginningless cycle of Samsāra will not come about unconsciously or automatically. Left to its own devices, Samsāra will not evolve into some climactic Omega state, nor will it culminate in an unchanging stasis, a paradisical unchanging eventless "Kingdom of God." This is because causes perpetually generate new conditions, which in turn generate new causes, and so the process goes on endlessly. Samsāra is not a closed finite system; the sources of its energy are inexhaustible.

But although there is no beginning and no end to Samsāra in its own terms, we can speak of the opposite of Samsāra as Nirvāna. If Samsāra signifies conditioned existence (Skt. samskrita-dharma), then Nirvāna means unconditioned existence (Skt. asamskrita-dharma). What is extinguished upon our entering into the state of Nirvāna are the very conditions which determine our limited and restricted existence, or to put this in more psychological terms, the karmic causes of our particular karmic vision which determine how we perceive reality are extinguished. If the cause of Samsāra in general is ignorance, then Nirvāna represents the opposite: knowledge or gnosis. In Tibetan the translation for the Sanskrit word avidyā meaning "ignorance" is *ma rig-pa*; and so the opposite of this is *rig-pa*, which is not knowledge in the sense of knowing this or that, but in the sense of "intrinsic awareness." It is the capacity of the nature of the mind to be aware and present. This is the special meaning of the term in the Dzogchen context, whereas usually in Tibetan it has the meaning of "intelligence" or "science." It is this *rig-pa*, this intrinsic awareness, which is the actual subject matter of this text by Guru Padmasambhava which we have here, and not some hypothetical metaphysical entity called "the One Mind."

But does the attaining of Buddhahood necessarily entail the extinction of our individuality? When discussing the condition of Buddhahood in the manifestation of its full fruition, the Mahāyāna speaks of the Two Bodies of the Buddha, the Dharmakāya and the Rūpakāya. Although this Sanskrit word kāya (sku) literally means "body," it also has the sense of "dimension," that is, an extension or manifestation in space. When we speak of our dimension, this indicates not just our physical body, but our immediate environment and all of the interrelations with the things which we encounter and experience there. In these terms, the Dharmakāya is the dimension of all existence. It is all-pervading and omnipresent, the same everywhere. It is uncreated and unending; its essence is emptiness, like the clear open unobstructed sky. All of the Buddhas of the three times have possessed this same Dharmakāya in common.

On the other hand, the Rūpakāya or "the Form Body" of the Buddha is something individual with each Buddha. This is because the Rūpakāya is the result of an immeasurable accumulation of meritorious karma from lifetimes extending over some three immeasurable kalpas.[23] Each Buddha has a unique and individual Rūpakāya, just as our own mortal human body is unique and individual due to our own particular karmic inheritance from past lives. This explanation is according to the Sūtra system of the Mahāyāna. For the understanding of Samsāra and Nirvāna according to Dzogchen, see the foregoing translation and commentary.[24]

But what of the Dharmakāya, the dimension of all of existence, the ultimate aspect of Buddhahood? It is not a personal God, God the Creator of heaven and earth who is known to the Biblical tradition of the West. Neither is it "the Brāhman of the Rishis, the Dreamer of Māyā, the Weaver of the Web of Appearances, the Outbreather and Inbreather of infinite universes," of which Evans-Wentz writes so eloquently. These concepts and images belong to the vocabulary of theistic Hinduism; it is a description rightly applicable to the Supreme God Vishnu in the Purānas and in the *Bhāgavad Gītā*. Such theological speculations were familiar to and were dealt with in refutations, at least in terms of the Buddhist perspective, by such eminent masters as Nāgārjuna, Śāntirakshita, and so on. But Evans-Wentz indiscriminately employs this theistic vocabulary, which he drew from his Hindu teachers and from English translations of Hindu scriptures, to elucidate the meaning of Dzogchen, without making any distinction between the Hindu and the Buddhist viewpoints. However, before we can honestly make such comparisons, we must first clearly determine what are the actual views of the traditions which we are comparing, and not blithely assume that they are all proclaiming the same doctrine.[25]

To speak of the individual as merging with and being absorbed into an ocean-like universal One Mind upon his realizing Nirvāna, "like a dew drop slipping into the shining sea," is not the view of Buddhism in general, nor of Dzogchen in particular.[26] Evans-Wentz mistakes the view of Mahāyāna Buddhism for that of modern popularized Advaita Vedānta and its talk of the individual self or Ātman merging into a universal Brāhman. This merging may constitute Moksha according to this one Hindu sect, which is only one among several schools of Vedānta, but it is not the Buddhist view of liberation. Although ultimately deriving from the extensive commentaries upon the teachings of the Upanishads by Śankarāchārya

(8 cen. CE), neo-Vedānta is a modern popularization and simplification of the ideas of this master and originated around the turn of the century in India with Vivekānanda, Rāma Tīrtha, and other English speaking Swāmis. Basically, neo-Vedānta was an attempt to present an ancient Hindu teaching, that of the Upanishads, in a form which would be meaningful in the context of modern life and society, especially in view of the undermining of traditional Hindu culture by the propaganda of Christian missionaries and the onslaught of modern industrial civilization. In this, neo-Vedānta was eminently successful.

As we have seen already, while resident in India Evans-Wentz spent a sizable amount of his time in the company of various Hindu teachers and masters, such as Swāmi Satyānanda of Rishikesh, Swāmi Śyamānanda of Vārānasī, Swāmi Kuladānanda of Puri, the Śankarāchārya of Puri, and so on. Compared to the very brief amount of time where he collaborated with Lama Kazi Dawa Samdup in 1919, the vast bulk of his time in India was spent investigating and taking teachings from these Hindu teachers. Thus, it is not surprising that he came to interpret Tibetan Buddhism as a species of Vedānta. This is, in fact, even today a widespread and popular notion in India that Prince Siddhārtha, who became the Buddha, was a Hindu and that His teaching represents what amounts to a Hindu reform movement. Therefore, the Buddha taught substantially the same doctrine as is found in the Upanishads and the Advaita Vedānta of Śankarāchārya.[27] But this notion has no basis in history or in tradition. Śankarāchārya, the founder of Advaita Vedānta, lived long after the time of the Buddha, nor is his interpretation of the Upanishads accepted by the majority of Vedāntists, who follow the interpretations of rival teachers such as Rāmānuja. Moreover, the majority of the Upanishads, although difficult to date precisely, appear to have come into existence after the time of the Buddha. Certainly, Śākyamuni Buddha was an Indian, but it is anachronistic to call Him a Hindu, since the religious phenomena we now know as Hinduism did not come into existence until centuries afterward.[28] And as a non-Brāhman, the Buddha was not party to the cult of Vedic sacrifice which did exist in His day.

4. The Law of Karma, the Human Condition, and Salvation

Nevertheless, we should take a look into what the Buddhist tradition actually says with respect to God. For his part, Evans-Wentz goes on to write:

> This yogic treatise [the translation we have here], like the Gospel of St. John, teaches that one needs only look within

himself to find the Truth ... the ancient teaching that the
Universe is the product of thought, that Brahmā thinks the
Universe and it will, when meditated upon, lead the medi-
tant to the realization that the only reality is Mind, the
One Mind, of which all the microcosmic minds throughout
the Cosmos are illusory parts, that everything conceivable
is, at root, idea and thought, and thus the offspring of
Mind.... [As for] the Sangsāric being, the dream-product
of the One Mind, its illusory reality is entirely relative;
when the One Mind no longer sustains Creation, its Creation ceases to be.... In the True State of the One Mind,
the pluralistic Universe has no existence....[29]

As we have said already, the Buddhist view may be described as non-
theistic. It does not assert that God, here called Brahmā, thinks or otherwise
brings the universe into existence as its Creator, or that his thinking sustains
its existence, or that, if he ceases to think (or dream or breathe, as the case
may be), his creation, the universe, ceases to exist. On the contrary, according to the Buddhist teachings found in both the Sūtras and the Tantras, our
universe is the aggregate result of the actions in their past lives of all the
sentient beings who inhabit our universe. When the world appears in the
same way to a group of sentient beings, such as the human race, for example, it is because all the members of that group share a common karmic
vision (las snang), that is to say, a particular way of perceiving things
determined by a karmic cause. To the first question found in the catechism,
"Who made the world?," the Buddhist teachings unhesitatingly reply, "It
is karma that has made the world."

What is the origin of our present condition? It has come about as the
result of the actions which we have committed in our previous lives. This
is known as the principle of karma (las), a Sanskrit word meaning literally
"action"; but in this context it also implies the effects, results, or fruits (Skt.
phala) of our actions (las rgyu 'bras-bu). It is said that their consequences
follow our actions as inevitably as the shadow follows the body. The causes
and consequences of karma are one of the principal themes for reflection
and meditation during the preliminary practices for Vajrayāna Buddhism.
This principle of karma is fundamental to the Buddhist view of life at all
levels. What is called wrong view (Skt. mithyā-drishti) primarily means
denying this teaching concerning karma. Indeed, the entire universe and all
its diversity in terms of both physical environments and living beings is
explained in terms of karma. According to the Abhidharmakośa,[30] "All the
diversity of the world is produced by karma." Again, as it says in the

Mahākaruṇāpuṇḍarīka Sūtra, "The world is created by karma; living beings are the result of and originate from it as a source; they are divided into types and states by it." And in the *Karmaśataka Sūtra*, it says, "Actions are of various kinds and through them the various modes of existence have been created."[31]

For example, the Buddhist teachings conventionally speak of the six destinies of rebirth ('gro-ba drug). The three higher destinies are those of the Devas or gods, the Asuras or titans (who are opponents of the gods, but otherwise quite similar to them), and the humans. The lower or evil destinies are rebirth among the animals, among the Pretas or hungry restless ghosts, and among the denizens of hell. How do we find ourselves reborn in any of these destinies? As the result of our actions in previous lives, our stream of consciousness becomes dominated by a particular passion, and thus with rebirth our consciousness finds itself in a space or situation which is structured in terms of that predominant passion. For example, a murderer who kills someone or a warrior who kills professionally will find that his stream of consciousness is infused and totally dominated by his thoughts of hatred and anger which are associated with his actions in the past. After death he will find himself reborn into an experience of hell, tormented by great heat or great cold in an exceedingly confined space. This space, which we call hell, was created for his consciousness by his habitual thoughts of hatred and anger. But when the energy of this accumulation of karma created by his angry hate-filled thoughts and aggressive violent actions is exhausted, then he will find himself reborn elsewhere, depending on what other unconscious propensities may exist beneath the surface of his stream of consciousness. In the same way, the propensities of greed, lust, desire, and attachment create a barren desert-like landscape of perpetually frustrated desires, where one wanders fruitlessly in search of satisfaction as a Preta, a ghost continuously afflicted with insatiable hunger and thirst. The propensities of delusion, confusion, bewilderment, and stupidity lead to rebirth in the animal realm, where one's existence is continuously dominated by irresistible instincts and the fear of being killed and eaten by others in the wild, or by servitude to mankind. The propensities of jealousy and envy creates the existence of the mighty restless titans known as Asuras, where one is continuously engaged without rest in warfare, struggle, and strife. The propensities of pride, arrogance, and ego-centricity lead one to be reborn among the Devas or gods of the realm of sensuous desire, where in a heavenly paradise they enjoy a very pleasant daydream-like existence. Attaining rebirth as an Asura or Deva also requires a great deal of meritorious karma and not just thoughts of envy or pride. But the thoughts of envy and pride determine in what way these states of existence manifest. They are, after all, states of consciousness. But even in these delightful Deva realms, one experiences suffering, because the Devas possess prescience or precognition; and so they suffer the fore-knowledge of their impending death and future rebirth elsewhere in much less pleasant circumstances. Thus the other side of the Deva's pride is anxiety and dread. The presence of all five passions or propensities simultaneously and in more or less equal measure leads one again into human rebirth.

In his way the Buddha employed the Indian mythology current in His day to illustrate the different psychological dimensions created by the passions and the actions of voice and body which follow from them. And in actual fact, all of these various destinies created by a predominance of one or the other of these passions in the stream of consciousness may be found within human existence here and now. It is therefore not necessary to look to some future life to find ourselves in a dimension created by one of these passions or obsessions. However, in terms of the traditional cosmology, since all of these types of beings spoken of above (infernal, ghostly, animal, titanic, divine, or human, possessing gross material bodies or bodies composed of some more subtle matter) are dominated by their sense desires, the dimensions of their existence are collectively known as the Kāmadhātu or the Desire World. Above this Desire World lie the planes of a purely mental existence in very subtle bodies of light. These planes are collectively known as the Rūpadhātu or the Form World. Beyond this, having no particular locations in space, but extending everywhere in our universe, are the planes of cosmic consciousness known as the Ārūpadhātu or the Formless World. In their totality these three worlds, the Tridhātu, comprise Saṃsāra, the beginningless cycle of death and rebirth.

But how is this karma transmitted from one lifetime to another? How can what we have done in a previous life effect us in this present life, especially in view of the well-known Buddhist doctrine of Anātman, that there exists no eternal or abiding self in persons? The principle involved here is interdependent origination: one event occurs and this is followed by another event dependent on the occurrence of the first, and so on *ad infinitum*.[32] The energy generated by our actions and stored in our stream of consciousness cannot be fully exhausted in a single lifetime and so this leads to the arising of experiences in future lives. We can speak of this process in a more psychological fashion by adopting the organic model used in the Yogāchāra school. Although there exists no permanent unchanging entity or substance called "the self," still there exists a vijnāna-santāna or "stream of consciousness," an unceasing flow of states of consciousness. This stream of consciousness flows through many different lifetimes like a river flowing through many different landscapes; it is the same river throughout its course, and yet it changes from moment to moment. The surface of the river, with its ever-changing ripples and eddies, represent the ordinary waking state of consciousness; but there also exist great depths in the river far below the surface and deep running currents which are normally not visible. This continuity of the stream in the depths is called the Ālaya (kun gzhi), "the foundation of everything," and is normally quite unconscious as a whole; but when its contents impinge on consciousness, we refer to this as the ālaya-vijnāna or "store consciousness." Being analogous to a receptacle, in the Ālaya are deposited the traces or residual memories of all of our past actions of a karmic nature. These residues or traces are known as vāsnās (bag-chags). Originally this term meant a trace of something, such as the residual scent left behind in a room when a lovely lady wearing perfume has passed through it. The residues of our actions are deposited in seminal form in the Ālaya, just as a gardener might plant his seeds in the dark humus earth in the autumn with the expectation that they would germinate and sprout in the spring. In the same way, when the requisite secondary causes are present in some future lifetime, then the karmic seed will germinate and sprout, manifesting to one's consciousness as some inexplicable impulse or samskāra, as some desire or passion or emotion or idea or perception, as the case may be. In this way, our psychic life is dominated by samskāras or "karmic formations," and as the result of these impulses we enter into action and thus again into transmigration.

The teachings giving an extensive analysis of karma and how it works from the point of view of the Sūtras are found in a collection of treatises collectively known as the Abhidharma, which supplement the Sūtras. According to these Abhidharma teachings, our actions may be classified into three types. First, there are those actions which are wholesome or virtuous (dge-ba) or meritorious (bsod-nams). These are actions leading in general to a happy rebirth in the Desire World, whether among the gods or among human beings. And among such wholesome and meritorious actions, those of generosity and of not harming others are emphasized. In the Sūtras there are found many examples of individuals who went on to reap in their future lives the benefits of their past generous and helpful actions. For example, the Brāhman Krika in prehistoric times practiced such extravagant deeds of generosity and of benefit to others that as the result of the great meritorious karma which he accumulated, he was reborn in heaven as the god Indra.

Secondly, there are actions that are unwholesome or non-virtuous (mid dge-ba) or non-meritorious (bsod-nams ma yin-pa). These are actions in general leading to an unhappy rebirth within the three evil destinies, that is, rebirth among the animals, the Pretas, or the denizens in hell. Among these non-virtuous or vicious actions, killing, stealing, and raping are considered to be the worst. Traditionally we speak of the ten wrong deeds (mi dge-ba bcu), namely, the three wrong actions of body—taking life, stealing, and rape: the four wrong actions of speech—telling lies, slander, harsh speech, and engaging in gossip; and the three wrong deeds of mind—covetous thoughts, ill will, and wrong views. As we have said previously, wrong views consist primarily in denying the existence of the law of karma and denying the efficacy of the Three Jewels for salvation. For any of these wrong deeds to become a karma path invariably and inevitably leading to rebirth in the evil destinies, the action must be premeditated, actually committed, carried out successfully, and not regretted or repented afterwards. Again, there are many examples found in the Sūtras of the consequences of such unwholesome actions.

Finally, there are actions which are indeterminate in nature known as āninjya-karma (mi gyo-ba'i las). Here the reference is to the attaining of various levels of concentration in meditation practice and the consequent rebirth into the corresponding states of absorption on the higher mental planes of the Form World and of the Formless World. We will consider this in more detail below.

As for the results or consequences of karma, this is known as the fruit or phala ('bras-bu). In the Abhidharma, four kinds of consequences of karma are distinguished:

1. The fruition that is the ripening of one's karma (Skt. vipākaphala): The principle involved here is that the consequence of an action may not necessarily come about immediately, but will be experienced sometime later, either in this life or in some future life, when the requisite secondary conditions for its manifestation are present. The fruit takes time to ripen, so to speak.

2. The fruition where the consequence is similar to or in agreement with the cause (Skt. nishyanda-phala): Here the principle involved is that the original action and the result experienced correspond. For example, if an individual willfully kills someone in his present life, then in his next he will find himself killed by another and will have a very short life span.

3. The fruition that creates the individual (Skt. purushakāra-phala): Here the principle involved is that any karmic action will multiply and increase in terms of its consequences. One may find himself continuing in great misery through several successive rebirths as different individuals due to merely one single action. And then compounding one action with another, he will continue to wander through endless cycles of reincarnation.

4. The fruition that is collective in nature (Skt. adhipati-phala): This refers to the physical and social environment into which one is reborn. This environment comes into existence as the aggregate result of the karma of all of the sentient beings who inhabit that

environment. It is the result of collective karma. In terms of human history, this is not difficult to understand with reference to our social environment. Society and culture are the collective consequence of what human beings have thought and done in the past. But the Buddhist teachings equally apply the principle of karma to our physical environment. The material world, this fair planet earth, is the aggregate result of the karma of all of the sentient beings who inhabit this world system. Thus karma has both its individual and its collective aspects.

But does this belief in karma lead to passivity on the part of the individual, to a mere resigned acceptance of one's fate and to the way things are? Some Western critics claim that the belief in karma is merely a rationale for the status quo, for poverty and social inequality. According to Buddhist teaching, however, karma does not mean mere fatalism. Quite the contrary. In His own day Śākyamuni Buddha had to oppose the influence of the fatalistic doctrines of the Ajīvika sect. We are not just the passive victims of an omniscient fate, nor the unconscious participants in the divine plan of some distant, omnipotent God. While it is true that our present circumstances, including our own material body, are the result of our karma, at this very moment we are free to choose the course of our actions within the limitations of our capacities and external circumstances. Thus, by free moral choice in the present and its consequent actions, we create our own karma, whether meritorious or nonmeritorious, which will bear its fruit in future lives. In this sense, we are the creators of our own destiny, whether rebirth in heaven or hell, rebirth as a human or as an animal. All is determined by what we do now.

What are the necessary conditions for an action to create new karmic consequences? Do all of our actions automatically create karma? Most of the actions of our body, voice, and mind are not karma-creating because they are merely resultant or vipaka, that is, they are unconscious, automatic, habitual, instinctive, reactive, and so on. For an action to bear karmic consequences a certain degree of awareness must be present—a degree of free will and free moral choice. Automatic reflex actions do not create karma. According to the *Abhidharma-samuccaya*: "What is karma? It is motivation and what is motivated." The *Abhidharmakośa* clarifies the matter by saying, "Karma is motivation and what has come about thereby. Motivation is mental activity and what is set up by it are bodily and vocal actions."[33] The Sanskrit term chetanā (sems-pa), here translated as "motivation," also means "volition" or "will." What proceeds from this or what is motivated, chetayitvā (bsam-pa), are one's actions of body and voice.[34] This chetanā or volition is a conscious intention to do something specific, whether its goal is inspired by ignorance and craving, thereby leading one further into worldly entanglements and transmigration, or whether it is guided by prajñā or wisdom, an intelligent discriminating insight into reality. The Abhidharma defines chetanā as a mental activity of attention (yid kyi las), a turning of awareness to some object. But chetanā is far more than a mere awareness, for here there is a conscious intention to do something about the object upon which one's attention is focused. Chetanā has an energy of its own which brings a state of consciousness into being and binds together in that state a complex of mental factors, involving feelings, perceptions, emotions, judgments, memories, and so on. To be karma-creating, the act of apperception leading to an action that creates karmic consequences must include this element of volition.

This is why, from the very outset of the teachings, in what are called the preliminary practices, much importance is given to reflection upon the unique opportunity afforded by this precious human rebirth for our spiritual development.[35] Animal behavior is largely instinctual and reflective, with little conscious choice. It is in human existence that the opportunities for conscious growth and possibility of enlightenment are at maximum. Yet there are many people who would waste this unique opportunity, living an unaware, animal-like existence, neglecting the accumulation of positive karma and the accumulation of wisdom. Failing to do this, they may find themselves in their next rebirth in a situation where they have lost their human condition.

What we are speaking about here is conscious evolution, conscious development—only this will carry us to enlightenment and Buddhahood. Awareness (rig-pa) is the central theme of the Buddhist teaching, its essential point, without which everything in the teachings will not really be understood. Natural evolution, which is unconscious and automatic, what in Buddhist terms is called Pratītya-samutpāda or interdependent origination, will not bring us on its own to Buddhahood. Natural evolution belongs to Samsāra; it is ultimately cyclical in nature, as time itself is, when seen in the larger perspective. The path of spiritual development is something quite other than the natural evolution of the world as depicted by Darwin and in scientific textbooks. There is no law of inevitable progress operative in things that automatically assures us of evolving toward Buddhahood without regard to what we do in this lifetime. Although we all have the potentiality for Buddhahood, there are many secondary conditions for its realization. As it says in the text translated here, just as it is necessary to press the sesame seeds in order to obtain the oil and churn the milk in order to obtain the butter, so it is necessary to practice in order to realize Buddhahood.

In the time of Śākyamuni Buddha, there existed in northern India a sect of wandering mendicants known as the Ājīvikas, founded by Gośāla

Maskarin, an elder contemporary of the Buddha. This sage taught that it was necessary for every individual soul (Skt. jīva) to evolve through precisely eighty-four thousand successive rebirths as plants, animals, humans, and gods, until in one's last lifetime in this long series of rebirths, as an Ajīvika ascetic one would realize Nirvāna and escape from the round of rebirth. But these successive rebirths, which spiral upward progressively, are not determined by the actions of the individuals involved, but by a fixed plan or fate (Skt. niyati). Thus, no matter what one does in a particular lifetime, he cannot fall backward into a lower existence. For example, once having attained the threshold of human existence, one cannot fall backward again into animal existence. This Ajīvika doctrine has been revived in recent times by H.P. Blavatsky and other Theosophical writers. But as Sakyamuni pointed out in relation to the Ajīvika teachings of Gośāla Maskarin, this notion of inevitable progress in relation to the reincarnating soul in actuality negates the law of karma. In the Buddhist view, if through our meritorious actions we can progress and move upward to rebirth as a god, so equally through our non-meritorious actions we can again fall backward. The Tibetan teachings continually emphasize the preciousness of human existence, of its being something only gained after long ages of animal existence. It is not something to be wasted or squandered by neglecting the accumulations of meritorious karma and of wisdom.

In his introduction to his *Tibetan Book of the Dead,* Evans-Wentz claims to be privileged to certain "esoteric teachings" drawn from the clairvoyant vision and yogic insight of certain unnamed masters of his acquaintance, which conflict with the so-called popular exoteric views of Tibetans.[36] Reference is made to "the psychical seed of the life-flux which the eyes cannot see—if a human being, it cannot incarnate in or overshadow, or be intimately bound up with a body foreign to its evolved characteristics, either in this world, or in the Bardo, or in any realm of Sangsāric existence. This is the natural law governing the manifestation of life, as inviolable as the law of karma.... For a human life-flux to flow into the physical form of a dog, or fowl, or insect, or worm, is, therefore, held to be impossible...."[37] The source for this esoteric view is none other than the leaders of the Theosophical Society, as we have pointed out previously. All of these neo-theosophical speculations concerning life-fluxes, globes, rounds, root races, subraces, etc., everything occurring in groups of seven, have nothing to do with genuine Tibetan teachings.

In the context of Buddhist teaching, it is quite clear that there is no law of inevitable progress operative in our world. Samsāra, as conditioned existence, is cyclical in structure; the cycles of time and manifestation, what are called kalpas, roll on relentlessly from time without beginning. Universes are born and die in unending cycles, just as is the case with individuals. In

these terms, there is no inevitable or irreversible progress toward enlightenment in Samsāra, for enlightenment lies beyond and outside time. It is not
something that will be eventually realized in time and history as the Millen-
nium, a paradisical age of return to innocence at the end of time. Spiritual
progress toward liberation and enlightenment is something quite other than
nature, for the impulse of nature, of the Bhavachakra or cycle of existence,
is ignorance and the passions. In Tibetan paintings, the Buddha is depicted
as standing outside of this wheel held in the clutches of the black demon of
death, ignorance, and desire, where He indicates the path to liberation from
cyclical existence. This path to liberation is not instinctual; it requires a
conscious evolution, a discovery of and development of awareness (rig-pa).
It is interesting to note that in the West it was the spiritual teachers G.I.
Gurdjieff and P.D. Ouspensky who agreed with the Buddhists on the necessity of conscious evolution, on the developing awareness through practicing
self-observation and self-remembering, as against this neo-theosophical notion of inevitable progress through reincarnation. When Theosophy first
came into existence toward the end of the last century, theories of evolution
and Social Darwinism were all the vogue, and ideas of inevitable progress,
as well as European imperialist expansion, were at their height; so it is not
surprising that H.P. Blavatsky brought these popular notions of evolution
and inevitable progress into her writings on occultism and reincarnation.
Victorian England was heralded as the highest pinnacle of human evolution.
But since that day, history itself has made short work of this notion of
inevitable human progress.

5. The Buddhist View of God

To speak of karma creating the world is not to deny the existence of the
gods, which in Sanskrit are called the Devas. The gods are not the creators
of the world, but represent only one type of sentient existence within the
world. The Buddha was neither an atheist nor an agnostic in the modern
sense. On the contrary, since He was the Buddha, the enlightened one, He
was one who understood directly the nature of existence—not only human
existence, but the nature of the existence of all types of sentient beings. The
Devas have a different karmic vision than we do as humanity, resulting
from different karmic causes. The Devas, therefore, exist in a different
dimension than our conventional human reality. They are superior to human beings in a large number of respects, having great clairvoyant powers
and a much longer life-span, measured in divine years rather than human
terms. Nonetheless, they are samsaric beings; they are not enlightened beings, nor are they all-knowing or all-powerful.

Rebirth among the Devas on those planes of existence known as the Devalokas or "the heavens" is a possibility for the human being because the cause for such a rebirth is realizable within human existence in terms of meritorious karma. In the Buddhist Sūtras are found many stories of the rebirth of human beings in the heaven worlds of the Devas, in such celestial realms as Trayatrimsā, Tushita, and so on. But according to the Buddhist teachings rebirth as a Deva in heaven is not the ultimate goal, since that existence is conditioned by causes and is, therefore, impermanent. It belongs to the cycle of conditioned existence called Samsāra and will inevitably come to an end. Rebirth, whether in a heaven or a hell, is not the consequence of the arbitrary judgment of some Deity, but is the direct result of our past actions. Although this existence as a Deva may be exceedingly pleasant in terms of sensual delights, indeed, a veritable daydream existence, surrounded as one is by countless lush and voluptuous Devīs, still this condition is not an eternal salvation, just as there is no eternal damnation in hell. Nirvāna is something quite other than a rebirth in a heavenly paradise. It represents unconditioned existence and is in no way a part of Samsāra or cyclical existence. The Devas themselves, as much conditioned by their sensual desires (Skt. kāma) as are humans, animals, hungry ghosts, and denizens of hell, belong to the Kāmadhātu, the world or dimension of sensuous desires.

As for the existence of God, of the Creator of heaven and earth, this is the concept central to religion as we know it in the West. Was the Buddha an atheist or an agnostic in relation to the existence of a Supreme Being or God? The Buddha was a Tathāgata, a word which etymologically means "a speaker of the Truth," and He possessed an omniscient awareness of all the dimensions of existence and all their aspects.[38] However, usually He did not choose to speak about metaphysical speculations unrelated to the pursuit of the path to liberation, although in certain Sūtras He did speak on the origin of the world, the human race, and so on. And in order to understand His meaning, we must look at the traditional Buddhist cosmology.

Beings reborn in the Desire World or Kāmadhātu possess either a gross material body like humans and animals or else bodies of subtle matter like the Devas, Asuras, Pretas, and infernal beings. Beyond the Desire World, there exist the higher planes of a purely mental existence where one inhabits a subtle body of light. These various higher planes are collectively known as the Rūpadhātu, the Form World or dimension of pure forms. The sentient beings who inhabit these higher planes of existence are free of all gross sensuous desires and possess great auras of light. Here they remain, in human terms, for exceedingly long periods of time, absorbed in their abstract meditations. These higher gods are in general not called Devas, but Brahmās, "the pure ones." In the Buddhist usage, Brahmā is a generic term for a type of divine celestial existence and not the proper name of an individual Creator God, as is the case in Hinduism. Like the existence of a Deva, that of a Brahmā is conditioned by one's karma, although here it is known as indeterminate karma (Skt. āninjya-karma). Therefore, although we may remain in the existence of a Brahmā on the higher mental planes for a period of time, measurable only in cosmic terms, nevertheless, when our accumulation of karma is inevitably exhausted, we will find ourselves reborn elsewhere.

Moreover, these Brahmās, just as was the case with the Devas, are not enlightened beings, although many religions conceive of one of their number as being the all-knowing Creator God. Although being exceedingly wise and possessing great powers of clairvoyance and prescience, still they are not omniscient—they do not understand the real nature of existence. In this respect, the Buddha is infinitely superior to all of the gods of conventional religion, for all of them are but worldly gods, the *laukika-devāh*, that is to say, they are divinities who belong to cyclical existence. For example, in ancient Indian belief, Indra was the king of the gods or Devas and led the glorious hosts of Devas in battle against the Asuras who ruled over the nations. Moreover, Indra could create great storms with lightning and thunder to bring the fertilizing rains to the fields of the righteous, those who adhere to the moral and social law. But equally he could send his wrath in the form of thunderbolts to bring destruction to the rebellious and the unrighteous. Or again, there was Brahmā, also called Prajāpati, "the Progenitor, " who, it was believed, reigned over our entire world-system as its creator, law-giver, and revealer of the Vedas. Such were the mythological beliefs which existed in India in the time of the Buddha, and it is upon such similar myths that our religions in the West rest. But in previous kalpas, there have existed a long line of Indras, each of whom reigned for a time as king of the gods in his resplendent palace of Vijayanti on the summit of Mount Meru in the center of the world. And in the same way, there have existed an endless succession of such Brahmā Prajāpatis, each thinking that he was the God who created the universe. However, since they are conditioned beings and are therefore limited and ignorant, the Buddhist does not take refuge in them, but rather in the principle of enlightenment which is the Buddha. When Sakyamuni attained enlightenment beneath the Bodhi Tree, becoming the Buddha, the first beings who came to Him to offer their homage and petition Him to teach the Dharma for the benefit of all beings were the gods Indra and Brahmā.

In the Sūtras there is found a Buddhist account of Genesis.[39] In reply to questions from His disciples, the Buddha explained that the humanity found on this planet earth once inhabited another planetary system. Ages ago when the sun of that world went nova and the planet was destroyed in the ensuing solar eruptions, the bulk of its inhabitants, as the result of their arduously practicing the Dharma for ten thousand years, were reborn on one of the higher planes of the Form World or Rūpadhātu, a plane of existence known as Ābhāsvara or "clear light." Here they enjoyed inconceivable bliss and felicity for countless aeons. Then, when their great store of past karma came onto maturity, our own solar system and planet earth began to evolve and some among their numbers were reborn on the lower planes of the Rūpadhātu in the vicinity of the nascent earth. This plane of existence where they found themselves reborn is known as Brahmāloka. The first of these beings to reawaken and be reborn, upon seeing the solar system evolving below him, exclaimed in his delight "I am the Creator!" In this way, he came to believe that he was the actual creator of the universe which he saw about him, for he did not remember from whence he came and was born without any parents. But in actuality the manifestation of this universe was due to the collective karma of all in that company and his own individual manifestation, which was a case of apparitional birth, was due to his own great stock of meritorious karma coming into maturation at that time because the requisite secondary conditions were present. Nevertheless, he persisted in his delusion, in this idea that he was the actual Creator of the universe because he was the first born within the evolving solar system and he saw no others there before him. But this belief was only his limitation and his obscuration, a primordial ignorance of his true origin, and so he fell victim to his own pride. This was the first appearance of the ego or the belief in the real existence of a self, in our universe. However, although he believed himself to be self-originated, actually his appearance in the center of our world-system was the fortunate consequence of his karma. And because he was the first among the Brahmās to be reborn out of Ābhāsvara, he became known as Mahābrahmā or God.

Then after existing by himself alone in solitary splendor for many aeons as the solar system evolved, he came to experience loneliness and thought that how nice it would be if there were only others in existence who might reflect his magnificence. And just at that precise moment, due to their own karma ripening, a large number of other beings from Ābhāsvara were reborn in Brahmāloka as Brahmās. When Mahābrahmā saw them, he thought that they must have appeared just then in space before him because of his desire. So he exclaimed proudly, "I am God, your Creator!"—even though, in actual fact, all of these exalted beings before his throne were reborn at that time because of their own karma maturing and not because of any desire of his. Then Mahābrahmā organized these myriads of beings who were appearing in the space about him into well-ordered celestial hierarchies. The first born and most radiant among them were grouped below his throne as his own personal priests and ministers known as the

Brahmāpurohitas, whereas those who were reborn later became his entourage known as the Brahmākāyikas. In this way, he surrounded himself, filling all the tiers of heaven with celestial hierarchies, believing all the time that he was their Lord and Creator, since he was ignorant of their own, as well as his own, real origin. Gradually, as time wore on, due to the presence of a series of secondary causes, some of these Brahmās entered into the cycle of material existence and began to be reborn on the surface of the newly evolved earth, first as animals and then later as human beings.

The foregoing account of Genesis is also called upon to explain a number of types of mystical experience. In the *Trividyā Sūtra*, when some Brāhman youths came to the Buddha and asked Him about the mystical experience of the state of Brāhman reported in the Vedas, experiences said to be both blissful and luminous, the Buddha explained that these mystical experiences were due to the memories the Brāhman sages possessed, although usually repressed, of their past existence as Brahmās on the Brahmāloka planes.[40]

Thus, according to the Buddhist view, the realization of Brāhman, is not the ultimate goal. It is not Nirvāna. It merely represents another type of conditioned existence within Samsāra, even though we may choose to call it "cosmic consciousness." Indeed, nowhere do Tibetan teachers speak of "the One Cosmic Mind as alone real, " as being the sole reality, as Evans-Wentz would have us believe. However, this does not mean that the Buddhist teachers are unaware of transpersonal and collective states of consciousness. Śākyamuni Buddha was quite familiar with the experience of cosmic consciousness, of merging one's individual finite consciousness for a time in the totality of nature or in the infinity of space. He referred to these transpersonal experiences in the *Brahmājāla Sūtra*, the *Trividyā Sūtra*, and elsewhere; but nowhere does He say that such transpersonal experiences are the ultimate goal of human evolution, as some current writers on transpersonal psychology would have us believe. The Dharmakāya is not cosmic consciousness, any more than it is Brāhman.[41] In fact, the Buddha specifically cautioned against pursuing the goal of rebirth among the long-lived gods, whose state of cosmic consciousness is still conditioned (Samsaric).

Sakyamuni Himself had direct experience of these transpersonal and mystical states of consciousness, which He came to reject as less than the ultimate goal. When Sakyamuni set out upon His quest for enlightenment, He found two masters living in the forests of northern India under whom He became a disciple. From the first of these teachers, Arāda Kamala, He learned how to practice meditation by fixating His attention upon an object of meditation. Through this He attained the state of concentration known as *samādhi/samādhi*. Within this there are distinguished four levels of concentration called dhyānas. The first dhyana has five constituent factors which define it as an experience, namely, applied thinking, analytical thinking, rapture, pleasurable feeling, and one-pointedness of mind. With the second dhyana, the intellectual process, all applied thinking and analysis, are suppressed and what remains is the experience of rapture, pleasurable feeling, and one-pointedness. With attaining the third dhyana, rapture—the feeling of exhilaration and exaltation—is eliminated, so that one remains pleasurably evenminded, mindful, and clear. And finally in the fourth dhyana all of these factors, including pleasurable feeling, are eliminated, leaving only one-pointedness of concentration. Herein the meditator remains in the utter purity of equanimity and mindfulness, having attained a calm state of mind. But upon returning to ordinary daily experience, Sakyamuni found Himself disillusioned after having explored these states of consciousness, thinking that there must be something higher than this.[42]

And so He went to a second master, Udraka Rāmaputra, who taught the young Bodhisattva how to meditate by fixating attention not on a concrete object but on empty space. Practicing in this way, He came to realize the state of concentration known as *nirvikalpa-samādhi*. Here, as before, there are distinguished four levels of concentration known as samāpattis or "attainments." While in a condition of meditation, by means of passing beyond all perceptions of concrete forms and by not attending to an awareness of diversity, one integrates into limitless space and remains in the attainment of the state of infinite space. This is the first samapatti. Then proceeding to the second, transcending limitless space and integrating into limitless consciousness, one remains in the attainment of the state of infinite consciousness. This is the formal definition of the second samapatti. This and the preceding state, that is, the state of integration into infinite space and the state of integration into infinite consciousness, are what Western writers understand by "cosmic consciousness." The last two attainments are known as the state where there is nothing whatever in consciousness and the state where there is neither perception nor nonperception.[43] These final two states of "cosmic consciousness," so to speak, are erroneously thought to represent extinction. Some believe that they represent the attainment of Nirvāna by the Arhat. But in actual fact, all of these samāpattis are conditioned states of consciousness and when their karmic causes are exhausted, one again comes into manifestation and has an awareness of perceptions. As was the case before, upon returning to ordinary daily experience, after having thoroughly explored these states, Sakyamuni became disillusioned and asked His master, "Is that all you have to teach Me? Can you not teach Me the way which leads beyond all illness, old age, and death?" His master replied in the negative.

Birth, illness, old age, and death are the four great sorrows afflicting human existence, an awareness of which originally motivated the young prince Siddhārtha to set out on His quest for liberation and enlightenment. Failing to find satisfaction in the teachings of either Arāda Kamala or Udraka Rāmaputra, He retired into the trackless forest in order to practice austerities. At the end of six years, abandoning mortification of the flesh as a means to win liberation from rebirth, He broke His fast and accepted food from a local village girl. Then crossing the Niranjana river, He entered into the precincts of enlightenment at Bodh Gaya, and, taking a seat beneath the Bodhi Tree, He vowed not to move from that spot until He realized enlightenment. He entered into a state of abstract concentration, and, during the course of the night as He sat in meditation beneath the tree, He came to a direct realization and understanding of the interdependence and emptiness of all existing things. Precisely with the first light of dawn, He entered into the state of enlightenment and became a fully manifest Buddha. By exhausting and completely annihilating all pollutants in His mind stream, such as sensuous desires, belief in existence, wrong views, and ignorance, He passed beyond conditioned existence and the cycle of death and rebirth or Samsāra. This is the account of the enlightenment of the Buddha according to the Sūtra system.

We must make a careful distinction between Nirvāna, unconditioned existence, and Samsāra, conditioned by karmic causes, including various states of consciousness, cosmic and otherwise. If, unlike the Buddha, "He who has awakened," one should die when absorbed in one of these abstract meditative states, the dhyānas or the samāpattis, then one will find himself reborn in the state of existence corresponding to that state of meditation. According to the Abhidharma, there exist seventeen mental planes belonging to the Rūpadhātu, correspondingly inhabited by seventeen classes of gods. To the first dhyana correspond the mental planes of Brahmākayika, Brahmāpurohita, and Mahābrahmā. These three planes comprise the Brahmāloka of which we spoke previously. To the second dhyana correspond the mental planes of Parīttabha, Aprāmanābha, and Ābhāsvara. To the third dhyana correspond the mental planes of Parīttaśubha, Aprāmanaśubha, and Śubhakritsna. And to the fourth dhyana correspond the eight highest cosmic planes of Anabhraka, Punyaprasava, Brihatphala, Avriha, Atapa, Sudriśa, Sudarśana, and Akanistha. Collectively these exalted cosmic planes are known as Śuddhāvāsa, "the pure abodes," inhabited by the Gods of the Pure Abodes. The last among them, Akanistha ('og-min) is known as the highest plane of existence. Beyond this is Mahākanistha, the plane of existence at which the Sambhogakāya aspect of the Buddha manifests itself.

In addition, there are four formless states of consciousness which have no specific location in space, but are "cosmic" in their dimensions. To the first formless attainment or samapatti corresponds the state of infinite

space; to the second samapatti corresponds the state of infinite consciousness; to the third samapatti corresponds the state of nothing whatever in
consciousness; and to the fourth samapatti corresponds the state of neither
perception nor nonperception. Even though these exalted states, as we have
said, represent the attainment of an experience of cosmic consciousness,
nonetheless, they are conditioned states of being.

A sentient being at the end of his life, due to his karma which may be
meritorious, nonmeritorious, or indeterminate, will inevitably find himself
reborn somewhere in the three worlds, in some dimension of existence in
the Desire World, the Form World, or the Formless World. And when that
accumulation of karma which is the cause of his being reborn in that
dimension of existence is exhausted, he will find himself reborn elsewhere.
Sakyamuni, as the result of His own personal experience and practice, came
to realize that all of these states of consciousness without exception, including the dhyānas and samāpattis, no matter how rarefied, exalted or "cosmic" these states might be, are but different forms of conditioned existence.
And being conditioned by causes, these states are not permanent or eternal.
Their attainment, no matter how blissful and felicitous this may be, is not
something everlasting and does not represent liberation from Samsāra.
Since all conditioned states are impermanent, even the attainment of cosmic
consciousness does not represent salvation or escape from Samsāra. This is
not the way which lies beyond birth and death. To think otherwise, is to
mistake the reflections for the mirror.

6. Dzogchen and Mahāmudrā

Elsewhere, in his book *Tibetan Yoga and Secret Doctrines*, Evans-Wentz
writes in such a way as to identify Mahāmudrā, "the Great Symbol," with
Dzogchen. There he writes:

> The mind in man is inseparable from the All-Mind. The
> object of yoga is to bring about the joining, or at-one-
> ment, of the human and the divine aspects of the mind. . . .
> Step by step the disciple is led to the realization that, simi-
> larly, all the innumerable aspects of the mind and intellect
> are but rays of the One Mind and Intellect. This attainment
> is not, however, of finality, but merely of knowledge in its
> microcosmic character. Not until the finite mind becomes
> the Infinite Mind and "the dew drop slips into the Shining
> Sea" in the state of Supramundane Consciousness, is the
> Nirvanic Goal reached. . . . When sangsāric thoughts, and
> passions born of these thoughts, are transmuted by the
> alchemy of the Great Symbol, they merge in at-one-ment

with the Dharma-kāyic Mind. The yogin, when realization comes, knows that thoughts instead of being inimical as he took them to be at first, are, as phenomena, existing things which are inseparably related to the thoughts of the Universal Mind. Then by a retrospective and reversive process, the yogin . . . allows the interminable flow of thoughts to go on unimpeded or naturally. And when he does so, the thoughts automatically assume a rhythmic vibration, in tune with the vibration of the thoughts of the Infinite Mind, of which the cosmic creation is the phenomenal fruit. . . . All sangsāric things have no existence apart from the Supramundane Mind; to the Hindu it is the Dream of Brahmā. . . . Who is the Spectator? It is the Super Intellect, the Supramundane Consciousness. Whence did the Super Intellect arise? From the One Mind, where all minds are in at-one-ment.[44]

However, this is no more the view of Mahāmudrā than it is the view of Dzogchen. But it is very much the view of modern neo-Theosophy. As we pointed out previously, the Buddhist teachings do not present Nirvāna as the merging or absorption of the finite human mind into some sort of oceanic Cosmic Mind, nor is the Dharmakāya conceived as being some sort of universal Over-Mind. In terms of the psychology of Dzogchen, a crucial distinction is made between the nature of the mind (sems nyid) and the mind (sems) or the mental process which is continuously constructing and fabricating things with its concepts. Thus the mind enters into speculations and judgments, thereby falsifying the existence of the unenlightened individual. Therefore, merely getting in tune with the vibrations of some Cosmic Mind, whether this mind is awake or dreaming, does not represent an authentic enlightenment or genuine liberation. It is simply letting oneself get caught up in delusion at another level, albeit a divine one rather than a human one. And again, as we explained previously, thoughts occurring at the level of cosmic consciousness, whether they occur in the mind of Mahābrahmā or in the mind of some other divine entity, are still thoughts which occur in time and therefore represent conditioned states of mind belonging to Samsāra.

While on the other hand, an enlightened being, whether thoughts are occurring or not, continuously remains in a state of contemplation, which is characterized by a primal awareness or gnosis which is just pure presence (rig-pa'i ye-shes). Thus an enlightened being, and this is what the term Buddha means, lives in the condition of the mirror which has the capacity to reflect everything, and yet is itself in no way modified or changed by this reflecting of things, whereas an unenlightened conditioned being, whether human or divine, lives in the condition of the reflections. Therefore, enlightenment, the attainment of Nirvāna, is not a question of merging a finite human self into some greater self, like pouring a bottle of water into the ocean.

When we consider Mahāmudrā and Dzogchen in terms of view, meditation, conduct, and fruition, it is seen that the view and the goal are the same, but there exist some differences with reference to meditation and conduct. This is because Mahāmudrā exists in the context of Tantric practice, that is to say, the path of transformation, and represents the culmination and final stage of this process. Dzogchen on the other hand, represents the path of self-liberation and may be practiced in its own terms without any prerequisite antecedent practice of transformation. This is because the principle here in Dzogchen is *ye-nas lhun-grub*, "spontaneously self-perfected from the very beginning," and so there is nothing which needs to be transformed.

There also exists a small difference between Mahāmudrā and Dzogchen with regard to view. The Mahāmudrā asserts that all appearances (snang-ba) are mind, that the nature of mind is empty, and that emptiness is the Clear Light ('od gsal). Although this explanation is basically the same as that in Dzogchen, still in Dzogchen it is not said that appearances are mind. Rather, in Dzogchen, it is said that appearances are the manifestations of mind (sems kyi snang-ba). They represent the inherent potency of awareness (rig-pa'i rang rtsal), in the same way as the rays of light coming from a lamp illuminate a dark room, or rainbow lights are projected from a crystal placed in the sunlight. Thus, appearances are the ornaments of mind (sems kyi rgyan), but are not the mind itself. For example, when the sun rises in the east at dawn, the sky also becomes light in the west, although there is no sun rising there. So we find nothing here of the metaphysical speculations to which Evans-Wentz alludes.

To state, as Evans-Wentz does, that the text here translated represents "the root teachings of Mahāyānic transcendentalism concerning Reality," blithely ignores the way distinctions are made within the teachings themselves with regard to view and practice. The text in question belongs to Dzogchen and not to the Sūtra system of the Mahāyāna. One must be careful not to confuse the different levels of view and practice in the Buddhist teachings; otherwise we make a complete muddle of things as Evans-Wentz does. As we have said before, the Buddhist teachings can be classified according to the means or methods employed to realize liberation. The Sūtra system represents the path of renunciation, the Tantras represent the path of transformation, and Dzogchen represents the path of self-realization. One cannot explain the higher teachings strictly in terms of the lower teachings. On the other hand, these respective levels of view and practice do not necessarily exclude each other, on the principle that the higher level includes the lower ones. Dzogchen gives a new perspective, which is both profound and vast, to the methods of renunciation, purification, and transformation. It is able within its own sphere to use any of the practices and meditations which belong to these lower levels as may prove useful. Dzogchen is beyond all limitations. And in Dzogchen, there is nothing to be renounced or purified or transformed because the Primordial State of the individual is pure from the very beginning and spontaneously self-perfected.

One cannot say that all views really teach the same thing, because individuals differ in their capacities and levels of understanding and spiritual maturity. For this reason, Śākyamuni Buddha taught many different kinds of doctrines and practices during His career—not because He changed His mind or was contradicting Himself, but because His disciples differed in their capacities for understanding the Dharma, and so He tailored the teaching to the individual, and not the individual to the teaching. For example, Sakyamuni taught that the world was flat and on its surface are found Mount Meru and the four great continents, that the sun and moon and stars all revolve around Mount Meru, and so on. This is seen by consulting the *Abhidharmakośa* and many Sūtras. Yet if the Buddha was all-knowing, as Buddhists believe, then certainly He knew that the earth is a spherical body revolving around the sun, as part of a solar system that is but a speck in a great galaxy of stars. However, if He spoke of these things in a strictly scientific manner as we can well do nowadays, no one in His own time, sixth century northern India, would have comprehended Him. Thus He had to teach people in terms of the conventional cosmology and mythology of the time, with its Meru mountain and the rest, in order to be understood by them. In any case, the principal point of His teaching was not cosmology, but the path to liberation.

7. C.G. Jung's "Psychological Commentary"

Moreover, this fundamental misunderstanding of the viewpoint of Dzogchen on the part of Evans-Wentz led Dr. Carl Jung in his "Psychological Commentary" to assert as fact a number of conclusions regarding Tibetan Buddhism which are reflections more of prejudice than of insight. Although they had corresponded previously and in addition Dr. Jung had written a "Psychological Commentary," published in the German edition of *Das Tibetanische Totenbuch* (1935), Evans-Wentz had not yet met the doctor in person. This occurred at Oxford in 1938 at the Tenth International Medical Congress for Psychotherapy.

In conversations ranging over two days between them, Dr. Jung admitted that up until that time he had not been able to solve for himself satisfactorily the problem of reincarnation. He told Evans-Wentz a number of his dreams touching on this matter. Then the notion that the Oriental or Eastern conception of reality is neither scientific nor philosophical was raised. Dr. Jung contended that the world is made up of psychological images; illusory thought is our immediate reality. He went on to assert that the Eastern approach to reality is indefinite and intangible, whereas that of the West is definite and tangible, being mediated through the world of form and matter. The Orientals, the Indian and the Tibetan live in a dream-like world, one that is very different from our concrete Western reality. Jung emphasized the point that, on the fundamental level, the unconscious of the West is the equivalent to the Superconscious or Cosmic Conscious of the East, suggesting that the principal difference between them is that we Westerners strive for individual awareness and autonomy, while the Oriental does not. Moreover, Jung was adamantly opposed to any wholesale importation of Eastern spiritual techniques, such as yoga, into the West. He felt that it would be very psychologically damaging for Westerners to attempt to practice Hindu and Buddhist methods of meditation because our Western psychic history and our Judaeo-Christian heritage is so different from the psychic history of the East.[45]

Nevertheless, Dr. Jung promised Evans-Wentz that he would provide a "Psychological Commentary" to *The Tibetan Book of the Great Liberation*, which the latter now had in manuscript form, the result of several weeks of editing in 1935–36 at Ghoom monastery and in Calcutta. Dr. Jung wrote his "Psychological Commentary" in 1939 and it was published with the Evans-Wentz book when it came out in 1954.[46]

My own book here deals with the view expounded in Dzogchen, as represented by a specific Tibetan text, the *Rig-pa ngo-sprod gcer-mthong rang-grol*, and this Addendum deals with the misunderstanding and misrepresentation of Dzogchen by a well-intentioned Evans-Wentz. Dr. Jung used the occasion of the invitation extended to him by Evans-Wentz to write a "psychological commentary" to the so-called "Tibetan Book of the Great Liberation" in order to present his own views concerning analytical psychology.[47] However, Dr. Jung's views, although provocative and stimulating in themselves, have nothing to do with Dzogchen. More than half of Jung's commentary is devoted to his own psychological theories, and throughout the commentary he footnotes his insights to his own writings. To deal with Jung's views regarding the psyche is beyond the scope of this book.

Dr. Jung considered himself first and foremost a "psychologist, " in the sense of being a psychotherapist or healer of souls. As such he was primarily concerned with symbols and their transformations, as they spontaneously manifest from out of the unconscious. These manifestations are held to be indicative of the psychic affliction of the patient, but also of the process of healing or becoming whole which he called individuation; hence his emphasis on the integration of opposites. But fundamentally Jung did not understand the meaning of the "nondual state" which in Buddhism is called samādhi and advayajnāna (gnyis-med ye-shes).[48] He understood nonduality as a conjunction of opposites, as, for example, in his discussions of the significance of the mandala. But this is not what nonduality means in the context of Buddhism and Vedānta. A critique of Jung's views in general regarding the East and its psychology may be found elsewhere.[49] So I shall limit what I have to say to Dr. Jung's specific comments on the Evans-Wentz translation.

Misled by this translation, Dr. Jung had no way to know what the Tibetan text was actually talking about, and this may be clearly seen by comparing the translation and commentary in this present book with those in Evans-Wentz's *The Tibetan Book of the Great Liberation*. In effect, what Dr. Jung was commenting upon in his "Psychological Commentary" is not the psychic reality of the East but the psyche as represented by Evans-Wentz. Nonetheless, I think a few things in general must be said here regarding the points raised by Dr. Jung.

In his commentary, Dr. Jung writes, for example:

> It is perhaps not superfluous to mention that the East has produced nothing equivalent to what we call psychology, but rather philosophy and metaphysics. Critical philosophy, the mother of modern psychology, is as foreign to the East as to Medieval Europe. Thus the word "mind" as used in the East, has the connotation of something metaphysical. Our Western conception of mind has lost this connotation since the Middle Ages, and the word has come to mean "psychic functioning. . . . " We do not assume that the mind is a metaphysical entity or that there is any connection between an individual mind and a hypothetical Universal Mind. Our psychology is, therefore, a science of mere phenomena without any metaphysical implications. The development of Western psychology during the last two centuries has succeeded in isolating the mind in its own sphere and in severing it from its primordial oneness with the universe. . . . We only know that there is no evidence for, and no possibility of proving, the validity of a metaphysical postulate such as "Universal Mind. . . . "

Even a superficial acquaintance with Eastern thought is sufficient to show that a fundamental difference divides East and West. The East bases itself upon a psychic reality, that is, upon the psychic as the main and unique condition of existence. It seems as if this Eastern recognition were a psychological or temperamental fact rather than a result of philosophical reasoning. It is a typically introverted point of view, contrasted with the equally typical extroverted view of the West.... [50]

More specifically, with regard to interpreting the meaning of the text which Evans-Wentz presented as a translation, he writes:

The "seeing of reality" clearly refers to Mind as the supreme reality. In the West, however, the unconscious is considered to be a fantastic irreality. The "seeing of the Mind" implies self-liberation. This means, psychologically, that the more weight we attach to unconscious processes the more we detach ourselves from the world of desires and of separated opposites, and the nearer we draw to the state of unconsciousness with its qualities of oneness, indefiniteness, and timelessness. This is truly a liberation of the self from its bondage to strife and suffering. "By this method, one's mind is understood." Mind in this context is obviously the individual's mind, that is, his psyche. Psychology can agree in so far as the understanding of the unconscious is one of its foremost tasks.... It is psychologically correct to say that At-one-ment is attained by withdrawal from the world of consciousness. In the stratosphere of the unconscious there are no more thunderstorms, because nothing is differentiated enough to produce tensions and conflicts. These belong to the surface of our reality.... Self-knowledge is here definitely identified with "knowing the One Mind," which means that knowledge of the unconscious is essential for any understanding of one's own psychology.... Even if one wishes "to know the mind as it is, one fails." The text again stresses how hard it is to gain access to the basic mind, because it is unconscious.... [51]

Here in his commentary, Dr. Jung is being rather patronizing regarding Asians, and he asserts a number of generalizations regarding the psychology of Eastern peoples which Oriental scholarship and anthropology show to have no validity.[52] It is the same with his assertions that Eastern peoples have produced no critical philosophy or psychology.[53] When making these assertions, clearly Dr. Jung has gotten out of his domain. A psychoanalyst is not necessarily a good anthropologist, and one is reminded that Malinowski's work among the Melanesians of the South Seas refuted many of Dr. Freud's armchair anthropological theories, including the universality of the Oedipus complex.[54] Dr. Jung's warnings to Westerners of the dangers inherent in our practicing Eastern spiritual disciplines and methods of mind training rest principally upon Dr. Jung's understanding of the meaning of psychology and of the task of psychotherapy. One reason for his opposition was that Jung's method relied on the practice of allowing symbols to spontaneously emerge from the unconscious, so that the analyst may interpret them and help his patient to do this also in order to understand what is going on in that patient's unconscious psyche. One aspect of this method he called "active imagination." He felt that Oriental methods such as yoga and the Tantric visualizations of Tibetan Buddhism would inhibit or even repress this process, thereby causing injury to the psyche. But this is a complex question and certainly cannot be dealt with here at any length.[55]

In his "Psychological Commentary" Dr. Jung interprets Evans-Wentz's "the One Mind" as the unconscious. This is made clear when he writes, "This section shows very clearly that the One Mind is the unconscious, since it is characterized as 'eternal, unknown, not visible, not recognized. . . . ' Should there be any doubt left concerning the identity of the One Mind and the unconscious. . . . "[56] As I have been at pains to point out previously this "One Mind" is not found in the original Tibetan text. Buddhism does not assume that the mind is a metaphysical entity or that there is a connection between an individual mind and a hypothetical Universal Mind; all this represents the speculations of Evans-Wentz, in line with his understanding of Neo-Platonism and Vedānta. Thus Dr. Jung's remarks in his commentary do not apply to Dzogchen at all. Rather Dr. Jung is discussing his own understanding of the unconscious psyche. He is not concerned with Dzogchen, but with symbols and their transformations—which is, in fact, in Buddhist terms, the province of Tantra, the path of transformation (sgyur lam). According to the Dzogchen teachings, in the tripartite division of our existence into Body, Speech, and Mind, the methods of Sūtra correspond to Body, those of Tantra to Speech, and those of Dzogchen to Mind. Here "speech" (gsung) means the entire field of energy of the individual, both vital and psychic, and the manifestations of the individual's energy. It is with this level of the individual's existence that Jung's psychology is concerned.[57]

Furthermore, Dr. Jung writes, "By means of the transcendent function we not only gain access to the One Mind and here he means the unconscious but also come to understand why the East believes in the possibility of self-liberation."[58] Again Dzogchen is not about gaining access to the unconscious psyche as such, and the liberation of which Jung speaks here is clearly not what self-liberation (rang-grol) means in the context of Dzogchen, as we have seen above.

In Buddhist terms, what Dr. Jung is talking about when he speaks of the unconscious is the Ālaya or Kunzhi (kun-gzhi), "the receptacle or storehouse of consciousness." Within this Ālaya are stored the psychic traces (avarana) of all past karmic actions. When the appropriate secondary conditions arise in the individual's life, these latent propensities manifest to consciousness as samskāras, that is, as impulses, emotions, intuitions, extraneous thoughts, and so on. These samskāras or "formations" are what emerge out of the unconscious and then become objects of awareness for the conscious mind (vijnāna). The conscious mind (manas) as a coordinating and integrating function is suspended between an internal unconscious (ālaya) and external sense experience (panchdvāra-vijnāna), which represents the so-called real world outside of the individual.

But this Ālaya is not just a receptacle, a kind of dust bin of the mind, passively receiving and preserving contents from past experiences; rather, it is something dynamic in its function—a process that continually organizes, integrates, and structures the individual's experience of himself and of his reality. Ālaya is translated into Tibetan as Kunzhi, "the foundation or basis (gzhi) of everything (kun)." This Ālaya or Kunzhi corresponds to what Jung calls the unconscious. It is out of this Ālaya that all of the symbols which normally give meaning to our existence arise.

But this Ālaya or Kunzhi is not the ultimate reality according to the Dzogchen teachings. The specific consciousness connected with the contents of the Ālaya or unconscious is known as the Ālayavijnāna (kun-gzhi rnam-shes), and this term consciousness (vijnāna, T. rnam-par shes-pa) always implies a dualistic distinction between subject and object. Therefore consciousness is an awareness or knowing of something (shes-pa) that is separate or discursive (rnam-par). It is a subject knowing or apprehending something (gzung), whether external or internal, as an object that is apprehended ('dzin). According to the Tantra system, there exist eight (tshogs brgyad) or nine types of consciousness, and these comprise five levels:

1. the five sense consciousnesses which are like five doors to the external world (panchdvāra-vijnāna),
2. mind consciousness, what we usually think of as "mind" (manovijnāna),
3. the defiled or the ego consciousness (klishta-manovijnāna),
4. one's consciousness of unconscious contents (ālaya-vijnāna), and
5. immaculate consciousness (amala-vijnāna).

Through the practice of the sādhana each of these is transformed into the corresponding gnosis or primordial awareness. In this way, the Ālaya-vijnāna is transformed into the mirror-like primordial awareness (ādarśa-vijnāna), therefore the Ālayavijnāna remains polluted and obscured. As it stands, the mind of the individual is limited and constricted in its operation due to inherited past karma; its vision of reality is distorted, functioning as a dualistic consciousness (vijnāna, T. rnam-shes); when liberated the mind functions without limitations as gnosis or primordial awareness (jnāna, T. ye-shes).[59]

Admittedly, the term Ālaya or Kunzhi is not always used in an unambi-guous way in Tibetan texts, and the different Tibetan schools treat it as a concept in various ways. The elucidation of the meaning of the term in the Tantra system goes beyond the Sūtra system which follows the Indian Yogāchārin school. Among the Nyingmapas, a distinction is made between the nature of the mind (sems nyid) and the Ālaya. The nature of the mind is totally unobscured; its very nature is luminous clarity, an imageless Clear Light ('od-gsal). Then because of its inherent potency or potentiality (rang rtsal) this interior luminosity (nang gsal) manifests as rays of light ('od zer) in five rainbow colors. The example given in the Dzogchen teachings is the placing of a crystal in the sun light, whereby various rainbows manifest spontaneously. Thus out of the colorless and imageless clear light inherent in the crystal manifest the rainbow-colored rays of light. Admittedly the example of the crystal is not perfect, but this example points to the process whereby images arise out of the imageless.[60]

Unlike the nature of the mind, the Ālaya is already subtly obscured with these colors. Some texts speak of the Ālaya or Kunzhi as if it were the same as the *sems-nyid* or nature of the mind, while others distinguish them. Thus some Nyingmapa writers speak of two Ālayas, the Ālaya meaning the nature of the mind which is primordially pure and the Ālaya which is the receptacle consciousness and which is obscured.[61]

In his commentary, Dr. Jung paraphrases "the Obeisance" translated by Evans-Wentz:

> The unconscious is the root of all experience of oneness (Dharmakāya), the matrix of all archetypes or structured patterns (Sambhogakāya), and the *conditio sine qua non* of the phenomenal world (Nirmānakāya).... The gods are the archetypal thought-forms belonging to the Sam-bhogakāya. Their peaceful and wrathful as-pects...symbolize the opposites. In the Nirmānakāya these opposites are no more that human conflicts, but in

the Sambhogakāya they are the positive and negative principles united in one and the same figure.[62]

Here Dr. Jung tells us much about his own insights into the interdependence of God and the Devil, but not much about Dzogchen; for although he is using certain Buddhist terms, the meanings he imparts to them are not those found in their usage in Buddhist texts or tradition. The "oneness" he speaks of here is not nonduality (advaya, T. gnyis med) as understood by Buddhism or Vedānta, but rather a pre-cosmic primordial chaotic all-embracing totality in which all kinds of opposites co-exist without being transcended. This is "the deep" (tehom) in the first chapter of the book of Genesis, not the Buddhist śūnyatā or the Pedantic brāhman. On the contrary, the unconscious which is the root of all experience of oneness (and of plurality, for that matter) is the Ālaya or Kunzhi, the basis of everything, which has a unity like the primordial ocean. Moreover the Ālaya is also the matrix of all archetypes or structured patterns. Since the Ālaya is obscured consciousness, it is not the Sambhogakāya let alone the Dharmakāya.

Tantra makes a distinction between pure and impure vision. A vision of the gods in their celestial paradise of Trayatrimsā, however beautiful and exalted the vision, is nevertheless obscured. It is still impure vision because the visionary, as well as the gods and goddesses whom he perceives, belong to the realm of the Desire World or Kāmadhātu. The vision of the dimension of the Sambhogakāya, on the other hand, represents pure vision (dag snang), where one has transcended or transformed his impure karmic vision (las snang), i.e., one's psychic inheritance. In the Tantras, the term deva or "god, deity" is a bit ambiguous, for it can refer to the worldly gods (laukika-devāh) still caught up in Samsāra or it may refer to the manifestations of the Sambhogakāya, whether these be peaceful or wrathful or joyous. It is to these latter that the "obeisance" or verse of homage at the beginning the text refers. These latter visions are truly archetypal in the Jungian sense because their spontaneously perfected manifestations are transformative. The transformative power of these visions is the source and the subject matter of the Tantras.[63]

It is precisely with this spontaneous emergence of images or symbols out of the nondual imageless Clear Light ('od-gsal) in the Bardo states that the Zhi-khro or "Tibetan Book of the Dead" cycle is concerned. Here one must make a careful distinction between the pure visions in the Chos-nyid Bardo, the Bardo of Reality, and the impure visions in the Srīd-pa Bar-do, the Bardo of existence representing the rebirth process. The former corresponds to the Sambhogakāya, while the latter to the Nirmānakāya.[64] But the elaboration of this process of the arising of visions or symbols goes beyond the scope of my present book.

In all fairness it must be admitted that it was the misinterpretations that Evans-Wentz gives in his translations, his introductions, and his lengthy footnotes, speaking repeatedly of "the One Mind," that led Dr. Jung astray, and the latter had no opportunity to deal with Dzogchen as it is understood and practiced by the living masters of this tradition. Had he enjoyed such contact, he might have revised his view, expressed in *Psychology and Religion* (1938) and elsewhere, of the unsuitability of Western people practicing "Eastern" methods of meditation and spiritual development. The cultural contents of individual minds may differ due to different historical circumstances, but the nature of the mind (sems nyid) is everywhere the same. The mirror has the capacity to reflect whatever is presented before it, yet its nature as mirror remains the same. Although Dr. Jung had not had the opportunity in his day, there are now, at least since 1959, living masters of Dzogchen tradition accessible to us—and so a fruitful dialogue could be brought about between Western psychology and Buddhist psychology.[65]

Although Evans-Wentz was not a professional Buddhologist or Tibetologist, he nonetheless performed a great service by introducing this and other Tibetan texts in translation to the West for the first time. Much of what he was writing in his introductions and notes was Comparative Religion or Comparative Philosophy, both of which are valid intellectual pursuits on their own. However, in order to make such comparisons, we must first come to see what the actual practitioners of Dzogchen, both ancient and contemporary, understand by their own tradition and its literature. Until we know what Dzogchen is actually saying, and this means not imposing on it an entirely artificial interpretation of a neo-Vedantic sort, we cannot compare the view of Dzogchen with that of Plotinus or any other religious or philosophical system.

Nor should we take a translation of a Tibetan text, lifting it out of the context of its own tradition, and use it to justify some personal philosophy of our own. This is not fair to one's readers who do not know the Tibetan language and have no means to judge whether the translation and the use to which it is put is accurate or not. Translation and comparative philosophy should be kept distinct, and it should be clearly demarcated as to which is which—otherwise great confusion and misunderstanding will result. It is the grossest arrogance for a Western scholar to sit in his university office, with his Tibetan-English dictionary in hand, and think that he understands better the original intent and meaning of these texts than do the living practitioners of the tradition who have been trained in it since childhood. There exists a rich oral tradition of interpretation in circulation among Tibetan Lamas which needs to be drawn upon for the accurate translating of the Tibetan texts, even texts which are quite ancient. Happily, this has been, in general, a trend for the last decade or so in Tibetan scholarship, that is to say, the collaboration between Western translators and learned Tibetan Lamas in the making of translations. And in this case, what is important at this primary level is to discover what the masters of the Dzogchen tradition actually say about their own tradition.

Appendix II

The Tibetan Text (with Corrections)

Here below will be found the transcription of the Tibetan text, a wood-block print obtained in Nepal some years ago, which was used as the basis of the foregoing translation. Lama Tharchin first went over the block print and suggested certain corrections. At a later point, I went over the text and the draft of the translation in some detail with Prof. Namkhai Norbu, and he also indicated certain corrections of the reading of the text. These are noted below by superscript numbers in the text and corrections at the end of the text.

1a zab chos zhi-khro dgongs-pa rang grol las
   rig-pa ngo-sprod gcer mthong rang-grol zhes bya-ba bzhugs-so

1b rig-pa rang gsal sku gsum lha la phyag 'tshal-lo
   zab chos zhi-khro dgongs-pa rang-grol las
   rig-pa ngo-sprod gcer mthong rang-grol bstan
   'di ltar rang gi rig-pa ngo-sprod kyis
   legs-par dgongs cig skal-ldan rigs kyi bu
   SAMAYA   rgya rgya rgya
   e-ma-ho
   'khor 'das yongs la khyab-pa'i sems gcig-po

2a ye nas rang-bzhin yin yang ngo ma shes
   gsal rigs rgyun-chad med kyang zhal ma mjal[1]
   'gag med cir yang 'char te ngos ma zin
   'di nyid rang ngo shes-par bya-ba'i phyir
   dus gsum rgyal-bas chos sgo brgyad khrid dang
   bzhi stong la sogs bsam gyis mi khyab-pa
   gsungs-pa thams-cad 'di nyid rtogs-pa las
   gzhan du ci yang rgyal-bas gsungs-pa med

2b gsungs-rab nam-mkha' mtha' mnyam dpag-med kyang
   don la rig-pa ngo-sprod tshig gsum-mo
   rgyal-ba'i dgongs-pa mngon-sum ngo-sprod 'di
   snga phyi med-par 'jug-tshul 'di-ka yin

kye-ho
skal-ldan bu dag tshur nyon dang
sems zhes zer-ba'i yongs sngags sgra che'o
'di nyid ma rtogs log rtog phyogs rtogs dang
yang dag ji-bzhin nyid du ma rtogs-pas
grub-mtha'i 'dod-pa bsam gyis mi khyab 'byung
de yang so-so'i skye-bo tha-mal-pas
ma rtogs rang ngo rang gis ma shes-pas
khams gsum rgyud drug 'khyams zing sdug-bsngal spyod
de yang rang sems 'di nyid ma rtogs skyon

3a   nyong-mongs rang-rgyal phyogs tsam bdag med-par[2]
      rtogs-par 'dod kyang ji-bzhin 'di ma rtogs
      gzhan yang rang rang gzhung dang grub-mtha' yis
      'dod-pas bcings-pas 'od-gsal mi mthong zhing
      nyon-mongs rang-rgyal gzung 'dzin zhen-pas bsgribs[3]
      dbu-ma bden gnyis mtha' la zhen-pas bsgribs
      bkri yog bsnyen grub mtha' la zhen-pas bsgrigs[4]
      mahā anu dbyings rig zhen-pas bsgrigs[5]
      gnyis-med don la gnyis su phye-bas gol
      gnyis-med gcig tu ma gyur sangs mi rgya
      thams-cad rang sems 'khor 'das dbyer med la
      spangs dang 'dor len theg-pas 'khor-bar 'khyams

3b   de phyir byas chos bya bral kun bcud la[6]
      'di ltar rig-pa gcer mthong rang-grol du
      bstan-pas chos kun rang-grol chen-por rtogs
      de phyir rdzogs-pa chen-por kun kyang rdzogs
      SAMAYA   rgya rgya rgya
      sems zhes zer-ba'i rig rig thur-thur-po
      yod ni cig kyang yod-pa ma yin te
      byung ni 'khor'das bde sdug sna-tshogs byung
      'dod ni theg-pa bcu gcig ltar du 'dod
      ming ni bsam gyis mi khyab so-sor btags
      la la dag ni sems-nyid sems-nyid zer
      mu-stegs la la bdag zhesming du btags
      nyon-thos-pas ni gdam-ngag gdam-ngag zer[7]
      sems-tsam-pas ni sems zhes ming du btags

4a   la-las shes-rab pha-rol phyin-pa zer
      la-las bde-gshegs snying-po'i ming du btags
      la-las phyag-rgya chen-po'i ming du btags
      la-las thig-le nyag gcig ming du btags

la-las chos kyi dbyings zhes ming du btags
la-las kun-gzhi zhes-pa'i ming du btags
la-las tha-mal zhes-pa'i ming du btags[8]
'di nyid don gsum 'jug-tshul ngo-sprod na
'das-pa'i rtog-pa rjes med gsal-por stong
ma 'ongs rtogs-pa ma skyes so-ma la
da-lta bzo-med rang-lugs gnas-pa'i dus
tha-mal rang gis dus kyi shes-pa la
rang gis rang la gcer gyi bltas-pa'i tshe

4b   bltas-pas mthong rgyu med-pa'i gsal-le-ba
rig-pa mngon-sum rjen-pa hrig-ge-ba
cir yang grub-pa med-pa'i stong sang-nge
gsal stong gnyis su med-pa'i yer-re-ba
rtag-pa ma yin cir yang grub-pa med
chad-pa ma yin gsal-le hrih-ge-ba
gcig tu mayin du-mar rig cing gsal
du-mar ma grub dbyer-med ro-gcig dang
gzhan nas med-pa rang rig 'di nyid ni
dngos-po'i gnas-lugs don gyi ngo-sprod 'di
'di la sku gsum dbyer-med gcig la tshang
ci yang ma grub stong-pa chos kyi sku
stong-pa'i rang mdangs gsal-ba longs-sku yin
'gag-med cir yang 'char-ba sprul-pa'i sku
gsum-ka gcig tu tshang-ba ngo-bo nyid

5a   'di nyid 'jug-tshul btsan thabs ngo-sprad na
da-lta rang gi shes-pa 'di-ka yin
ma bcos rang gsal 'di-ka yin-pa la
sems-nyid ma rtogs bya-ba ci la zer
'di la sgom rgyu ci yang med-pa la
bsgoms-pas ma byung bya-ba ci la zer
rig-pa mngon-sum 'di-ka yin-pa la
rang sems ma rnyed bya-ba ci la zer
gsal rig rgyun-chad med-pa 'di-ka la
sems ngo ma mthong bya-ba ci la zer
yid kyi bsam-mkhan kho-rang yin-pa la[9]
btsal yang ma rnyed bya-ba ci la zer
'di la bya rgyu ci yang med-pa la
byas-pas ma byung bya-ba ci la zer
ma bcos rang sar bzhag-pas chog-pa la

5b   gnas su ma btub bya-ba ci la zer

byar-med cog-ge zhag-pas chog-pa la
de la ma nus bya-ba ci la zer
gsal rig stong gsum dbyer-med lhun-grub la
bsgrubs-pas ma 'grub bya-ba ci la zer
rgyu rkyen med-par rang byung lhun-grub la
rtsol-bas ma nus bya-ba ci la zer
rtog-pa shar grol dus mnyam yin-pa la
gnyen-pos ma thub bya-ba ci la zer
de lta'i shes-pa 'di-ka yin-pa la[10]
'di la mi shes bya-ba ci la zer
sems-nyid stong-pa gzhi-med yin-par nges
rang sems dngos med nam-mkha' stong-pa 'dra
'dra'am mi 'dra rang gi sems la ltos
stong-pa chad-chod lta-ba ma yin-par
rang-byung yeshes ye nas gsal-bar nges
rang-gyung rang la nyi-ma'i snying-po 'dra

6a   'dra'am mi 'dra rang gis sems la ltos[11]
rig-pa ye-shes rgyun-chad med-par nges
rgyun-chad med-par chu'i gzhung dang 'dra
'dra'am mi 'dra rang gi sems la ltos
sna-tshogs rgyu 'dran ngos zungs med-par nges
'gyu-ba dngos-med bar-snang ser-bu 'dra
'dra'am mi 'dra rang gi sems la ltos
cir snang thams-cad rang snang yin-par nges
snang-bar rang snang me-long gzugs-brnyan 'dra
'dra'am'mi 'dra rang gi sems la ltos
mtshan-ma thams-cad rang sar grol-bar nges
rang-byung rang-grol bar-snang sprin dang 'dra
'dra'am mi 'dra rang gi sems la ltos
sems las ma gtogs gzhan na chos med-do

6b   sems la bhai-ba bhai rgyu ga na yod
sems las ma rtogs gzhan na chos med-do
spyod-pa spyod rgyu gzhan na chos med-do
sems la ma rtogs gzhan na chos med-do[12]
dam-tshig bsrung rgyu gzhan na chos med-do
sems las ma rtogs gzhan na chos med-do
'bras-bu sgrub rgyu gzhan na chos med-do
yang ltos yang ltos rang gi sems a ltos
phyi-rol nam-mkha'i byings su phar bltas-pas
sems ni 'phro-ba'i 'phros mi 'dug na

nang du rang gi sems la tshur bltas-pas
rtog-pas 'phro-ba'i 'phro-mkhan mi 'dug na
rang sems phra phro med-pa'i gsal-le-ba
rang rig 'od-gsal stong-pa chos kyi sku
spring-med dwangs-pa nam-mkha'i nyi shar 'dra

7a   rnam-par mi mnga' cir yang sa-ler mkhyen
'di don rtogs dang ma rtogs khyad-par che
gdod nas ma skyes rang byung 'od-gsal 'di
pha ma med-pa'i rig-pa'i khye'u chu tshar[13]
sus kyang ma byas rang byung ye-shes tshang
skye ma myong zhing 'chi rgyu med-pa tshar[14]
mngon-sum gsal kyang mthong-mkhan med-pa'i tshar[15]
'khor-bar 'khyams kyang ngan du-ma'i gro mtshar
sangs-rgyas mthong yang bzang du mi 'gro msthar
kun la yod kyang ngo mi shes-pas mtshar
'di gzhan 'bras-bu gshan cig re-ba mtshar
rang nyid yin kyang gzhan du rtsal mtshar
e-ma da-lta'i rig-pa dngos-med gsal-ba 'di

7b   'di-ka lta-ba kun gyi yang rtse yin
dmigs-med khyab-brdal kun dang bral-ba 'di
'di-ka sgom-pa kun gyi yang rtse yin
ma bcos 'jig-rten lhug-par brjod-pa 'di
'di-ka spyod-pa kun gyi yang rtse yin
ma btsan ye nas lhun gyis grub-pa 'di
'di-ka 'bras-bu kun gyi yang rtse yin
nor-ba med-pa'i theg chen bzhi bstan-pa
lta-ba nor-ba med-pa'i theg chen 'di
da-lta'i shes-pa gsal-le 'di yin-pas
gsal-le ma nor-bas na theg zhes bya[16]
bhai-ba nor-ba med-pa'i theg chen 'di
da-lta'i shes-pa gsal-can 'di yin-pas
gsal la mi nor-bas na theg zhes bya
spyod-pa nor-ba med-pa'i theg chen ni
da-lta'i ye-shes gsal-can 'di yin-pas
gsal la mi nor-bas na theg ces bya

8a   'bras-bu nor-ba med-pa'i thig can ni[17]
da-lta'i shes-pa gsal-le 'di yin-pas
gsal la mi nor-bas na theg ces bya
mi 'gyur-ba yi gzer chen gzhi brtan-pa[18]
lta-ba 'gyur-ba med-pa'i gzer chen 'di

da-lta'i shes rig gsal-le 'di-ka yin
dus gsum bstan-pa'i phyir na gzer zhes bya'o
sgom-pa 'gyur-ba med-pa'i gzer chen ni
da-lta'i shes rig gsal-le 'di-ka yin
dus gsum bstan-pa'i phyir na gzer zhes bya'o
spyod-pa 'gyur-ba med-pa'i gzer chen ni
da-lta'i shes rig gsal-le 'di-ka yin
dus gsum bstan-pa'i phyir na gzer zhes bya'o

8b   'bras-bu 'gyur-ba med-pa'i gzer chen ni
da-lta'i shes rig gsal-le 'di-ka yin
dus gsum bstan-pa'i phyir na gzer zhes bya'o
dus gsum gcig tu bstan-pa'i man-ngag ni
sngar rjes mi spyad 'das-pa'i 'du-shes-par
phyis mdun mi bsu yid kyis 'brel thag-bcad
da-lta 'dzin-med nam-mkha' ngang la gzhag
sgom du med de ci yang mi sgom zhing
yengs su med de yengs-med dran-pas bstan
bhai-med yengs-med ngang la gcer gyis ltos
rang rig rang shes rang gsal lhang-nge-ba
shar-ba de-ka byang-chub sems zhes bya'o
bhai du med de shes bya'i yul las 'das
yengs su med de ngo-bo nyid kyi gsal
snang stong rang-grol gsal stong chos kyi sku

9a   sangs-rgyas lam gyis mi sgrub mngon-gyur-pas
rdo-rje sems-dpa' dus 'di mthong-ba yin
mtha' drug zad sar skyel-ba'i gdams-pa ni
lta-ba mi mthun rgya-che grangs mang yang
rang rig sems 'di rang-byung ye-shes la
'di la lta-bya lta-byed gnyis su med
lta'am lta na lta-ba'i mkhan-po tshol
lta-mkhan kho-rang btsal-bas ma rnyed-pas
de'i tshe lta-ba zad sar skyel-ba yin
lta-ba'i phugs kyang de-ka rang la thug
lta-ba lta rgyu ci yang med-pa la
ye med stong-pa phyal-bar ma song-bas
da-lta rang rig shes-pa gsal-le-ba
rdzogs-pa chen-po'i lta-ba de-ka yin
rtogs dang ma rtogs de la gnyis su med

9b   bsgom-pa mi mthun rgya-che grangs mang yang
rang rig shes-pa tha-mal zang-thal la

bhai-bya bhai-byed gnyis su med-pa la
bhai dang mi bhai'i mkhan-po tshol
bhai'i mkhan-po btsal-bas ma rnyed na
de'i tshe sgom-pa zad sar 'khyol-ba yin
bhai-ba'i phugs kyang de-ka rang la thugs
bhai-bya bhai rgyu ci yang med-pa la
gti-mug 'thib rgod dbang du ma song-bar
da-lta ma bcos shes-pa gsal-le-ba
ma bcos mnyam-par bzhag-pa bsam-gtan yin
gnas dang mi gnas de la gnyis su med
spyod-pa mi mthun rgya-chen grangs mang yang
rang rig ye-shes thig-le nyag-gcig la
spyad-bya dang ni spyod-byed gnyis su med

10a   spyod-pa ma spyod spyod-mkhan ded kyi tshol
spyod-mkhan de nyid btsal-bas ma rnyed na
de'i tshe spyod zad sar 'khyol-ba yin
spyod-pa'i phugs kyang de-ka rang la thug
spyod-pa bya rgyu ye nas med-pa la
bag-chags 'khrul-pa'i dbang du ma song-bar
da-lta'i shes-pa ma bcos rang gsal la
bcos slad blang dor gang yang mi byed-par
de-ka rnam-par dag-pa'i spyod-pa yin
dag dang ma dag de la gnyis su med
'bras-bu mi mthun rgya-che grangs mang yang
rang rig sems-nyid sku gsum lhun-grub la
bsgrub-bya dang ni sgrub-byed gnyis su med
sgrub-kkhan de nyid btsal-bas ma rnyed na
'bras-bu sgrub-mkhan de nyid nged kyi tshol

10b   bsgrub-mkan de nyid btsal-bas ma rnyed na
de'i tshe 'bras-bu zad sar 'khyol-ba yin
'bras-bu'i phugs kyang de-ka rang la thug
'bras-bu ci yod sgrub rgyu med-pa la
spang blang re dogs dbang do ma song-bar
da-lta'i shes rig rang gsal lhun-grub la
mngon'gyur sku gsum rang la rtogs-pa nyid
ye sangs-rgyas-pa'i 'bras-bu nyid nyid-do
rtags chad mtha' brgyad bral-ba'i rig-pa 'di
gang gi mthar ma lhung-ba'i dbu-ma zer
dran rig rgyun-chad med-par rig-pa zer
stong-pa rig-pa'i snying-po-can yin-pas

de phyir bde-gshegs snying-po'i ming du btags
'di don shes na kun gyis rab tu phyin
de phyir shes-rab pha-rol phyin yang zer

11a blo 'das mtha' dang ye nas bral-ba'i phyir
de phyir phyag-rgya chen-po'i ming du btags
de phyir rtogs dang ma rtogs khyad-par las
'khor 'das bde sdug kun gyi gzhi gyur-pas
de phyir kun-gzhi zhes-pa'i ming du btags
bzang med tha-mal rang mkhar gnas dus kyis
shes-pa gsal-le hrig-ge 'di nyid la
tha-mal shes-pa zhes-pa'i ming di btags
bzang rtog snyan ming man-po ci btags kyang
don a da-lta'i shes rig 'di-ka las
'di man gzhan las lhag-pa su 'dod-pa
glang-po rnyed kyang rjes 'tshol ji-bzhin-no

11b stong gsum thag tu dran kyang rnyed mi srīd
sems las ma rtog sangs-rgyas rnyed mi srīd
'di ngo ma shes phyi-rol sems btsal yang
rang gis gzhan 'tshol rang nyid ci phyir rnyed
dper na glen-pa cig gis mi mang khrod
ltad-mos byas-pas rang nyid dor nas su
rang ngo ma shes bzhin du 'tshol-ba yang
rang gis gzhan du 'khrul-pa de bzhin-no
dngos-po gshis kyi gnas-lugs ma mthong-bas
snang-ba sems su ma shes 'khor-bar grol
rang sems sangs-rgyas ma mthong myang 'das sgribs
'khor 'das gnyis la rig dang ma rig gis
skad-cig gcig gis bar a bye-brag med
rang gis sems la gzhan du mthong-bas 'khrul

12a 'khrul dang ma 'khrul ngo-bo gcig-pa ste
'gro la sems rgyud gnyis su ma grub-pas
sems-nyid ma bcos rang sar bzhag-pas grol
'khrul-pa de nyid sems su ma rig ni[19]
chos-nyid don de nam yang mi rtogs-pas
rang shar rang-byung rang gis rang la blta
snang-ba 'di dag dang-po gang las byung
bar du gang las gnas shing mtha' mar gar 'gro-ba
bltas-pas dper na rdzing gi bya rog bzhin
rdzing nas phur kyang rdzing las log-pa med
de bzhin snang-ba sems las shar-ba bzhin

rang gis sems las shar zhing sems su grol
sems-nyid kun shes kun rig stong gsal'di

12b gdod nas gsal stong dbyer-med nam-mkha' ltar
rang-byung ye-shes mngon-sum gsal-ba ru
gtan la phebs-pa de-ka chos-nyid-do
yin-pa'i rtags ni snang-srīd thams-cad kyang
rang gi sems su rig cing sems-nyid 'di
rig cing gsal-bas nam-mkha' lta-bur rtogs
chos-nyid mtshon-pa'i nam-mkha' dper bzhag kyang
re-zhig phyogs tsam mtshon-pa'i brda tsam ste
sems-nyid rig bcas stongs-pa cir yang gsal
nam-mkha' rig med stong-pa bem stongs te
de phyir sems don nam-mkha' mtshon du med
yengs su med kyis de-ka'i ngnag la bzhog
snang-ba kun-rdzob sna-tshogs 'di dag kyang

13a gcig kyang bden-par ma grub 'jigs-pa bzhin
dper na snang-srīd 'khor 'das thams-cad kun
rang gi sems-nyid gcig-pu'i mthong snang yin
gang tshe rang gi sems rgyud 'gyur tsam na
phyi ru 'gyur-ba de'i mthong snang 'byung
des na thams-cad sems kyi mthong snang ste
'gro-ba rigs drug so-sor snang-bar mthong
phyi ru mu-stegs rtag chad gnyis su mthong
theg-pa rims dgu so-so'i lta-bar mthong
sna-tshogs mthong zhing sna-tshogs gsal-ba bzhin
tha-dad bzung-bas so-so'i zhen-pas 'khrul
snang-ba thams-cad sems su rig-pa ni
mthong snang shar yang 'dzin-med sans-rgyas yin

13b snang-ba ma 'khrul 'dzin-pas 'khrul-pa yin
'dzin rtog sems su shes na rang gis grol
cir snang thams-cad sems kyi snang-bas yin
snod kyi 'jig-rten bem-por snang-ba'ang sems
bcud kyi sems-can rigs drug snang-ba'ang sems
mtho rigs lha mi'i bde-ba snang-ba'ang sems[20]
ngan-song gsum gyi sdug-bsngal snang-ba'ang sems
ma rigs nyon-mongs dug lnga snang-ba'ang sems[21]
rang-byung y-shes rig-pa snang-ba'ang sems
bzang rtog mya-ngan 'das shing snang-ba'ang sems
bdud dang 'dre'i bar-chad snang-ba'ang sems

lha dang dngos-grub legs-par snang-ba'ang sems
rnam-par dag-pa sna-tshogs snang-ba'ang sems

14a mi rtog rtse gcig gnas-par snang-ba'ang sems
dngos-po mtshan-ma'i kha-dog snang-ba'ang smes
mtshan-med spros-pa med-pa snang-ba'ang sems
gcig dang du-ma gnyis-med snang-ba'ang sems
yod med gang du ma grub snang-ba'ang sems
sems las ma rtogs snang-ba gang yang med
sems-nyid ma 'gags snang-ba gang yang 'char
shar yang rgya-mtsho'i chu dang chu-rlabs bzhin
gnyis su med de sems kyi ngang du grol
btags bya ma 'gags ming 'dogs ci btags kyang
don la sems ni gcig las yod ma yin
gcig-po de yang gzhi-med rtsa-bral yin
gang gi phyogs su mthong-ba gcig kyang med
dngos-po ma mthong cir yang grub-pa med
stong-par ma mthong rig cing gsal-ba'i mdang

14b so-sor ma mthong gsal stong dbyer-med dang
da-lta rang gi shes-pa gsal hrig-ge
yin-par byas kyang de nyid byed mi shes
rang-bzhin med kyang nyams su dngos su myong
'di nyid nyams su blangs na kun grol te
dbang-po dag la blo brtul med-par rtogs
til dang 'o-ma mar gyi rgyu yin kyang
ma bslu gam-pa rtsir khu-ba mi 'byung ltar[22]
'gro kun sangs-rgyas snying-po dngos yin kyang
nyams su ma blangs sems-can sangs mi rgya
nyams su blangs na ba-lang rdzi yang grol
bshad mi shes kyang mngon-sum gtan la phebs
rangs gis kha ru myong-ba'i bu-ram la
gzhan gyis de'i ro bshad mi dgos shing
'di nyid ma rtogs pandita yang 'khrul
theg dgu'i bshad-pa shes bya mkhas gyur kyang

15a ma mthong rgyang gi gtam rgyud bsnyegs-pa bzhin
sangs-rgyas la ni skad-cig nyer ma reg
'di nyid rtogs na dge sdig rang sar grol
'di nyid ma rtogs dge sdig gang spyad kyang
mtho rigs ngan-song 'khor-ba las mi bsags[23]
rang sems stong-pa ye-shes rtogs tsam na
dge sdig phan-yon gang yang ma grub-bo

bar-snang stong-par chu mig chags-pa bzhin
stong-pa nyid la dge sdig yul ma grub
des na rang rig mngon-sum gcer mthong du
gcer mthong rang-grol 'di nyid rab tu zab
de phyir rang rig 'di nyid 'dris-par bgyi
zab rgya
e-ma rig-pa ngo-sprod gcer mthong rang grol te

15b   ma 'ongs phyi-rab snyigs-ma'i sems-can don
rgyud lung man-ngag rang gi mod-pa kun
dgos-pa mdor bsdus nyung-ba 'di sbyar-ro
da-lta spel yang rin-chen gter du sbas
ma 'ongs las 'phro-can dang 'phrad-par shog
SAMAYA   rgya rgya rgya
rig-pa mngon-sum ngo-sprod-pa'i bstan-bcos
gcer mthong rang-grol zhes bya-ba
o-rgyan gyi mkhan-po padma 'byung 'gnas kyi sbyar-ba
'khor-ba ma stong bar du ma rdzogs

Corrections to the Text

1 gsal rig rgyun-chad med kyang zhal ma mjal
2 nyan-thos rang-rgyal phyogs tsam bdag med-par
3 nyan-thos rang-rgyal gzung 'dzin zhen-pas bsgribs
4 kri yog bsnyen grub mtha' la zhen-pas bsgrib
5 maha anu dbyings rig zhen-pas bsgribs
6 de phyir byas chos bya bral kun bskyung la
7 nyan-thos-pas ni bdag-med gdam-ngag zer
8 la-las tha-mal shes-pa'i ming du btags
9 yid kyis bsam-mkhan kho-rang yin-pa la
10 da-lta'i shes-pa 'di-ka yin-pa la
11 'dra'am mi 'dra rang gi sems la ltos
12 sems las ma rtogs gzhan na chos med-do
13 pha ma med-pa'i rig-pa'i khye'u-chung mtshar
14 skye ma rmyong zhing 'chi rgyu med-pa mtshar
15 mngon-sum gsal kyang mthong-mkhan med-pa'i mtshar
16 gsal la ma nor-bas na theg zhes bya
17 'bras-bu nor-ba med-pa'i theg-can ni
18 mi 'gyur-ba yi gzer chen bzhi bstan-pa
19 'khrul-pa de nyid sems su ma rig na
20 mtho-ris lha mi'i bde snan-ba'ang sems
21 ma rig nyon-mongs dug lnga snang-ba'ang sems
22 ma bslu snum rtsir khu-ba mi 'byung ltar
23 mtho-ris ngan-song 'khor-ba las ni bsags

Notes

Notes to the Introduction

[1]For an explanation of the titles of the text and of its Terma cycle, see the Commentary in this volume. The transliteration of Tibetan terms, when required or useful, will be put in parentheses after the term as it is nowadays more or less pronounced, or after its English equivalent, as for example, Bardo (bar-do), view (lta-ba), etc. If the corresponding Sanskrit term is also given, this is indicated by "Skt.," except where it is given alone without the Tibetan term, with or without parentheses. Written Tibetan has many pre-initial and final consonants which are no longer pronounced in the modern official Lhasa dialect, although presumably they were once pronounced when the written script of the language was developed in the seventh century of our era. Thus the name of the teaching with which we are concerned here is pronounced "Dzogchen" but written *rdzogs-chen*, or in its full form *rdzogs-pa chen-po*. The Tibetan names for persons and places, etc., are also given in their approximate pronunciation, as for example, the name of the Tibetan king Tisong Detsan which would be transliterated as *Khri-srong lde'u-btsan* and the name of the first Buddhist monastery in Tibet, Samye, which would be transliterated as *bSam-yas*. But when an exact transliteration of the Tibetan is required, as for example, with book titles, the transliterated term or title is italicized. Thus, we have Rigpa, but here it is *Rig-pa ngo-sprod*. The transliteration of Tibetan terms follows the Wylie system, and the transliteration of Sanskrit terms is a simplification of the usual system. A glossary of most of the Tibetan technical terms relating to Dzogchen in this text has been provided.

[2]For the traditional account of Padmasambhava, see the translation of a portion of the *bKa-thang gser-phreng* in *The Tibetan Book of the Great Liberation*, W. Y. Evans-Wentz (Oxford University Press, London 1954), pp. 105-192; and the translation of the *Padma bka'-thang* in *The Life and Liberation of Padmasambhava* (two vols.), K. Douglas and G. Bays (Dharma Press, Emeryville 1978) an English version of the original French translation by Gustave-Charles Toussaint in his *Le Dict de Padma* (Librairie Ernest Leroux, Paris 1933). On the early history of Tibet, see *A Cultural History of Tibet*, David Snellgrove and Hugh Richardson, London 1968. The dates given in this introduction and elsewhere in the book are generally those determined by H. Richardson, with whom I had the privilege of studying Tibetan history.

[3]There exist various kinds of *gter-ma* or hidden treasures. A *sa-gter* or "earth treasure" is a text or sacred object discovered as an actual physical thing, in contrast to a *dgongs-gter*, "mind treasure" and to a *dag-snang*, "pure vision." On Termas in general, see *Hidden Teachings of Tibet*, Tulku Thondup (Wisdom Publications, London 1986).

[4]This interpretation of the meaning of the term Rigdzin was given by Namkhai Norbu Rinpoche (oral communication).

[5]See *The Rise of Esoteric Buddhism in Tibet*, Eva Dargyay (Motilal Banarsidass, Delhi 1977), pp. 151-153.

[6]Phowa ('pho-ba, Skt. vijnāna-samkrānti) is the practice of projecting the consciousness (rnam-shes, Skt. vijnāna) of the individual out of the physical body at the time of death and transferring it into another dimension of existence in order to consciously choose one's condition of rebirth. This is usually rebirth in Sukhāvatī (bde-ba-can), the pure realm of the Buddha Amitābha in the west, but it could be rebirth in any human or celestial dimension. Properly, the actual Phowa or transfer is only accomplished at the precise moment of death; to do so before then would constitute suicide. But it is necessary to perform a preliminary practice before the time of death in order to master the technique, and this is combined with long life practice (tshe grub) in order to prevent the premature leakage of vital energy (srog). One of the physical signs that the preliminary practice has succeeded is that a small hole opens at the top of the head, an aperture in the skull, and this may be certified by inserting a blade of grass into this opening. This Phowa process, if thoroughly mastered, allows the individual to circumvent the usual Bardo experience described in the "Tibetan Book of the Dead."

[7]The six abhijnās or clairvoyant powers (mngon-shes drug) are clairvoyance or the divine eye (lha'i mig gi mngon-shes), clairaudiance or divine hearing (lha'i rna-ba'i mngon-shes), telepathy or knowledge of the thoughts of others (gzhan sems shes-pa'i mngon-shes), psychokinesis (rdzu-'phrul gyi bya-ba shes-pa'i mngon-shes), recollection of past lives (sngon gyi gnas rjes dran-pa'i mngon-shes), and knowledge of the exhaustion of one's inner pollutants (zag-pa zad-pa shes-pa'i mngon-shes).

[8]If a Terton discovers a complete cycle of Terma teachings, he must then meet with his secret consort (gsang yum) in order to pursue certain secret practices; and if a monk, generally he will have to give up the robe and become a Ngagpa (sngags-pa) or Tantric yogin.

[9]*Kar-gling zhi-khro* is the abbreviated title for the *Zab-chos zhi-khro dgongs-pa rang-grol* cycle of Terma teachings. *Zhi-khro* is the general designation for this genre of literature which deals with the practices and visions associated with the Bardo or afterdeath experience; *zhi-khro* (pronounced "shi-tro") is short for *zhi-ba dang khro-bo'i lha tshogs*, "the hosts of Peaceful and Wrathful Deities."

[10]On the Nine Vehicles see the Commentary.

[11]Dzogchen (rdzogs-pa chen-po) is so called because it is complete and perfect (rdzogs-pa) in itself, there being nothing lacking in it, and because

it is great (chen-po) in the sense that there is nothing greater than it or beyond it. This designation "the Great Perfection" refers to the Primordial State (ye gzhi) of the individual, to use the terminology of Namkhai Norbu Rinpoche. And it is also called *kun-bzang dgongs-pa*, "the Primordial State of Samantabhadra." In the system of Old Tantras followed by the Nyingmapa school, Samantabhadra (kun tu bzang-po) is the name for the Primordial Buddha (Skt. ādibuddha), or more precisely, the State of Primordial Buddhahood. But here Samantabhadra does not mean some distant transcendent Deity, but the very essence of Buddhahood immanent in every sentient being, although at present unrecognized. This essence of Buddhahood, which is empty and devoid of any inherent nature, has existed from time without beginning, uncreated and indestructible. It does not evolve or undergo change. It is primordially perfected (ye rdzogs) and has never actually been caught up in Samsāra or in time and conditioning, for it is beyond the mind, beyond all time and conditioning, and therefore primordially enlightened. In the Dzogchen Tantras, especially in the *rDzogs-chen Sems-sde* series of Tantras, those ancient texts which are the earliest literary sources of the Dzogchen teachings, this Primordial State is called the Bodhichitta (byang-chub sems), the enlightened nature of mind. In this context the term Bodhichitta has a very different sense than it does in the Sūtra system of Mahāyāna Buddhism. Here the word *sems* in *byang-chub sems* means *sems nyid*, the nature of mind. In the Mahāyāna Sūtras the Bodhichitta means the resolute intention to attain enlightenment (bodhi) of a supremely perfect Buddha in order to liberate all sentient beings from the suffering experienced in the cycle of death and rebirth (Samsāra). Thus, although the Bodhichitta represents the beginning of the spiritual career of the Bodhisattva, being like a seed in need of nourishment and cultivation, Buddhahood is still a very distant goal, something to be realized only in the far future after incalculable lifetimes. But in Dzogchen the term signifies a primordial enlightenment which is ever-present in full manifestation at the core of every sentient being, even though it may be obscured at present, as the face of the sun may be obscured by the clouds. The face of the sun may go unrecognized by those walking about the surface of the earth, but if it were not fully present in the sky, there would be no light at all in the world. It is the same with the individual's intrinsic Buddha-nature; if it were not fully present from the very beginning, there would be no awareness at all, no illumination of existence. For a consideration of these questions see the Commentary and Addendum.

[12]Here I follow the exposition of Namkhai Norbu Rinpoche. See *The Crystal and the Way of Light*, Namkhai Norbu and John Shane (Routledge and Kegan Paul, London 1986).

[13]*The Tibetan Book of the Great Liberation*, W. Y. Evans-Wentz (Oxford University Press, London 1954), pp. 202-239.

[14]Oral communication from Dudjom Rinpoche.

Notes to the Commentary

[1]The Evans-Wentz translation in *The Tibetan Book of the Great Liberation* renders the title as "Here follows the (Yoga of) knowing the Mind, the Seeing of Reality, called Self-Liberation, from the Profound Doctrine of Self-Liberation by Meditation upon the Peaceful and Wrathful Deities." (pp. 202-240)

[2]*Kar-gling zhi-khro* "(the cycle of teachings on contemplating) the Peaceful and Wrathful Deities according to Karma Lingpa," is the abbreviated title for this entire Terma cycle. The texts contained in this cycle are generally known, rather inaccurately, as "The Tibetan Book of the Dead," due largely to the efforts of Evans-Wentz. He was undoubtedly inspired to give it this title by the Wallis Budge translation called *The Egyptian Book of the Dead*. The actual title for the two principal texts found in this Evans-Wentz edition is the *Bar-do thos grol*, "Liberation through hearing while in the intermediate state." The Tibetan term Bardo, Skt. antarābhava, means "intermediate state." There are many of these intermediate states and not just the afterdeath experience. This is what is wrong with calling this entire cycle of Terma teachings "a book of the dead." In his edition of *The Tibetan Book of the Dead* (pp. 71-72, note 1), Evans-Wentz speaks of seventeen treatises contained in the so-called "Book of the Dead." He gives a list of their titles, but only in translation. But in fact, there is nothing canonical about this list of seventeen. It just happened that the Tibetan blockprint of the *Kar-gling zhi-khro* purchased in Gyantse, Tibet, in 1919 by Major W.L. Campbell, then the official British Resident in Tibet, and subsequently presented to Evans-Wentz in Darjeeling, happened to contain only these seventeen texts—among them the text that is retranslated here. An edition of the *Kar-gling zhi-khro* published by Dodupchen Rinpoche in Gangtok, Sikkim, contains twelve of these texts and an edition published in Vārānasī by Kalsang Lhundup contains thirteen texts. In addition, there are many ritual and liturgical texts, often quite short, which belong to the cycle. One recent edition printed in India includes fortythree such texts.

[3]The six Bardos or intermediate states are as follows:

1. skyes-gnas bar-do   the Bardo of the ordinary waking state,
2. rmi-lam bar-do   the Bardo of the dream state,
3. bsam-gtan bar-do   the Bardo of meditation,
4. 'chi-kha'i bar-do   the Bardo of dying,
5. chos-nyid bar-do   the Bardo of Reality,
6. srīd-pa bar-do   the Bardo of rebirth.

The last three Bardos refer to dying, the after-death experience, and the rebirth process respectively. Thus these teachings do not deal only with death and dying, and this Terma cycle should not be thought of as being just "a book of the dead."

[4]Literally the term *thugs-rje* means "compassion, " and it clearly has this meaning in the Sūtra system. But in the Dzogchen context, it has the special meaning of the "Energy" of the Primordial State of the individual, which is unobstructed, uninterrupted, and all-pervading.

[5]The explanation of the Trikāya in Evans-Wentz (p. 202, note 1) is not the view elucidated in Dzogchen.

[6]Evans-Wentz (p. 202, note 4) says that *samāyā* means "thorough perception, infallible knowledge" which is clearly wrong. Nor is *samāyā gya gya gya* a mantra meaning, as he says, "Vast vast vast is Divine Wisdom!"

[7]Evans-Wentz mistranslates this line as "All hail to the One Mind that embraces the whole of Sangsara and Nirvāna" (p. 203).

[8]For a fuller explanation of these Three Statements of Garab Dorje, there is the commentary on them by Patrul Rinpoche known as the *mKhas-pa srī rgyal-po'i khyad-chos*; see *"The Special Teaching of the Wise and Glorious King,* together with a commentary on it by Patrul Rinpoche," translated with notes and introduction in *The Golden Letters* by Vajranātha. Forthcoming from Station Hill Press.

[9]Personal communication from Dudjom Rinoche.

[10]Here the text has *rgyud drug* "the six streams (of consciousness)" for the more usual *'gro drug* "the six destinies."

[11]For the Buddhist teaching on how one's individual karma relates to rebirth in these different dimensions of existence, see Appendix I, section 4.

[12]The text has *nyon-mongs* which makes no sense, whereas the reading should be *nyan-thos*, "Sravaka."

[13]Evans-Wentz mistranslates this line as "They are overwhelmed by suffering and are in darkness because of the suffering, " whereas actually the line translates as "the Śrāvakas and Pratyekabuddhas are obscured by their attachments to subject and object."

[14]Since they separate these two, Space and Awareness (dbyings rig), the Tantric practitioners fall into error or deviation (gol-sa) whereas they are in fact nondual (gnyis-med) from the very beginning. Evans-Wentz mistranslates this line, "There being really no duality, pluralism is untrue. Until duality is transcended and at-one-ment realized, Enlightenment cannot be attained." The line actually translates as "If these two do not become one without duality, you will not attain Buddhahood." Evans-Wentz confuses the meaning here with Plotinus' *Enneads*, V.VI.6, saying that divine at-one-ment means absorption into the One Mind.

[15]Evans-Wentz (p. 207) translates this line as "The whole of Sangsara and Nirvāna, as an inseparable unity, are one's mind"; and he interprets this to mean in his note (n. 1), "This aphorism expounds most succinctly the

ultimate teaching of the Mahāyāna . . .the One Mind being the Cause of All Causes, the Ultimate Reality, every other aspect of the whole, visible and invisible, and all states or conditions of consciousness, are inseparable parts of the One Mind. . . . "

[16]Here, with respect to these Eleven Vehicles (theg-pa bcu-gcig), the meaning is not quite certain since the usual system is that of Nine Vehicles (theg-pa dgu) as outlined previously. Occasionally a tenth vehicle is distinguished, the Vehicle of Gods and Men (lha mi'i theg-pa), where the principal teaching is morality and the law of karma. This vehicle is enumerated before that of the Śrāvakas. Also the vehicle of Atiyoga is sometimes subdivided into three: Ati, sPyi-ti, and Yang-ti. These last two added to the usual nine would give eleven vehicles.

[17]Evans-Wentz translates sems nyid as "the Mind Self" which is completely wrong and un-Buddhist.

[18]Here the text reads gdams-ngag gdams-ngag zer, which makes no sense and in context it should read bdag-med gdams-ngag zer, "speak of the doctrine of anātman or no self." Evans-Wentz mistranslates this phrase as "the Essentiality of the Doctrine."

[19]The text has bde-gshegs snying-po, which is literally the Sanskrit Sugatagarbha, but we are using the variant form Tathāgatagarbha (de gshegs snying-po) here because it is more common and familiar. In any event, the meaning is the same.

[20]This term thig-le nyag-gcig has reference to Thodgal practice. Dzogchen is also called thig-le chen-po "the Total Sphere."

[21]tha-mal gyi shes-pa, "ordinary awareness"; some have translated it as "ordinary mind." Evans-Wentz mistranslates this line as "Other names, in ordinary language, are also given to it." The line actually translates as "Some simply call it by the name ordinary awareness." This awareness (shes-pa) is ordinary (tha-mal) because it is not rendered special by any particular mental activity. It is an awareness which is prior to and transcends the mind and its intellectual and emotional activities. Therefore, the term simply signifies Rigpa or intrinsic awareness.

[22]bzo-med rang-lugs gnas-pa, "remain in its own condition without any fabrication"; rang-lugs literally means "one's own system."

[23]The term ro-gcig (Skt. ekarasa) means "having a single taste or flavor" in the sense of being essentially identical.

[24]Evans-Wentz (p.214-215) translates these lines as "The One Mind being verily of the Voidness and without any foundation, one's mind is, likewise, as vacuous as the sky." The actual Tibetan translates as "It is certain that the nature of the mind is empty and without any foundation whatsoever; one's own mind is insubstantial like the empty sky." Nevertheless, Evans-Wentz goes on to interpret this in his note (n. 1), "The finite aspect of mind being a microcosmic reflex of the One Mind . . . it partakes of its vacuous and foundationless nature. Only in the highest trance state of samādhi, or divine at-one-ment, is the truth of this realizable. . . . "

[25]The text reads *snang stong rang grol gsal stong chos kyi sku*. However, it is usually said that the inseparability (dbyer-med) or unity (zung-'jug) of appearance and emptiness (snang stong) is what characterizes the Nirmānakāya, the inseparability or unity of clarity and emptiness (gsal stong) and of bliss and emptiness (bde stong) characterize the Sambhogakāya, and the inseparability or unity of awareness and emptiness (rig stong) characterizes the Dharmakāya. Clarity (gsal-ba) relates to the manifestation of light which is the dimension of the Sambhogakāya.

[26]Vajrasattva (rdo-rje sems-dpa') is the name for the Sambhogakāya aspect of the Buddha as a single individual; as a collectivity it is the five Dhyāni Buddhas (rgyal-ba rigs lnga). Seeing the face (i.e., the nature) of Vajrasattva means realizing the state of the Sambhogakāya. Vajrasattva is not the Adi Buddha as Evans-Wentz would have it.

[27]*sems rgyud*, "mind-stream," refers to the continuously changing stream of thoughts in one's mind (and inevitably calls for comparison with William James' "stream of consciousness"). But it is not just the association of ideas, as Evans-Wentz would have us believe, because unconscious factors are equally included in this stream.

[28]Evans-Wentz (p. 230) translates these lines as "The One Mind, omniscient, vacuous, immaculate, eternally, the Unobscured Voidness, void of quality as the sky, self-originated Wisdom, shining clearly, imperishable, is Itself the Thatness. The whole visible Universe also symbolizes the One Mind." And in his note (n. 2) he explains further, "As a homogeneous whole, the Universe symbolizes the undivided One Mind." On the contrary, these lines in Tibetan actually translate as "The nature of the mind, whereby one knows everything and is aware of everything, is empty and clear. Like the sky, its emptiness and its clarity are inseparable from the very beginning. This manifest self-originated primal awareness arises as clarity and, becoming systematically established, it is the Dharmatā, the nature of phenomena."

[29]Here the Tibetan text clearly indicates that what is meant is one's own (rang gi) single (gcig-pu) nature of the mind (sems nyid), which is the Primordial State of the individual, and not some cosmic universal Over-Mind as Evans-Wentz would have us believe.

[30]The presentation of Dzogchen by Evans-Wentz in *The Tibetan Book of the Great Liberation*, being a species of modern popularized Vedānta, is in fact an eternalist view from the standpoint of the Buddhist perspective. See the Addendum which follows.

[31]The external physical universe (snod kyi 'jig-rten), "the world which is a container," is likened to a container or a vessel (snod) and all living beings who inhabit the universe are likened to its contents which is, so to speak, the vital essence or nectar (bcud). Thus the compound term *snod bcud*, "the vessel and nectar," means the physical universe and its inhabitants.

[32]The Tibetan word *dge-ba* (Skt. kuśala) means a wholesome, healthy, or virtuous action. It is an action which produces meritorious karma and reaps fortunate and desirable results in the future. The reverse of this is a

nonvirtuous action (mi dge-ba) which creates nonmeritorious karma and brings unfortunate results in the future. In particular there exists a list of the ten nonvirtuous actions (mi dge-ba bcu): killing, stealing, rape, lying, slander, harsh speech, gossiping, covetous thoughts, ill will, and wrong views. Wrong deeds in general are called sdig-pa (Skt. pāpa). Often this term is translated as "sin." But it should be clearly understood that, in the Buddhist context, "sin" does not bear the sense of disobedience to some Supreme Deity. Fundamentally, sdig-pa is an action of selfish and ignorant motivation which causes harm and suffering to another sentient being.

[33]In terms of the practice of Thodgal (thod-rgal), there are four visions (snang-ba bzhi); the fourth and culminating vision among these is the exhaustion of all phenomena into the nature of reality (chos nyid zad-pa). In the Dzogchen Upadeśa series of teachings, it is Thekchod (khregs-chod) which introduces us to Rigpa and contemplation, whereas Thodgal has the purpose of developing this state of contemplation through vision.

[34]These Sanskrit terms refer to three types of texts which contain the Dzogchen teachings. A Tantra (rgyud) gives a rather elaborate presentation of the teaching, together with many explanations. Āgama (lung) gives an abbreviated explanation, usually dealing with particular points touched on in a Tantra. An Upadeśa (man-ngag) is the private and intimate instruction of a master to his disciples on how to enter into and continue the practice.

Notes to Appendix I

[1]The Tibetan Book of the Great Liberation, W. Y. Evans-Wentz (Oxford University Press, London 1954), pp. 202-239.

[2]For example, one only has to read the relevant sections in Austine Waddells The Buddhism of Tibet, or Lamaism (Luzac, London 1895), where he sees the Tibetan Lamas, much as the medieval Church saw witches and sorcerers, as pursuing the worship and propitiation of demons and fiendesses; and he makes out Dzogchen to be a subsect of the unreformed Red Hat Lamaist Church, a subsect particularly addicted to sorcery, necromancy, and other nefarious practices.

[3]Lama Anagarika Govinda agrees with this view of the Hindu and Theosophical influences on Evans-Wentz's interpretations of Tibetan Buddhism. See his Foreword (pp. v-ix) in Pilgrim of the Clear Light, the Biography of Dr. Walter Y. Evans-Wentz, Ken Winkler (Dawnfire Books, Berkeley 1982).

[4]Ibid.
[5]See the Foreword by Leslie Shepard (p. vii) in *The Fairy Faith in Celtic Countries*, W. Y. Evans-Wentz (University Books, New York 1966).
[6]*The Tibetan Book of the Dead*, W. Y. Evans-Wentz (Oxford University Press, London 1927), pp. 39-61. Here Evans-Wentz asserts that the Tibetan account of rebirth in the *Bar-do thos-grol*, in particular rebirth in the animal realms, is only symbolic and not the real esoteric teaching. He claims to have this from the highest authority, certain illuminated but unnamed masters, that once a soul evolves and attains a human rebirth, it cannot fall back again into an animal rebirth. Although he does not name his exalted and mysterious sources, it is quite clear that he was referring to the leaders of the Theosophical Society. This conception of reincarnation as an evolution through inevitable progress into higher forms is not Buddhist, for it contradicts the very principle of karma. Karma does not represent some sort of Divine Providence, evolution within a Divine Plan. Rather, this "esoteric" doctrine of reincarnation presented by Evans-Wentz represents a kind of spiritualized Darwinism. According to the Theosophical teachings, those souls who are now incarnated among the white Aryan race, and this means in particular the Teutonic subrace, represent the most highly evolved souls, in a spiritual sense, on our planet. The native Tibetans are a rapidly degenerating remnant of Atlantis and the Blacks—well, they are relegated to Lemuria and future extinction. The culmination of this present age will see the white Aryan race, in the form of a new subrace evolving now on the West Coast of America and in Australia, as dominant over the earth and destined to replace everywhere all other races as they become obsolete. Imagine a world ruled by Los Angeles and Sydney! Thus, at least on a theoretical level, Theosophy unites nineteenth century European racism with a theory of inevitable progress through evolution. It is not surprising that such ideas had wide appeal in turn-of-the-century America. For the Buddhist vs. the Theosophical view on reincarnation, see *The Buddhist Doctrine of Rebirth in Subhuman Realms*, Francis Story (Maha Bodhi Society, Calcutta, no date).
[7]*Pilgrim of the Clear Light*, pp. 39-40.
[8]We cannot here go into the question of the authenticity of these enigmatic and mysterious *Stanzas of Dzyan*, which Theosophists adamantly hold to be genuine and which no Orientalist or Buddhist scholar accepts as genuine. Madam Blavatsky, in her introduction to *The Secret Doctrine* (1888) declares that this small manuscript, which is the *ur-text* for all of the world's religious scriptures, can be found among the volumes of the *Kiu-ti* (presumably the *rGyud* or Tantra section of the Buddhist canon) which will be found in every Tibetan monastery. Blavatsky goes on to inform us that from the older form *Dzyan* comes the Sanskrit *dhyana*, and also the Chinese *ch'an-na* and the Japanese Zen. An interesting coincidence here is that one of the early synonyms of the word Dzogchen was Tibetan *bsam-gtan chen-po*, which would be Sanskrit *mahadhyana*. Dzogchen is *maha*, "great," because it is what lies beyond *dhyana*, "meditation." *The Stanzas*

of Dzyan, which is the root text in Blavatsky's *The Secret Doctrine,* deals with cosmogenesis and anthropogenesis. (For an account of the Genesis of the world and of humanity as found in the Dzogchen Tantras, see *The Pure Melodious Voice of the Dragon,* translated with introduction and notes by Vajranātha [forthcoming]). For a Theosophical view of the authenticity of these Stanzas in relation to Tibetan Buddhism, see *The Books of Kiu-te,* David Reigle (Wizards Bookshelf, San Diego 1983). Also *H. P. Blavatsky, Tibet and Tulku,* Geoffrey Barborka (The Theosophical Publishing House, Adyar 1966).

[9]Oral communication from Celtic scholar John Sharkey.

[10]For an account of Sardar Bahadur Laden La, see *The Tibetan Book of the Great Liberation* (pp. 86-89); and for the translation entitled "An Epitome of the Life and Teachings of Tibet's Great Guru Padmasambhava," see pp. 105-192 in the same volume.

[11]Alexandra David-Neel gives her account of Lama Kazi Dawa Samdup in *Magic and Mystery in Tibet* (University Books, New York 1958); or the first English edition, *With Magicians and Mystics in Tibet* (London 1931) in chapter one, where she soundly criticizes the Lama for his free and intemperate drinking habits.

[12]*Shrichakrasambhara Tantra* in *Tantrik Texts* no. 7 (London 1919). Despite the title, this is not a translation of the famous *Srī Chakrasamvara Tantra* (dPal 'khor-lo bde-mchog gi rgyud) found in the Kangyur, but of sādhana from the Sakyapa school for that same deity.

[13]*Tibetan Yoga and Secret Doctrines,* W. Y. Evans-Wentz (Oxford University Press, London 1935), pp. 108-109.

[14]Ibid. pp. xviii-xix.

[15]In general, the preliminary practices of Tibetan Buddhism are called *sngon-'gro,* "preliminaries," in the Nyingmapa and Kagyudpa schools. First there are the ordinary preliminaries known as the *blo ldog rnam bzhi,* the four meditations which bring about a change or reversal (ldog) in our attitude (blo) toward life. First there is the meditation on our precious human existence (mi lus rin-po-che) which affords us the unique opportunity (dal 'byor) for the practicing of the Dharma. Second there is the meditation on the impermanence of life (tshe mi rtag-pa). Third there is the meditation on the universality of suffering in Samsāra ('khor-ba'i nyes-dmigs). And fourth there is the meditation on the causes and consequences of karma (las rgyu 'bras-bu). These meditations are largely in aid of developing our motivation to practice the Dharma. Then follow the extraordinary preliminary practices which lay the actual foundation for the practice of the Vajrayāna. Their purpose is twofold, the purification of obscurations (sgrib sbyangs) and the accumulation of meritorious karma (dge bsags). These five practices constitute taking refuge in the Three Jewels (skyabs 'gro), producing the Bodhichitta (sems bskyed), the Varasattva meditation and mantra recitation (rdor-sems sgom bzlas), the mandala offering (mandal 'bul), and the Guru Yoga (bla-ma'i rnal-'byor).

The Gelugpa school calls the preliminaries by the name of *lam-rim*, or "stages of the path," and have their own explanations for these.

[16]See the Foreword by Lama Anagarika Govinda (pp. v-ix) in *Pilgrim of the Clear Light.*

[17]*The Tibetan Book of the Dead*, Francesca Fremantle and Chogyam Trungpa (Shambhala, Berkeley 1975). Also see *Secret Doctrines of the Tibetan Books of the Dead*, Detlef Ingo Lauf (Shambala, Boulder 1977).

[18]There exist several versions of the *Bar-do thos-grol* other than that text translated by Lama Dawa Samdup; this includes a Gelugpa version, which may have been the edition used by the Lama when compiling the dictionary.

[19]*The Tibetan Book of the Great Liberation*, p. 93.

[20]Ibid. pp. 1, 4, 12, 196.

[21]On the different types of Indian mysticism, where a plurality of eternal selves or souls is postulated as really existing (as in the case of Jainism, Samkhya, Yoga-darśana, Ajīvika, etc.), as against a purely monistic mysticism where only one substance (brāhman) exists and all plurality is illusory (as with Advaita Vedānta, etc.), see Heinrich Zimmer, *Philosophies of India* (Bollingen, New York 1951). Also see R.C. Zaehner, *Mysticism, Sacred and Profane: An Inquiry into Some Varieties of Praeternatural Experience* (Clarendon Press, London 1957); R.C. Zaehner, *Hindu and Muslim Mysticism* (Athlone Press, London 1960); and Geoffrey Parrinder, *Mysticism in the World's Religions* (Oxford University Press, London 1976).

[22]Op. cit. pp. 12, 175, 201.

[23]During his spiritual career, culminating in the realization of the enlightenment of a Buddha, the Bodhisattva must perfect the two accumulations: the accumulation of merit (bsod-nams kyi tshogs) and the accumulation of wisdom (ye-shes kyi tshogs). This he does through cultivation and practicing the six perfections of generosity, morality, patience, vigor, meditation, and wisdom. According to the Sūtra system, the Bodhisattva must strenuously pursue these six perfections during the course of countless lifetimes extending over three immeasurable kalpas before he will realize Buddhahood. One immeasurable kalpa (Skt. asamkhyeya-kalpa) is approximately the period of manifestation for a single universe. As the result of his accumulation of merit the Bodhisattva matures the Rūpakāya, and as the result of the accumulation of wisdom he comes to realize the Dharmakāya. Thus the Buddha has two aspects to His realization: the Dharmakāya which is impersonal and nonindividual and common to all Buddhas and the Rūpakāya which is particular to the manifestation of each Buddha. For example, the Nirmānakāya aspect of the Buddhas Dīpankara, Sakyamuni, and Maitreya, which manifest under different conditions in time and history, are not the same, yet in terms of Their essence which is the Dharmakāya, there is no difference.

[24]One can object to the application of the concept "individuality" to Buddhahood. On this question, Edward Conze writes, "Among all the tenets

of Buddhism none has occasioned more controversy and misunderstanding than the Anātman theory, which suggests that nowhere can a 'self' be apprehended. The prospect of complete self-extinction ... seems so bleak and arid to many students of the Dharma that they dream up a 'true self' which, they say, will be realized by the extinction of the false, empirical self. This misinterpretation has proved so popular in Europe that one may be tempted to regard it as either an expression of the typical concern of modern Europeans for 'individuality' and 'personality,' or as a remnant of the Christian belief in an immortal 'soul.'" (Edward Conze, *Buddhist Thought in India* [George Allen and Unwin, London 1962], p. 122. On the question in general, see Conze pp. 122-123.)

In the famous dialogue of Vatsagotra with the Buddha (*Samyukta Nikāya* VI, 400), the latter refused to commit Himself on the question of the real existence of a self (ātman), and on the question of the continued individual existence of a Tathāgata or Buddha after attaining final Nirvāna. This was not because the Buddha did not know, for the Buddha was sarvajñā or all-knowing of all things relating to the path and its fruit (see the *Abhisamayālankāra*), but such matters are inexpressible in words. Indeed, these questions He ranked among the unanswerable questions, because answering them is beyond the powers of human logic and reason which are dualistic and limited in outlook. Moreover, among the four perverted views (viparyāsa), there is the fault of attempting to perceive a self where there is no self, that is, attempting to superimpose a permanent self or unchanging entity on an ever-changing stream of consciousness.

In the Sūtra system one conventionally speaks of the individual attaining Buddhahood or Nirvāna or enlightenment. But this is meant in the conventional sense only, for in terms of Absolute Truth, there exists no individual to attain anything whatsoever. From the viewpoint of the Dharmakāya, there exist neither ignorant sentient beings in need of liberation nor enlightened Buddhas who have attained liberation, for they both lack any inherent nature (Skt. asvabhava). All phenomena (dharmas) in their inherent nature are empty (śūnya), and so one cannot speak of individuality in any absolute sense. Nonetheless, both ignorant sentient beings and enlightened Buddhas continue to manifest throughout our universe in numbers beyond counting. So, conventionally one speaks of individual sentient beings being led along the path to enlightenment and of individual Nirmānakāya Buddhas leading them to enlightenment. But none of this soteriological and eschatological activity is ultimately real. In itself, Buddhahood is not something which is attained; it is not an event which occurs in time and history, for it is the unconditioned (Skt. asamskrita-dharma), and therefore transcends time and causality. It has no cause, it does not come into existence, nor does it cease to exist. Thus, Buddhahood transcends all definitions of individuality and non-individuality, for it cannot in its essence be encompassed within the limitation of the Aristotelian logic of either/or.

What then is the inherent and essential difference between an ignorant sentient being and an enlightened Buddha? None. Both are equally empty (śūnyatā). Both possess the same Primordial Base, although they differ in terms of the Path (ignorance or enlightenment) and the Fruit (ordinary sentient being or enlightened being). In terms of this Primordial Base, one speaks of the Essence (ngo-bo) of the nature of mind as śūnyatā or emptiness, so attaining Buddhahood is not a question of one thing merging into another, like the dew drop slipping into the shining sea. Rather, the example given in Dzogchen is as follows: What is the difference between the space inside the clay pot and the space outside the pot? Then when one breaks the clay pot, where is the difference between these two spaces?

But śūnyatā is not a mere absence or an inert nothingness. Rather, it is potent and dynamic (rtsal) and this potentiality is called its Nature (rang bzhin) which is luminous clarity (gsal-ba). In the Sūtra system, one speaks of realizing the Rūpakāya or Form Body, which represents the individuality of a Buddha, by virtue of perfecting the accumulation of merit, and of realizing the Dharmakāya, which is the impersonal and universal aspect of the Buddha, by virtue of perfecting the accumulation of wisdom. Here the accumulation of wisdom (Skt. jnāna-sambhara) means the realization of the emptiness of all existence. But this "accumulating" and "attaining" is only something spoken of from the conventional viewpoint which exists within the limitations of linear time and causality. In terms of the Absolute Truth, there is nothing accumulated and no one who accumulates; there is nothing attained and no one who attains. All of this is paradoxical and transcends the limitations of conventional reason and logic. From the ultimate standpoint of the Dharmakāya, there are no Buddhas, but from the standpoint of the Rūpakāya, Buddhas manifest as individual Buddhas. But this manifestation of Buddhas is only a phantom show for the benefit of ignorant, deluded sentient beings, in aid of bringing them to self-recognition, to discovering for themselves what has been there all along.

[25]For a comparison of Buddhist views with various Western systems of philosophy, see *Thirty Years of Buddhist Studies*, Edward Conze (University of South Carolina Press, Columbia 1968), especially "Buddhist Philosophy and its European Parallels" (pp. 210-228) and "Spurious Parallels to Buddhist Philosophy" (pp. 229-242). Here Dr. Conze practices a wise, perceptive, and cautious Comparative Philosophy in contrast to Evans-Wentz.

[26]"Like a dew drop slipping into the shining sea" is a poetic conceit found at the conclusion of a famous poem on the life of a Buddha by Sir Edwin Arnold (1832-1904), entitled *The Light of Asia, or the Great Renunciation* (1879). This poem was much read and appreciated in Theosophical circles and often quoted in Theosophical books. However, even at the time of its publication, Oriental scholars complained that it gave a false impression of Buddhist teaching. On the other hand, the suggested anal-

ogy between the Buddha and Christ appealed to Theosophical readers, as much as it offended sectarian Christians.

[27]This was the personal experience of the translator while living for three years in a Hindu ashram in South India, as well as travelling about that region. There exist some similarities between Advaita Vedānta and Mahāyāna Buddhism in terms of view, but also differences, and especially so in terms of meditation and conduct.

[28]For a discussion of this problem, see *Hinduism*, Nirad Chaudhuri (Oxford University Press, Oxford 1979), and also *Brāhmanism, Buddhism, and Hinduism*, Lal Mani Joshi (Buddhist Publication Society, Kandy 1970).

[29]Op. cit. pp. 197, 201.

[30]*Abhidharmakośa* IV.I.

[31]The present account of how karma functions relies in part on chapter six of sGam-po-pa's *Thar-pa rin-po-che'i rgyan*. For a translation of this text, see *The Jewel Ornament of Liberation*, H.V. Guenther (Rider, London 1959), pp. 74-90. The passages which are quoted here will be found on p. 74 of that translation.

[32]Interdependent origination, Skt. *pratītya-samutpāda*, Tib. *rten-'brel*, is a key concept in Buddhism. It has been variously translated as dependent origination (Stcherbatsky), conditioned co-production (Conze), and so on. But this principle of causality may be understood at different levels: Hīnayāna, Mahāyāna, Vajrayāna, and Dzogchen. The Buddha, who possessed a clairvoyant prescience (Skt. abhijna) and omniscience (Skt. sarvajnā), did not have the same problem with causality that David Hume had.

[33]*Abhidharmakośa* IV.1-2.

[34]For this definition, see Guenther, ibid. p. 74.

[35]The preliminary practices of the Vajrayāna are introduced by four meditations which bring about our change in attitude toward life. See note 15.

[36]*The Tibetan Book of the Dead*, W. Y. Evans-Wentz (Oxford University Press, London 1927), pp. 39-61.

[37]Ibid. pp. 42-43.

[38]The Sanskrit term Tathāgatagarbha (de-bzhin gshegs-pa) is usually interpreted to mean he who has thus (tathā) gone (gata) as all other Buddhas have similarly gone into Nirvāna. But according to the *Mādhyavyutpatti*, the introduction to the first Sanskrit-Tibetan dictionary (8 cen. CE), an alternative etymology for this word is "he who speaks the truth (tathā)" and this is born out by Vedic material. The omniscience (Skt. sarvajnā) of the Buddha is analyzed into its various aspects by the *Abhisamayālankāra*.

[39]There are a number of places in the Buddhist sources where this account of Genesis is found, which in itself is very old and probably pre-Buddhist. It is found in both Sanskrit texts like the *Abhidharmakośa* and the *Sikshasamuccaya* and in Pāli texts like the *Dīghanikāya*, the *Anguttaranikāya*, and the *Visuddhimagga*.

[40]The *Trividyā Sūtra* is extant in the Pāli version as the *Tevijjā Sutta* (Dīghanikāya, Sutta 13). The title of this Sūtra, Trividya, literally "the threefold knowledge," refers to the three Vedas which are the sacred scriptures of Brāhmanism, namely, the *Rig Veda*, the *Sāma Veda*, and the *Yajur Veda*. In the time of the Buddha, only these three Vedas were considered canonical by the Brāhman priests. The *Atharva Veda* was added to their number at a later date.

In this Sūtra, two Brāhman youths named Vasishtha and Bharadvāja are arguing over the nature of Brahmā or God. They come to the Buddha in order to settle their dispute because He is reputed to have direct knowledge of these transcendental matters. The Buddha confirms this, saying to them, "For the Tathāgata, there is no difficulty in answering questions about Brahmāloka and the means to progress to that state. For He knows and understands Brahmā and the Brahmāloka, especially the means and methods of the path thereto. Accordingly, He has followed this path and was reborn at one time in that Brahmāloka. Therefore, He has knowledge of it."

In this discourse, the Buddha refutes the representatives of various Brāhmanical schools who claim that their teaching "is the straight path ... the direct way which makes for salvation, and leads him, who acts according to it, into the state of union with Brahmā (brahmasahavyatāya)." (13.4). These Brāhmans assert that all of their teachings lead to this same goal, for they say, "Just as near a village or a town, there are many and various paths, yet they all meet in the village, just in that same way are all the various paths taught by various Brāhmans." (13.10).

But for the Buddha, union with Brahmā could not be the ultimate goal of the spiritual path, and indeed none of these Brāhmans had themselves seen Brahmā, nor had they ever met or heard of anyone who had, or knew him by direct personal experience, or knew his origin or location. "So that the Brāhmans versed in the three Vedas have forsooth said thus: What we know not, what we have not seen, to a state of union with that we can show the way, and can say: This is the straight path, this is the direct way which makes for salvation and leads him, who acts according to it, into a state of union with Brahmā." To this the Buddha replies, "Now what think you, Vasishtha? Does it not follow, this being so, that the talk of the Brāhmans, versed though they be in the three Vedas, turns out to be foolish talk?" (13.14). For the Buddha, this philosophical speculation with its talk of union with Brahmā is a tale of the blind leading the blind (13.15). Salvation or liberation from Samsāra has nothing to do with such metaphysical speculations or with a metaphysical entity such as Evans-Wentz's "the One Mind."

Although the text reads Brahmā (masculine gender), it is obvious that the Buddha is referring to the speculations on the nature of Brāhman (neuter gender) which are found in the Upanishads, most of which were set down in writing after His time. The Buddha is not denying that one may attain the experience of the state of Brāhman, or that one may be reborn in Brahmāloka as a Brahmā; but He considers these to be conditioned states of existence, and therefore they do not represent liberation from Samsāra. He is pointing out that metaphysical speculation is not the path to salvation, which lies beyond the mind and its concepts. Admittedly Brāhman is not defined in this way in the Advaita Vedānta of Śankarāchārya, but the Buddha was addressing the Brāhmanical speculations regarding the nature of Brahmā/Brāhman current in His day.

The above quotes from the Sūtra are found in *The Comparison of Religions*, R.C. Zaehner (Beacon Press, Boston 1962) pp. 97-98; also in *Long Discourses of the Buddha*, A.A. Bennet (Chetanā, Bombay, no date).

[41]It appears that originally the Sanskrit term *brāhman* found in the Vedas meant some sort of miraculous magical power evoked through ritual activity. However, in the Upanishads, which were composed much later and constitute the so called wisdom or gnosis section (jnāna-khanda) of the Vedas, much space and ingenuity is devoted to the reinterpretation of ritual and sacrifice from a far more mystical and spiritual point of view. Often in the Upanishads, *brāhman* comes to designate the Ultimate Reality, in itself inexpressible and inconceivable, which is at the same time identical in substance with the "Self" or essence of the human individual, usually called the *ātman*. This term originally meant "breath." See *The Philosophy of the Upanishads*, Paul Deussan (T. & T. Clark, Edinburgh 1906). But except for certain demonstratively old texts, like the *Brihadāranyaka Upanishad* and the *Chāndogya Upanishad* most of the some odd one-hundred Upanishads were definitely composed after the time of the Buddha. Hence the futility of trying to derive the essential message of the Buddha found in the oldest Sūtras from Brāhmanist speculations. The Buddhist message originated in an entirely different milieu, namely, the Śramana Movement in 7-6 cen. BC eastern India, whereas the learning of the Brāhmans was centered far to the west in Taxila, found in modern day Pakistan. See *Brāhmanism, Buddhism, and Hinduism*, Lal Mani Joshi (Buddhist Publication Society, Kandy 1970).

Nonetheless, the views regarding *brāhman* found expressed in the Upanishads do not agree among themselves, but represent a variety of speculation based on the mystical experience of forest-dwelling sages. One such group of forest-dwelling Brāhman sages, the Jātilas, were encountered by the Buddha personally, and He greatly approved of them, the more so because they shared with Him a similar view of the law of karma—a key issue in the teachings of the Buddha. But He did not derive his teachings from these Brāhmans, nor were His own two masters, Arāda Kamala and Udraka Rāmaputra, regarded as Brāhmans. Rather, they were Śramanas or non-Brāhman ascetics, as was the Buddha Himself. Indeed, in the early days the followers of the Buddha were not called Bauddhas, i.e., Buddhists, but Śākyaputriya-śramanas, "ascetics who follow the Son of the Śākyas." Thus, to call the Buddha a "Hindu reformer" is anachronistic. Sectarian Hinduism largely developed with the writing of the Purānas, all of which were composed long after the time of the Buddha. See *Hinduism*, Nirad Chaudhuri (Oxford University Press, 1979). The interpretation of the Upanishads according to Advaita Vedānta, found in the brilliant commentaries of Śankarāchārya (788-820), came almost a thousand years after the time of the Buddha. And indeed, Sankara himself was accused by his Brāhman critics, such as Mādhva, of being a "crypto-Buddhist." Certainly there exist many similarities to be found in these various nondualist philosophies. But a comparison of the nondualist views of Dzogchen with those of Advaita Vedānta or of Kashmiri Śaiviasm or of more modern Advaitins, such as Ramakrishna or Ramana Maharshi, is beyond the scope of my present book. However, it should be remembered that general similarities with respect to certain aspects of a philosophical system do not establish identity in every regard—nor do similarities necessarily offer proof of historical derivation or influence.

[42] On these states of meditation, see *Buddhist Meditation*, Edward Conze (George Allen and Unwin, London 1956), pp. 113-118.

[43] Ibid. pp.117-118.

[44] Evans-Wentz, op. cit., p. 134 n.3, p. 136 n.1, p. 138 n.4, p.141 n. 3, p. 143 n.2.

[45] *Pilgrim of the Clear Light*, pp. 56-57.

[46] Op. cit. pp. xxix-lxiv.

[47] For example, when Dr. Jung comes upon the term "self" in the Evans-Wentz translation, he immediately assumes that this "self" has the same significance as his own use of the term in German. In his commentary he writes, "The text goes on to say that the Mind is also called the 'Mental Self.' The 'self' is an important item in analytical psychology.... The Mind as 'the means of attaining the Other Shore' points to a connexion between the transcendent function and the idea of the Mind or Self. Since the unknowable substance of the Mind, i.e., of the unconscious, always represents itself to consciousness in the form of symbols—the self being one such symbol—the symbol functions as a 'means of attaining the Other Shore,' in other words, as a means of transformation. In my essay on *Psychic Energy* I said that the symbol acts as a transformer of energy. My interpretation of the Mind or Self as a symbol is not arbitrary; the text itself calls it 'The Great Symbol.'" Op. cit. pp. lvii-lviii.

However, the term "Mental Self" has been coined by Evans-Wentz and is not found in the Tibetan text. "The means of attaining the Other Shore" is Evans-Wentz's mistranslation of Prajñāpāramitā, which the text is equating with the nature of the mind. Literally this term means the perfection of wisdom or the wisdom which has gone beyond. It is the insight into the nature of reality which perceives that all phenomena or dharmas are empty in their inherent nature, and this insight goes beyond all metaphysical concepts and mental constructions. There is nothing here about psychological symbols. The term Mahāmudrā (phyag-rgya chen-po) may indeed be translated as "the Great Symbol," but here Jung gives it a meaning out of context with its significance in the text. The Mahāmudrā is the final stage in the process of transformation in Tantra and transcends both the visualization process (bskyed-rim) and the perfection process (rdzogs-rim). It is called great (chen-po), not because it is a symbol of the "Self," but because it is a state of realization beyond all symbols in the process of transformation.

[48]As an example of Jung's not understanding the meaning of nonduality, he writes in his "Psychological Commentary": "Whenever there is a lowering of the conscious level we come across instances of unconscious identity, or what Levy-Bruhl called 'participation mystique.' The realization of the One Mind is, as our text says, the 'at-one-ment of the Trikāya'; in fact it creates the at-one-ment. But we are unable to imagine how such a realization could ever be complete in any human individual. There must always be somebody or something left over to experience the realization, to say 'I know at-one-ment, I know there is no distinction.' The very fact of the realization proves its inevitable incompleteness. One cannot know something that is not distinct from oneself. Even when I say 'I know myself,' an infinitesimal ego—the knowing 'I'—is still distinct from 'myself.' In this as it were atomic ego, which is completely ignored by the essentially nondualist standpoint of the East, there nevertheless lies hidden the whole unabolished pluralistic universe and its unconquered reality." Op. cit. p. lx.

[49]See *Yoga and Psychotherapy: the Evolution of Consciousness*, Swāmi Rama, R. Ballentine, S. Ajaya (Himalayan Institute, Glenview 1976), pp. 104-138.

[50]Op. cit. pp. xxix, xxxv.

[51]Op. cit. pp. li-lii, liv.

[52]Here in the foregoing quotation, the term "the East" is, in fact, a fictional entity created by Western intellectuals and writers, having no historical or cultural reality. What is the East? Is it the Arab countries and Islamic civilization? Or is it Hindu India? Or is it China and Japan in the Far East? These regions have totally different religions, cultures, and histories, and were only belatedly united as the East in the nineteenth century as the result of European imperialist expansion. Even if we restrict this appellation to India and the Far East, the only religious and cultural complex that these nations all share in common before modern times is Buddhism. What is meant by "the East" is a stereotype concocted by certain Western writers from a superficial understanding of the Upanishads in translation and from recent popular presentations of Advaita Vedānta. By this I mean such sentiments as "the world is unreal," "life is only a dream," and so on. The East comes to be characterized as mystical, other-worldly, woolly-minded, dreamy, irrational, intuitive, pessimistic, life-negating, and so on. With this, the West is usually contrasted as being realistic, practical, outward-looking, progressive, life-affirming, and so on. What this amounts to is a stereotyping of Asians and of non-Europeans in

general, as being "a lesser breed without the Law." This becomes, especially in the nineteenth and twentieth centuries, a rationalization for European imperialist expansion as "the white man's burden." "They" are different from us and this difference implies their inferiority. The same stereotyping was also used to demonstrate the moral and practical superiority of Christianity over such "Eastern" religions as Hinduism and Buddhism.

The writings of Albert Schweitzer is one case that comes to mind. See his *Indian Thought and Its Development* (Beacon Press, Boston 1936), where he characterizes the Western Biblical religions as "life-affirming," whereas Eastern religions are "life-denying." According to Schweitzer, Hindu and Buddhist yogins, because of their pessimistic and life-denying philosophies which exalt the delights of the next world over against this world which is but a veil of tears, ignore the plight of humanity in this present life and just sit around in mountain caves, caught up in personal ego-centric reveries as they contemplate their navels. They are like so many lumps of gold in a dung pile. Whereas Christian missionaries, such as Schweitzer himself in Africa, nobly and "unselfishly" set out for distant heathen lands to spread the Word of God in order to uplift the lesser breeds and bestow upon them the blessings of civilization.

To employ Jungian terminology, the so-called "East" is in reality a projection of the shadow side of the Western European psyche. Western Europe saw in the East everything that it denied in itself—the East is dark, sensual, passionate, corrupt, mystical, dreamy, irrational, feminine. Jung himself, otherwise a very wise and perceptive man, fell victim to this projection, having had little direct contact with Asians personally. Jung's autobiographical writings, such as *Memories, Dreams, Reflections*, Ed. Aniela Jaffe (Random House, New York 1961, pp. 238-288), suggest that the experiences he encountered during his visit to India and especially during his brief visit to black Africa, were very traumatic for him personally and that he was unable to integrate the conditions he experienced there. It was almost as if India and Africa gave rise within him to some primordial fear.

On the other hand, anyone who has lived for some time among the Tibetans resident in India and Nepal since 1959 has found them to be no more introverted, mystical, and dreamy than any comparable group of Westerners. Despite having a religion that does in fact place a great deal of emphasis on the practice of meditation, the average Tibetan is quite cheerful and extroverted, worldly wise and practical, as much so as any American, the extrovert among extroverts. It is only a small handful of Tibetans nowadays who devote their lives exclusively to the *via contemplative*, and this was also true in the past. The Milarepas are exceedingly rare among the Tibetans, as are the St. Anthonys among practicing Christians. So we cannot simply dismiss the East, and Tibet in particular, by setting up this strawman and then knocking him down with self-congratulating arguments.

[53]Also in the foregoing quotation, Dr. Jung asserted that the East has produced no critical philosophy comparable to the West, but only metaphys-
ics, and that it has produced no psychology. Here Dr. Jung is simply
moving out of his domain—he was not himself an Orientalist nor did he
know any Oriental language. He relied principally upon translations in
Western languages of selected Oriental texts for his evidence. That these
were not necessarily reliable translations has already been shown by our
discussion of Evans-Wentz.

In contrast to what Dr. Jung writes here, we have only to observe that
in the early centuries of our era, the Indian masters of the Mādhyamaka
tradition, such as Nāgārjuna, Aryadeva, and Chandra-kīrti, were in the
forefront of developments in India in forging a critical philosophy that,
like the sword of Manjuśrī, would cut through the veils of intellectual
illusion and demolish every metaphysical system. The Buddhist master
Dignāga and Dharmakīrti carried the development of logic to new
heights. In the Abhidharma literature is found a psychology of the phe-
nomenology of consciousness which uses introspection or self-observation as its principal method of investigation. The procedures and results
are reminiscent of the investigations originally undertaken by Wilhelm
Wundt in Germany and William James in America, the two fathers of
modern experimental psychology at the turn of the century.

[54]See *The Sexual Life of Savages*, Bronislaw Malinowski (Harcourt Bracing,
London 1929).

[55]Personally I have always found Dr. Jung's writings to be very stimulating,
insightful, and thought-provoking. However, it has always puzzled me
that he was so categorical and vehement in opposing the practice by
Westerners of Eastern methods of spiritual development. As a psychologist, Dr. Jung, although he was appreciative at a distance of Yoga and
Zen and other spiritual disciplines, was strongly opposed to importing
Oriental techniques of mind training into the West. He asserted that,
although Buddhism and Buddhist techniques of meditation may be very
good for a few rather eccentric individuals, their value as a whole for
Western people is rather dubious. Jung held that the mental outlook and
the education necessary for the real practice of Buddhism, as well as other
Oriental systems, is lacking in the West and that a direct transplant of
this exotic orchid into the hot-house of the West is neither desirable nor
could it possibly succeed. Buddhism has its roots deep in an Oriental
tradition that is totally alien to the West; therefore, a slavish initiation of
Buddhist practices by Westerners is bound to be fruitless, if not dangerous.

As Dr. Jung writes in his *Psychology and Religion*, "If I remain so
critically adverse to yoga, it does not mean that I do not regard this
spiritual achievement of the East as one of the greatest things the human
mind has ever created. I hope my exposition makes it sufficiently clear
that my criticism is directed solely against the application of yoga to the
peoples of the West. The spiritual development of the West has been

along entirely different lines from that of the East and has therefore produced conditions which are the most unfavorable soil one can think of for the application of yoga. Western civilization is scarcely a thousand years old and must first of all free itself from its barbarous one-sidedness. This means, above all, deeper insight into the nature of man. But no insight is gained by imitating methods which have grown up under totally different psychological conditions. In the course of the centuries the West will produce its own yoga, and it will be on the basis laid down by Christianity." (p. 537, *The Collected Works of Carl G. Jung*, vol. 11 [Routledge and Kegan Paul, London 1958]).

Granted that slavish imitation of Oriental methods by Westerners who have not penetrated to their real meaning and principle is something less than desirable. However, Dr. Jung had no personal experiences with these methods and had little or no contact with Asian masters of these various traditions. Many thousands in the West have by now practiced these Eastern methods belonging to Hinduism, Buddhism, Sufism, and Taoism to no ill effects. This is not to deny that some of these methods should not be practiced by people with severe emotional problems or that some Asian teachers have abused their position in the West. I see no problem with the practice of these methods by Western individuals of maturity and emotional stability. Buddhism, for example, assumes the common structure and the common psychic functioning of all human minds, despite cultural differences. It successfully exported its meditation methods to China and Japan, both cultures very different from India, though, of course, this process took several centuries. Because of the existence of a common human foundation, these meditation methods are, therefore, equally applicable in the East and in the West. The experimental verification and the therapeutic value of these Buddhist techniques of meditation and mind training is increasingly becoming evident as Westerners take them up, understand them properly, and practice them.

Dr. Jung was principally concerned with the emergence of symbols from the unconscious, and from his psychoanalytical background he came mistakenly to regard yoga as largely a matter of suppressing the contents of mind, whether conscious or unconscious. Some yoga texts make this appear to be the case, but it is impossible to entirely suppress the arising of discursive thoughts in the mind, since their continuous emerging is a part of the very nature of the mind—as is made clear, at least, in Zen, Mahāmudrā, and Dzogchen. Meditation is not a matter of repressing the emotions, but rather of letting them be and observing them in a detached and mindfully aware manner. To try to suppress them, or any discursive thought, only feeds them more energy. Detachment (vairāgya) does not mean repression. Nor does Tantric yoga seek to chain or banish the latent psychic energies of the unconscious, but rather it seeks to transform and alchemically transmute these energies through a symbolic process in order to use them in more effective and creative ways in one's life. This is what it means in the Tantra when it says that through the practice of sādhana one will develop siddhis.

Dr. Jung calls his method "active imagination," that is, letting the contents of the unconscious psyche arise to consciousness as symbols so that they may be interpreted and integrated—and this is only proper in the therapeutic context. But the yogin is not doing psychotherapy. Although he makes no effort to suppress these symbols arising in the mind, the yogin does not allow himself to be glamorized by them or be distracted by these discursive thoughts (rnam-rtog). They are experiences (nyams). But he does not fixate on them and hold them in consciousness, because his purpose is not psychoanalysis—it is yoga. Yoga, Zen, Mahāmudrā, Dzogchen, and so on, are not psychotherapies in themselves, although they may touch on psychotherapy in many places because they also are working with the human mind. But the relationship between Western psychotherapies and Eastern spiritual disciplines is too large a question to be dealt with here in this note. Alan Watts in his *Psychotherapy East and West* (Pantheon Books, New York 1961) has done us no service by equating and confusing the two.

Nor does it do any service for Dzogchen or any other Eastern spiritual path, or for the Christian religion itself for that matter, to simply explain these paths in terms of psychotherapy. This is a case of trying to explain the higher in terms of the lower—the same kind of reductionism any psychologist resents when some writers assert that the functioning of the psyche can be explained as so much chemical and electrical activity in the human brain.

At times Dr. Jung seems to suggest that, because of their different cultural histories, the symbolic processes in Eastern and Western psyches are fundamentally different. For this reason, he appears to indicate that any Western spiritual methods must be based on the Christian tradition. As he says, "In the same way, Western man is Christian, no matter what denomination his Christianity.... You cannot mix fire and water. The Eastern attitude stultifies the Western and vice versa...." (op. cit. p. xxxvi) Certainly one may think this, but Christianity is not the only Western spiritual and symbolic system. Dr. Jung himself during the later part of his career extensively investigated medieval alchemy, itself an Oriental system deriving from Egypt.

Moreover, Christianity itself was originally an Eastern or Oriental religion, originating among first century Jews residing in Palestine in the East. Peter and Paul were Jews. Jesus Christ himself was a Jew, indeed a Jewish rabbi. He was most certainly not the tall, slender, blue-eyed, blond-haired Nordic depicted in Protestant Sunday school lessons. This foreign Eastern religion was brought to Europe, to Greece and Rome, by missionaries and converts such as Peter and Paul who were Orientals. Nevertheless, the archetypal figures of Zeus, Jupiter, Wotan, Taranis, and Perun inhabiting the collective unconscious of the Greeks, Romans, Germans, Celts, and Slavs respectively, did not prevent these nations from adopting a religion alien to their indigenous paganism. The Judaeo-Christian heritage of present day Americans, Canadians, Europeans, and so on, will no more prevent them from becoming genuine Buddhists or Vedantins or Sufis than European paganism prevented their ancestors from becoming Christians.

At times, Dr. Jung seems to indicate that symbolisms are somehow hereditary—they are embedded in our psychic history, in our racial unconscious. As he says, "The trouble is that Western man cannot get rid of his history as easily as his short-legged memory can. History, one might say, is written in the blood" (op. cit. p. lvi). Dr. Jung may or may not at the end of his life have accepted the idea of reincarnation. But if rebirth is the case, as the Buddhist teachings maintain, then racial memories are not so important, since one is not always reborn in the same nation or race or sex. Rather, Buddhists say that it is our individual karma that is all important in this matter. Indeed, there may be some of us, although we now inhabit Western bodies, who may never have been Christians in any of our past lives. On the contrary, if in this present life one is attracted to the Buddhist teachings and comes into contact with the opportunity to practice them and with realized masters who can transmit them, this would seem to suggest that in the past one has lived many times as a Buddhist.

In my own studies and in my own experience of years in the East, I have found that there is no fundamental difference between East and West. Yes, cultures vary from place to place, but everywhere human beings are the same. I have found no fundamental conflict between Eastern and Western spiritual paths. If we take Protestant Christianity as the cultural and spiritual norm, then, of course, Buddhism will appear very strange and foreign indeed. The differences between Christianity, especially Biblically oriented Protestant Christianity, and Buddhism, on the exoteric level , are certainly very marked, although this does not preclude the possibility of dialogue. But I have found that, on the esoteric level, it is quite another matter. In the mystical theology of the Greek Church and especially in Christian Gnosticism I have found a real communality of spirit with esoteric Buddhism. This matter I have dealt with elsewhere in *Illumination in Gnosticism and Buddhist Tantra*, unpublished dissertation.

[56]Op. cit. pp. li, lxi.

[57]A parallel is found in the distinction made in Greek between Nous and Psyche. As a psychologist, Dr. Jung is dealing with Psyche rather than Nous. The psyche may perceive the Nous as pneuma (spirit), but pneuma is not a level of existence (hypostasis) in Neo-Platonic thought. Rather the term belongs to a Christian and Gnostic milieu as exemplified by Paul of Tarsus' tripartite division of the human being into pneuma, psyche, and sarx (spirit, soul, and flesh). Here there is a certain correspondence with the Buddhist triad of Body, Speech, and Mind, but this should not be

pushed too far since the Buddhist understanding of this triad is different than the Christian.

There exists this question of the psyche or soul as against the spirit and of the opposing of the psychotherapeutic cure of souls to the spiritual disciplines. This very interesting question is too large to be dealt with in a note here, for it would require a much more thorough examination of Jungian thought.

[58]Op. cit. p. xlvi.

[59]The usual list of the eight consciousnesses is:

1. sight or eye consciousness (chakshur-vijnāna),
2. hearing or ear consciousness (śrotra-vijnāna),
3. smell or nose consciousness (ghrāna-vijnāna),
4. taste or tongue consciousness (jihvā-vijnāna),
5. touch or body consciousness (kāya-vijnāna),
6. mind consciousness (manovijnāna),
7. defiled mind (ego) consciousness (klishtha-manovijnāna), and
8. store consciousness (ālaya-vijnāna).

To these eight are sometimes added in the Tantras a ninth:

9. immaculate consciousness (amala-vijnāna).

The first five are collectively known as the consciousnesses of the five gates or doors (pancha-dvāra-vijnāna). These nine are then grouped into five levels of consciousness which through the practice of Tantric sādhana are purified and transformed into the corresponding gnosis or primordial awareness (jnāna):

1. the five sense consciousnesses (panchdvāra-vijnāna) are transformed into the all-accomplishing gnosis (krityanusthāna-jnāna),
2. mind consciousness (manovijnāna) is transformed into the discriminating gnosis (pratyavekshana-jnāna),
3. defiled mind consciousness (klishtha-manovijnāna) is transformed into the gnosis of identity (samatā-jnāna),
4. the store consciousness (ālaya-vijnāna) is transformed into the mirror-like gnosis (adarsa-jnāna), and
5. the immaculate consciousness (amala-vijnāna) is transformed into the gnosis of the Dharmadhātu (dharmadhātu-jnāna), the primordial awareness of the dimension of all existence.

[60]See *The Crystal and the Way of Light*, Namkhai Norbu and John Shane (Routledge and Kegan Paul, London 1986).

[61]Oral communication from Dudjom Rinpoche.

[62]Op. cit. p. 1.

[63]In our world the principal source of revelation of the Tantras are the visions or experience of the transformation of energy which occurred to various Mahāsiddhas in ancient India.

Jung was opposed to Westerners practicing Eastern methods such as Tibetan visualization techniques. In this context, the question could be asked whether a Westerner when he dies will have the visions of the

Peaceful and Wrathful Deities precisely as described in the *Bar-do thos-grol*, "the Tibetan Book of the Dead." This is unlikely, unless that individual has had Tantric training in his present life or in his previous life. Probably he would have visions of a radiant white-robed figure, such as are reported in many near death experiences, or else visions of choirs of angels. (See *Life After Life*, Raymond Moody [Bantam Books, New York 1975]). But according to many Tibetan Lamas, to whom I have presented this question, if that Western individual has practiced in this life the sādhana of the *Zhi-khro*, then indeed he would have the vision of the Peaceful and Wrathful Deities in the Bardo after death. Is this a case of the conscious mind sending suggestions to the unconscious or of its programming the computer in the unconscious psyche? Perhaps. Jung apparently denied that this was possible. Yet in the West there exist a number of esoteric or occult groups, working with ceremonial magic, which do precisely this. Dion Fortune (Violet Firth) was one Jungian analyst who worked with these symbolic ritual methods, as her voluminous writings testify.

The Dzogchen teachings explain the matter a little differently. Through certain practices like a dream yoga or the practice of the natural Clear Light, the practitioner comes to experience directly the Clear Light at the moment of falling asleep and before the onset of the dream state. This experience is known as "the son Clear Light." The processes of falling asleep, experiencing the Clear Light, and dreaming are analogous to the three Bardos. Having practiced this method while yet alive, then at the time of death, the practitioner, having already had a foretaste, so to speak, then immediately recognizes the manifestation of the Clear Light and integrates with it, thereby attaining liberation. This is known as the meeting of the "the son Clear Light" with "the mother Clear Light." See *The Cycle of Day and Night*, Namkhai Norbu, Tr. John Reynolds (Station Hill Press, Barrytown 1987).

[64]The experiences of the Clear Light ('od gsal) in the '*Chi-kha'i Bar-do* or immediately following it correspond to the Dharmakāya.

[65]For a recent attempt to compare Jung's psychological theories with Tibetan Buddhism, see *Jung's Psychology and Tibetan Buddhism: Western and Eastern Paths of the Heart*, Radmila Moacanin, London 1987. Also see *Jung and Eastern Thought*, Harold Coward, Albany 1985.

Glossary of Tibetan Buddhist Terms

Note: The Tibetan terms are listed in the order of the Tibetan alphabet. (DZ) indicates a special usage in the context of Dzogchen. Capitalization is also used at times to indicate a special technical usage. For example, *thugs-rje* (Skt. karuna) ordinarily means compassion, but in the Dzogchen context this term has the special meaning of "Energy," i.e. the energy of the Primordial State of the individual which is the nature of the mind.

ka-dag	primordial purity, primordially pure
kun khyab	all-pervading
kun rdzob	relative
kun-gzhi	Ālaya, the basis of everything
kun rig	aware of everything
kye-ho	listen
klong	vast expanse (of space)
klong-sde	the Space Series of Dzogchen teachings
bka'-ma	"traditional teachings" handed down through an unbroken lineage of masters and disciples
skal-ldan	fortunate, one possessing good karma
sku	Body, body, dimension
sku gsum	Trikāya, the Three Bodies of the Buddha
bskyed-rim	Generation Process, visualization process, the stages of production or development, utpattikrama
khrid	an explanation giving guidance
'khrul-pa	error, delusion, erroneous
gol-sa	deviation

dgongs brgyud	direct transmission (in a mind to mind fashion)
dgongs-pa	intention, state of contemplation, to contemplate; the Primordial State of the individual (DZ)
'gro drug	the six destinies of rebirth
rgya	seal
sgyur lam	path of transformation
sgrib-pa	obscuration, to be obscured
bsgom-pa	meditation
bsgrub-mkhan	one who has realized, the realizer
nges don	certain meaning, real meaning
ngo-sprod	introduction, to introduce
ngo-bo	essence, Essence (DZ)
ngo ma shes-pa	not recognize, unrecognized
ngo shes-pa	recognition, to recognize
dngos-po gshis kyi gnas-lugs	the natural condition of the real disposition of things
dngos-po 'gnas-lugs	the natural condition of things
dngos med	immaterial
dngos-gzhi	principle practice, principle section
sngags-lugs	the Mantra system
sngon-'gro	preliminaries, preliminary practice, preliminary section
cir yang grub med	not created by anything
gcer grol	liberation through bare attention
gcer mthong	to see with naked awareness, to see nakedly
chos	dharma(s), phenomena
chos nyid	Dharmatā, the nature of reality
chos dbyings	Dharmadhātu, the dimension of existence
ji bzhin nyid	the state of being just as it is
ji bzhin nyid du ma rtogs-pa	not understanding the real condition of things just as they are
'jug tshul	methods for entering (into practice)
rjes thob	subsequent realization, post-meditation experience
nyan-thos-pa	Sravaka, a Hīnayāna disciple

nyams	experience, meditation experience
nye brgud	short lineage of transmission
nyon-mongs	passion, defilement, kleśa
gnyis med	nonduality, nondual
gnyis 'dzin	grasping at duality
gnyen-po	antidote
mnyan-bzhag	state of contemplation, samahita
snyan brguy	oral transmission
bsnyen-grub	sevā-sādhana, the practice of visualizing thedeity and reciting its mantra
ting-nge 'dzin	samādhi, contemplation, state of contemplation
gter-ston	treasure master, discoverer of a hidden treasure
gter-ma	hidden treasure, a text hidden in ancient times and rediscovered at a later date
rtag chad	eternalism and nihilism
rten-'brel	interdependent origination, pratityasamutpada, an auspicious conjunction of events
rtogs-pa	understanding, to understand
lta rgyu	is looking, one who is looking
lta-ba	view, viewpoint, to look
stong-pa nyid	emptiness, śūnyatā
brtan-pa	stability, stable, firm
tha-mal gyi shes-pa	ordinary awareness
thig-le	sphere, bindu
thig-le nyag-gcig	the Unique Sphere
thugs-rje	compassion, Energy (DZ)
theg-pa dgu	the nine vehicles to enlightenment
mtha' bral	unlimited, free of limitations or of extremes
da-lta'i shes rig	immediate present awareness
dag snang	pure vision
dam-tshig	samāyā, Tantric vow
drang don	conventional meaning
dran rig	mindful awareness
gdod nas ma skyes	uncreated from the very beginning

bdag	self, ego, I; the doctrine of Ātman
bdag med	without a self; the doctrine of Anātman
bdag-'dzin	grasping at a self, grasping at the reality of
bde-stong	bliss and emptiness
mdangs	transparent radiance
mdo-lugs	the Sūtra system
'dod-chags	greed, desire, raga
brda brgyud	symbolic transmission
nang brgyud	the Inner Tantras
gnas-pa	calm state; to abide, be established, remain
gnas-lugs	natural condition
rnam-rtog	a thought, discursive thought, vikalpa
snang-ba	appearance; to appear, manifest
snang srīd	all phenomenal existence, everything which appears and exists
dpyod-pa	analysis, to analyze
spong lam	path of renunciation
spyod-mkhan	one who acts
spyod-pa	conduct, behavior
sprul-pa	emanation, to emanate
spros-bral	free of intellectual elaborations, without conceptions
phyi rgyud	the Outer Tantras
'phro-ba	to emanate, project
'phro-ba'i 'phro-mkhan	the projectionist who projects
bag-chags	karmic traces of residues, inherited predispositions, vāsnās
bar-do	the intermediate state between death and rebirth
bar-do thos-grol	liberation through hearing while in the Bardo, (Tibetan title of "the Book of the Dead")
bar-do drug khrid	explanations giving guidance for the six Bardos
bhai rgyu	is meditation, one who is meditating
bhai-ba	meditation, to meditate
bhai-ba'i mkhan-po	meditator
bhai med	without meditation

byang-chub	enlightenment, Bodhi
byang-chub sems	Bodhichitta, the thought of enlightenment, the Primordial State of the individual (DZ)
bya bral chos	inactive dharmas, actions which are not done
byas chos	active charmas, actions which are done
bla-ma	master, Guru
dbyings	space, dimension
dbyer med	inseparable
ma 'gag-pa	unobstructed
ma bcos-pa	unfabricated, without modifications
ma yengs-cig	do not be distracted
ma rig-pa	ignorance, lack of awareness
man-ngag	upadeśa, secret oral instruction
man-ngag gi sde	Secret Instruction Series of Dzogchen teachings, the Upadeśa Series
dmigs med	without conceptions, without visualization
rtsa-rlung	the yoga of the channels and the energies
rtsal	potency, creativity, skill; the external manifestation of energy (DZ)
tshig gsum gnad brdeg	the three statements which strike the essential point
'dzin med	without grasping
rdzogs-pa chen-po	Dzogchen, Atiyoga, the Great Perfection
rdzogs-rim	Perfection Process, stages of completion, nishpannakrama
zhi-khro	the Peaceful and Wrathful Deities
zhe-sdang	hatred, anger, dvesha
gzhi	base, foundation
gzhi-med rtsa-bral	without a base and without a root
zag bcas	polluted, āsrava
zad sar 'khyol-pa	exhausted and overthrown
zab chos	profound teaching
zung-'jug	union, unified, inseparable, yuganaddha
gzer	nail, essential point

bcos med rang lugs gnas-pa	remain in its own condition without any modification
'od gsal	the Clear Light
yin-pa'i rtags	the sign of its existence
ye-nas med-pa	not exist from the very beginning
ye-shes	primal awareness, primordial awareness, gnosis, wisdom, cognition, jnāna
yengs med	without distraction, undistracted
yer-re-ba	authentic, unadulterated
rang grol	self-liberation
rang grol lam	path of self-liberation
rang rgyal	Pratyekabuddha
rang ngo shes-pa	self-recognition
rang mdangs	inherent transparent radiance
rang snang	self-manifested
rang byung	self-originated
rang byung 'od gsal	self-originated Clear Light
rang byung ye-shes mngon-sum	manifest self-originated primordial awareness
rang byung rig-pa	self-originated awareness
rang-bzhin	nature, inherent nature, Nature (DZ)
rang-bzhin med	without inherent nature
rang rig	one's own intrinsic awareness
rang sar grol	liberated into its own condition
rang sar bzhag-pa	settle into its own condition
rang sems	one's own mind
rig-stong	awareness and emptiness
rig-pa	intrinsic awareness, pure presence (DZ); intelligence
rig-pa ngo-sprod	introduction to one's intrinsic awareness
rig-pa rjen-pa	naked awareness
rig-pa mngon-sum	manifest intrinsic awareness
rig-'dzin	Vidyādhara, knowledge-holder
rig-pa'i rtsal	the potency of intrinsic awareness
rig rig thur-thur-po	sparkling awareness

rigs kyi bu	son of a noble family, kulaputra
ring brgyud	long lineage of transmission
ro-gcig	of a single flavor, identical in essence
lung	authorization, tradition, traditional knowledge, āgama
las 'phro-can	one whose karma has ripened
shar grol	liberation as soon as it arises
shes-pa	to know, be aware
shes-rab	discriminating wisdom, Wisdom, prajñā
shes rig	awareness which knows
gshis	disposition, real disposition
sang-nge-ba	immaculately pure
sems	mind, thought(s)
sems-rgyud	mind-stream, stream of consciousness
sems nyid	the nature of the mind
sems nyid gcig-po	a single nature of the mind
sems-sde	the Mind Series of Dzogchen teachings
bsam-gtan	concentration, level of concentration, dhyana
gsal-stong	clarity and emptiness
gsal-ba	clarity, luminous clarity, clear, to elucidate
gsal rig	clarity and awareness, clear awareness
gsal rig stong gsum	clarity, awareness, and emptiness
gsal-le-ba	lucidly clear
gsal-le hrig-ge-ba	lucid and present
hrig-ge-ba	present, aware
lhun-grub	spontaneously self-perfected
e-ma-ho	how marvelous

Bibliography

Barborka, Geoffrey. *H.P. Blavatsky, Tibet, and Tulku.* The Theosophical Publishing House, Adyar, 1966.

Bennet, A. A. *Long Discourses of the Buddha.* Chetanā, Bombay, no date.

Chaudhuri, Nirad. *Hinduism.* Oxford University Press, Oxford, 1979.

Conze, Edward. *Buddhist Meditation.* George Allen and Unwin, London, 1956.

———. *Buddhist Thought in India.* George Allen and Unwin, London, 1962.

———. *Thirty Years of Buddhist Studies.* University of South Carolina Press, Columbia, 1968.

Coward, Harold. *Jung and Eastern Thought.* SUNY Press, Albany, 1985.

Dargyay, Eva M. *The Rise of Esoteric Buddhism in Tibet.* Motilal Banarsidass, Delhi, 1977.

David-Neel, Alexandra. *Magic and Mystery in Tibet.* University Books, New York, 1958.

Dawa Samdup, Kazi. *Shrichakrasambhara: A Buddhist Tantra.* Tantrik Texts No. 7, (ed.) Arthur Avalon, Luzac, London, 1919.

Deussan, Paul. *The Philosophy of the Upanishads.* T. & T. Clark, Edinburgh, 1906.

Douglas, K. and Bays, G. (tr.). *The Life and Liberation of Padmasambhava.* Dharma Press, Emeryville, 1978.

Evans-Wentz, W. Y. *The Fairy Faith in Celtic Countries.* University Books, New York, 1966.

———. *The Tibetan Book of the Dead.* Oxford University Press, London, 1927.

———. *The Tibetan Book of the Great Liberation.* Oxford University Press, London, 1954.

———. *Tibetan Yoga and Secret Doctrines.* Oxford University Press, London, 1935.

———. *Tibet's Great Yogi Milarepa.* Oxford University Press, London, 1928.

Freemantle, Francesca and Trungpa, Chogyam. *The Tibetan Book of the Dead.* Shambhala, Berkeley, 1975.

Guenther, Herbert V. *The Jewel Ornament of Liberation*. Rider, London, 1959.

Joshi, Lal Mani. *Brāhmanism, Buddhism, and Hinduism*. The Buddhist Publication Society, Kandy, 1970.

Jung, Carl G. *Memories, Dreams, Reflections*, (ed.) Aniela Jaffe. Random House, New York, 1961.

———. *Psychology and Religion* in *The Collected Works of Carl G. Jung*, (vol. 11), (ed.) Sir Herbert Read, etc. Routledge and Kegan Paul, London, 1958.

Lauf, Detlef Ingo. *Secret Doctrines of the Tibetan Books of the Dead*. Shambhala, New York, 1977.

Malinowski, Bronislaw. *Sex and Repression in Savage Society*. Harcourt Brace, New York, 1927.

Moacanin, Radmila. *Jung's Psychology and Tibetan Buddhism*. Wisdom Publications, London, 1987.

Moody, Raymond. *Life After Life*. Bantam Books, New York, 1975.

Norbu, Namkhai. *The Crystal and the Way of Light*, (ed.) John Shane. Routledge an Kegan Paul, London, 1986.

———. *The Cycle of Day and Night, Where One Proceeds Along the Path of the Primordial Yoga*, (ed., transl.) John Myrdhin Reynolds. Station Hill Press, Barrytown, New York, 1987.

Parrinder, Geoffrey. *Mysticism in the World's Religions*. Oxford University Press, London, 1976.

Reigle, David. *The Books of Kiu-te*. The Wizard's Bookshelf, San Diego, 1983.

Schweitzer, Albert. *Indian Thought and Its Development*. Beacon Press, Boston, 1936.

Snellgrove, David and Richardson, Hugh. *A Cultural History of Tibet*. George Weidenfeld and Nicolson, London, 1968.

Toussaint, Gustave-Charles. *Le Dict de Padma*. Librairie Ernest Leroux, Paris, 1933.

Tulku Thondup. *Hidden Teachings of Tibet*. Wisdom Publications, London, 1986.

Waddell, Austine. *The Buddhism of Tibet, or Lamaism*. Luzac, London, 1985.

Watts, Alan. *Psychotherapy East and West*. Pantheon Books, New York, 1961.

Winkler, Ken. *Pilgrim of the Clear Light*. Dawnfire Books, Berkeley, 1982.

Zaehner, R. C. *Hindu and Muslim Mysticism*. Athlone Press, London, 1960.

————. *Mysticism Sacred and Profane*. Clarendon Press, London, 1957.

————. *The Comparison of Religions*. Beacon Press, Boston, 1962.

Zimmer, Heinrich. *Philosophies of India*. Bollingen, New York, 1951.

Index of Tibetan Buddhist Terms

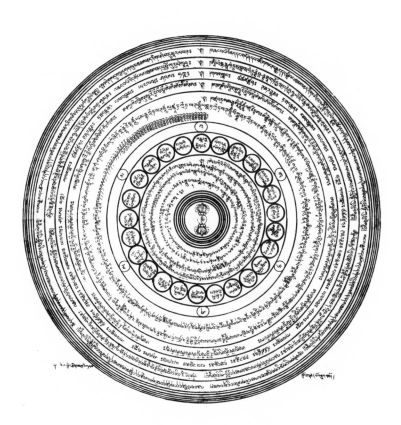